# The Trolley Problem Mysteries

# The Berkeley Tanner Lectures

The Tanner Lectures on Human Values were established by the American scholar, industrialist, and philanthropist Obert Clark Tanner; they are presented annually at nine universities in the United States and England. The University of California, Berkeley became a permanent host of annual Tanner Lectures in the academic year 2000-2001. This work is the ninth in a series of books based on the Berkeley Tanner Lectures. The volume includes a revised version of the lectures that F. M. Kamm presented at Berkeley in March of 2013, together with the responses of the three invited commentators on that occasion—Judith Jarvis Thomson, Thomas Hurka, and Shelly Kagan—and a final rejoinder by Professor Kamm. The volume is edited by Eric Rakowski, who also contributes an introduction. The Berkeley Tanner Lecture Series was established in the belief that these distinguished lectures, together with the lively debates stimulated by their presentation in Berkeley, deserve to be made available to a wider audience. Additional volumes are in preparation.

MARTIN JAY
R. JAY WALLACE
*Series Editors*

Volumes Published in the Series

JOSEPH RAZ, *The Practice of Value*
Edited by R. JAY WALLACE
With Christine M. Korsgard, Robert Pippin, and Bernard Williams

FRANK KERMODE, *Pleasure and Change: The Aesthetics of Canon*
Edited by ROBERT ALTER
With Geoffrey Hartman, John Guillory, and Carey Perloff

SEYLA BENHABIB, *Another Cosmopolitanism*
Edited by ROBERT POST
With Jeremy Waldron, Bonnie Honig, and Will Kymlicka

AXEL HONNETH, *Reification: A New Look at an Old Idea*
Edited by MARTIN JAY
With Judith Butler, Raymond Guess, and Jonathan Lear

ALLAN GIBBARD, *Reconciling Our Aims*
Edited by BARRY STROUD
With Michael Bratman, John Broome, and F.M. Kamm

DEREK PARFIT, *On What Matters: Volumes 1 & 2*
Edited by SAMUEL SCHEFFLER
With T.M. Scanlon, Susan Wolf, Allen Wood, and Barbara Herman

JEREMY WALDRON, *Dignity, Rank, and Rights*
Edited by MEIR DAN-COHEN
With Wai Chee Dimock, Don Herzog, and Michael Rosen

SAMUEL SCHEFFLER, *Death and the Afterlife*
Edited by NIKO KOLODNY
With Susan Wolf, Harry G. Frankfurt, and Seana Valentine Shiffrin

# The Trolley Problem Mysteries

## F. M. KAMM

*With Commentaries by*
JUDITH JARVIS THOMSON
THOMAS HURKA
SHELLY KAGAN

*Edited and Introduced by*
ERIC RAKOWSKI

# OXFORD

UNIVERSITY PRESS

Oxford University Press is a department of the University of
Oxford. It furthers the University's objective of excellence in research,
scholarship, and education by publishing worldwide.

Oxford   New York
Auckland   Cape Town   Dar es Salaam   Hong Kong   Karachi
Kuala Lumpur   Madrid   Melbourne   Mexico City   Nairobi
New Delhi   Shanghai   Taipei   Toronto

With offices in
Argentina   Austria   Brazil   Chile   Czech Republic   France   Greece
Guatemala   Hungary   Italy   Japan   Poland   Portugal   Singapore
South Korea   Switzerland   Thailand   Turkey   Ukraine   Vietnam

Oxford is a registered trademark of Oxford University Press
in the UK and certain other countries.

Published in the United States of America by
Oxford University Press
198 Madison Avenue, New York, NY 10016

© The Regents of the University of California 2016

"The Trolley Problem Mysteries" by F. M. Kamm was delivered as a Tanner Lecture
on Human Values at the University of California, Berkeley, March 2013. Printed with
the permission of the Tanner Lectures on Human Values,
a corporation, University of Utah, Salt Lake City.

Library of Congress Cataloging-in-Publication Data
Kamm, F. M. (Frances Myrna)
The trolley problem mysteries / F.M. Kamm ; with commentaries by Judith Jarvis
Thomson, Thomas Hurka, Shelly Kagan ; edited and introduced by Eric Rakowski.
pages cm. — (The Berkeley Tanner lectures)
Includes index.
ISBN 978–0–19–024715–7 (hardcover : alk. paper)
1. Consequentialism (Ethics)   2. Dilemma.   3. Decision making—Moral
and ethical aspects.   4. Responsibility.   I. Title.
BJ1500.C63K36 2015
171'.5—dc23
2015000999

For Barbara Herman, Judith Thomson, and
Philippa Foot (in memoriam)
With gratitude and respect.

# Contents

## REPLIES TO COMMENTATORS

# Contributors

THOMAS HURKA is Chancellor Henry N. R. Jackman Distinguished Professor of Philosophical Studies at the University of Toronto. He previously served as professor of philosophy at the University of Calgary and as a visiting fellow at Oxford. He is a member of the Canadian and American Philosophical Associations and an editorial board member of *Ethics*. Hurka's work centers on moral and political philosophy, with emphases on normative ethical theory and perfectionist moral theories. He has written on issues of punishment, population, nationalism, friendship, and war. Hurka's many contributions include two works on perfectionist moral theory: *Perfectionism* (Oxford University Press, 1993) and *Virtue, Vice, and Value* (Oxford University Press, 2001). He is also the author of *The Best Things in Life: A Guide to What Really Matters* (Oxford University Press, 2010) and *British Ethical Theorists from Sidgwick to Ewing* (Oxford University Press, 2015).

SHELLY KAGAN is Clark Professor of Philosophy at Yale University. Prior to his appointment at Yale, Kagan taught at the University of Pittsburgh and the University of Illinois at Chicago. Kagan's work focuses on moral philosophy, and more specifically on normative ethics. He has published widely, on topics including well-being, desert, mortality, and Kantianism. However, the main focus of his research has been consequentialism and its contrast with deontological moral theories. Kagan is the author of numerous influential works including *The Limits of Morality* (Oxford University Press, 1989), which offers a defense of consequentialism, *Normative Ethics* (Westview, 1997), *Death* (Yale University Press, 2012), and *The Geometry of Desert* (Oxford University Press, 2012).

F.M. KAMM is Lucius Littauer Professor of Philosophy and Public Policy, Kennedy School of Government, and Professor of Philosophy, Harvard University. Kamm's work focuses on normative ethical theory and applied ethics. She is the author of *Creation and Abortion* (1992), *Morality, Mortality*, vols. 1 and 2 (1993, 1996), *Intricate Ethics* (2007), *Ethics for Enemies: Terror, Torture, and War* (2011), *The Moral Target: Aiming at Right Conduct in War and Other Conflicts* (2012), and *Bioethical Prescriptions* (2013), all from Oxford University Press. She serves on the editorial board of *Philosophy & Public Affairs*, among other journals, and on the Faculty Advisory Committee of the Edmond J. Safra Ethics Center. She has held Guggenheim and National Endowment for the Humanities Fellowships and is a fellow of the American Academy of Arts and Sciences.

ERIC RAKOWSKI is Halbach Professor of Trust & Estates Law at the University of California at Berkeley. His philosophical work is concerned primarily with questions of distributive justice, deciding whom to aid when not all can be helped, and biomedical ethical problems. He is the author of *Equal Justice* (Oxford University Press, 1991).

JUDITH JARVIS THOMSON is Professor Emeritus of Philosophy at MIT. She has held visiting appointments at the Australian National University, the University of Pittsburgh, the University of California at Berkeley, and Yale Law School. Thomson is widely recognized for her work in metaphysics, the theory of action, causation, and ethics, where her writing on moral rights has earned special attention. Her books include *Acts and Other Events* (Cornell University Press, 1977), *Rights, Restitution, and Risk* (Harvard University Press, 1986), *The Realm of Rights* (Harvard University Press, 1990), *Moral Relativism and Moral Objectivity* (with Gilbert Harman) (Wiley-Blackwell, 1996), *Goodness and Advice* (Princeton University Press, 2003), and *Normativity* (Open

Court, 2008). Thomson has held fellowships from the National Endowment for the Humanities, the Guggenheim Foundation, and the Centre for Advanced Study at Oslo. She is also a member of the American Academy of Arts and Sciences.

# The Trolley Problem Mysteries

# Introduction

Eric Rakowski

What has come to be known as the trolley problem originated in Philippa Foot's inconclusive early essay on the morality of abortion. She there imagined, by way of comparison, a group of spelunkers deciding whether to dynamite a companion stuck in the only exit from a flooding cave, a judge hanging an apparently blameless suspect to save more innocents from a bloody-minded mob, a pilot whose airplane is going down choosing to aim for a more or less populated area, a doctor who could kill a healthy individual to produce a serum or obtain body parts to save several patients from death, and, fatefully, the driver of a runaway tram whose vehicle will strike and kill five workmen unless he steers it onto another track where it will kill only one workman. Foot thought that the driver should not hesitate to redirect the tram, whereas the doctor and the judge should not take the life of an innocent person. She was less sure about abortion.

Foot can be forgiven for not foreseeing how many journal pages and seminar hours would later be devoted to her examples. One can fairly ask whether that allocation of time and effort has been wise, or whether it might have been spent more profitably examining more common trade-offs between gains and risks.[1] The trolley problem has, however, proved a uniquely fascinating puzzle for moral philosophers for nearly forty years. That is largely owing to the imaginative and challenging work of two people: Judith Jarvis Thomson and Frances Kamm.

The trolley problem is a problem of moral justification. What accounts for the conviction that Foot's tram driver should, or at least may, turn his brakeless vehicle away from the five workmen, knowing that it will then kill a different worker, while simultaneously sustaining the belief that a doctor may not kill a healthy person to enable five dying patients to live? A multitude of justificatory principles could yield what seem the right answers in these cases. How ought one to choose among them?

The dominant approach to the trolley problem has been to vary the examples to see which of the candidate principles best match our intuitive reactions to the test cases and their variants, while themselves offering compelling expressions of our more fundamental moral beliefs. Suppose, for instance, that the trolley can be turned not by its driver but by a passenger. Or suppose that a bystander alone can do it. Does it make a difference if the trolley, once diverted, would loop back around and kill the five *unless* it hits and kills the lone workman? If the bystander may or should turn the trolley when he can, may he instead push a person onto the tracks, or cause a person to fall onto the tracks, if sending that person to his death is the only way he can stop the trolley and save the five? Does it matter who that possible victim is, whether on a side track or subject to being pushed—another worker, a foreigner, the bystander's friend, a personal enemy? And as for the doctor, is it significant whether it is his fault that five patients face death if he does nothing to help them at the cost of another person's life? If the five can be saved not by physically assaulting one other person but by using a machine that emits a gas that the doctor knows will fatally poison someone else nearby, may he proceed? Examples proliferate, the contours of the justificatory problem shift, and the job of tailoring moral principles to fit the cases grows exponentially more complex.

Almost singlehandedly at first, in clear, arresting prose, Thomson drew attention to Foot's puzzles, modified her cases to make them more analytically useful, and punched holes in possible justifications for what she thought were sound intuitive responses to evocative scenarios. She originated the term "the trolley problem," applying it, as this volume's exchange between Kamm and Thomson elucidates, in two separate articles to two distinct difficulties: first, the task of explaining why the *trolley driver* may direct the vehicle away from the five workmen even if it will thereby plow into another worker, whereas a surgeon ordinarily may not extract organs from one healthy person to save five lives; and second, the task of explaining why a *bystander* may switch the trolley from a track leading to five workers to a track leading to one, whereas the surgeon may not make an involuntary organ donor of the healthy patient to keep alive five terminally ill patients. Finally, it was Thomson who, after proposing and defending several solutions to the two trolley problems over the ensuing decades, at last concluded that the second version of the trolley problem—the one involving a bystander able to change the trolley's course—was no problem at all. The second problem dissolves, she argued, because on reflection a bystander may *not* spare the five workmen if switching the trolley's track would thereby kill a single workman who otherwise would live.

Thomson initiated and carried forward the inquiry Foot framed but never pressed. Philosophers' collective thinking about the trolley problem and many other life-or-death decisions, however, owes as much today to Kamm's writing. Her ingenious examples, designed to expose the implications of making or forgoing some moral commitment, and her tenacious interrogation of competing views, have earned her envy and respect. First tackling the trolley problem in the 1980s, Kamm returned to it and to her preferred solution again and again, refining her arguments and defenses. Nobody else has added nearly as much to our understanding of the normative commitments that rival approaches to the trolley problem entail.

This skeletal summation fails to do justice to the wealth of contributions by others to discussions of the trolley problem and the wrongness of killing or letting die in a myriad of actual and hypothetical cases.[2] Many of the world's leading moral philosophers have weighed in over the last thirty years. It does, however, spotlight the present volume's importance. In these Tanner Lectures, delivered at Berkeley in 2013, Kamm lays out in resplendent detail her current thinking on the trolley problem. In Lecture I, she seeks to explain the moral significance of *who* must decide whether to turn the trolley, or knock someone onto the track to halt its advance, or stop it using means, such as a bomb, that would kill somebody who otherwise would live. In Lecture II, Kamm focuses instead on the moral importance of *how* the trolley is turned, because in Kamm's view the permissibility of preventing a runaway trolley from killing five at the expense of one person who is not among the five depends on the nature of the link between the action and the harm suffered by the one. Actions that harm a person directly while serving as means to the greater good of keeping five alive, such as pushing the single person onto the track to stop the trolley from striking the five, she believes are impermissible. But actions that are, in a certain sense, identical with the good of saving five or some component of that good, such as a driver or bystander's altering the moving trolley's direction, are in Kamm's view permissible.

In setting forth and defending her complex approach to the trolley problem and a vast array of other cases in which an agent must decide whether to allow some to die when fewer other people might die instead, Kamm devotes a substantial part of both lectures to an extended critique of Thomson's views. In her commentary on Kamm's lectures, Thomson replies, trenchantly. She finds fault with a number of Kamm's arguments and restates the case for thinking that a bystander (as opposed to a trolley driver) may not redirect the trolley from five to one. Kamm then devotes even more space in her replies to meeting Thomson's criticisms, at the same time sharpening her dissent from Thomson's current view. This is a truly remarkable exchange between the two leading contributors to this moral philosophical debate. It makes these lectures, commentaries, and replies absolutely invaluable for future work on the trolley problem.

In addition to engendering discussion about what agents should or may do when they can either allow a harm to occur to one group of people or themselves harm another group instead, the trolley problem has sparked sharp disagreements about philosophical method. The foundation of the trolley problem is a pair of firm beliefs about moral duties or permissions in particular circumstances. The trolley driver *should*, or *may*, turn the trolley from five to one. The doctor *may not* remove parts of one person's body to save five other people. What moral principle or set of principles best accounts for these beliefs? We want the principles we endorse and our reactions to cases to cohere. As the cases become more complex and further from everyday experience, however, questions often arise as to whether we should honor our intuitive reactions to those cases and attempt to modify the principles we are inclined to accept in order to validate those reactions, or whether we should consider our reactions mistakes, given our allegiance to principles with which those reactions cannot convincingly be squared.[3] The commentaries by Judith Thomson, Thomas Hurka, and Shelly Kagan all criticize Kamm's ethical methodology. They allege that it unduly privileges intuitive responses to bizarre or overly complicated hypothetical test cases. They further contend, for different reasons, that the principle Kamm develops to handle trolley problem scenarios—the Principle of Permissible Harm—lacks the resonance with our deepest moral convictions that so crucial a principle should have. Hurka finds the account of causation implicit in Kamm's principle arbitrary and underdeveloped, and he thinks the Principle of Permissible Harm's implications are counterintuitive in a number of cases involving killing in wartime. Kagan argues that Kamm has failed to offer a compelling rationale for her principle, regardless of how successfully its implications match our intuitions in test cases. He suggests that we might be wise to adopt a more reformist approach to the trolley problem, elbowing aside at least some of our case-specific intuitions out of regard for more fundamental moral principles we think more surely are true. Kamm responds to these overarching doubts about method as well as to these targeted substantive criticisms in her replies to each of the commentators.

The present volume by no means spans the immense terrain of argument that Foot's imaginative hypotheticals opened up.[4] But it showcases some of the best of current thinking, by the leading voices in the field.

## Notes

1. See, for example, Barbara H. Fried, "What *Does* Matter? The Case for Killing the Trolley Problem (or Letting it Die)," *Philosophical Quarterly* 62 (2012): 505–529.

2. For an absorbing account of the trolley problem and related cases, including biographical sketches of key philosophical participants and brief accounts of some of the moral doctrines thought to bear on those cases, see David Edmonds, *Would You Kill the Fat Man? The Trolley Problem and What Your Answer Tells Us about Right and Wrong* (Princeton, NJ: Princeton University Press, 2014).

3. Philosophical arguments are appeals from an author to an audience to see or respond or understand in a certain way. They are not reports on opinion polls. Nonetheless, in trying to determine what each of us should conclude about the tug of intuitions or the robustness of tentatively held principles, we might be interested to learn what others think. One set of experiments, conducted between December 2009 and October 2011, tends to show that people are more certain that an innocent person should not be pushed onto the trolley tracks to save five than they are that a bystander may or should switch the trolley from five to one. And this difference in certainty can lead some who initially favored the bystander's turning the trolley to abandon that

view to achieve what they regard as greater consonance with their response to the pushing case. See Mark Kelman and Tamar Admati Kreps, "Playing with Trolleys: Intuitions About the Permissibility of Aggregation," *Journal of Empirical Legal Studies* 11 (2014): 197–226. Thomson's thinking has followed this same arc, for reasons she supplies in her commentary.

4. Consequentialist views are not discussed at any length, for example. My own approach to the trolley problem can be found in Eric Rakowski, "Taking and Saving Lives," *Columbia Law Review* 93 (1993): 1063–1156, reprinted in *Bioethics*, ed. John Harris (New York: Oxford University Press, 2001). It diverges markedly from both Kamm and Thomson's current views. I argue that an individual ordinarily may not be killed without her consent for the sake of others but that, in many instances, decision makers may justifiably rely on victims' hypothetical consent to a policy of maximizing the number of lives saved in choosing to save the larger group.

# The Trolley Problem Mysteries

# Lecture I

## Who Turned the Trolley?

**F. M. KAMM**

### 1.

Some philosophers, known as *act-consequentialists*, believe that insofar as the greater number of people surviving is the greater good, it is always right for anyone to do what brings about their survival.[1] Nonconsequentialists deny that it is always right to do whatever brings about the greater good, though they need not deny that consequences matter in some ways to the rightness of acts. As support for their view, nonconsequentialists have cited the Transplant Case: if a doctor kills a single healthy person, she will be able to use his organs to produce what we shall assume is the greater good, saving five fatally ill patients each of whom is equal in all morally relevant respects to the one healthy person. (See diagram 1. Diagrams of the various cases discussed in Lecture I and Lecture II appear on pages 103–109.) Yet, intuitively, it seems impermissible for the doctor to kill the one to save the five.

However, the philosopher Philippa Foot noted that even many nonconsequentialists think it is permissible to kill one to save five in the following case: A driver is driving a trolley (which Foot called a "tram") when it becomes clear that it is headed toward killing five people on one track and cannot brake. It can only be stopped from killing the five by the driver redirecting it away from them onto another track where it will kill one different person, who is equal in all morally relevant respects to each of the five.[2] (Trolley Driver's Two Options Case, represented in diagram 2, with the trolley symbolized by the short horizontal line. All diagrams should be understood to allow the trolley to be moved back from where it is and onto a different track.) Some nonconsequentialists find it mysterious that it is permissible to kill in this case but not in Transplant, even though in both it is a question of killing one to save five, and they think that explaining this mystery just is the trolley problem. (Indeed, when Judith Thomson introduced the title "the trolley problem," she applied it to the question of how to distinguish the permissibility of the driver turning his trolley in Foot's case from the impermissibility of killing in Transplant.[3])

However, this suggestion about what the trolley problem is should not be understood so narrowly that the problem concerns only these two cases rather than all cases that are structurally similar. For example, one might face the question of whether it is permissible to redirect the trolley off a track and onto a slope leading to someone far away from any track, even though one may not generally kill someone to stop a threat to others.[4] Similarly, the question might arise of whether it is permissible to redirect a flood or unmanned missile headed for a large city with many people toward a country town with few people in it, even if one may not kill people in some other way to stop the threat to the large city. We might face an analogous problem when lives are not at stake but only significant harm to either a larger or a smaller group of people. For convenience, I shall use the names "Transplant" and "Trolley Case" when they exemplify the general problem.

Even more broadly, we could see the trolley problem, understood as I have so far described it, as presenting a challenge to nonconsequentialists who, in some rough way, think there is what is called a side-constraint on harming nonthreatening people to produce greater goods. A side-constraint is not merely a factor that weighs against producing the greater good; it is supposedly a factor that has priority over producing the greater good. That is, we may produce the greater good only if doing so is consistent with respecting that constraint. One view is that side-constraints are individual rights giving rise to correlative duties owed to the right bearer by others and that they reflect fundamental aspects of our conception of persons and their status, which are the background to pursuing persons' good. The challenge is to explain exactly what the side-constraint on harming amounts to, and what its form is, if it does not exclude turning the trolley and thus killing one person to save five others.

On the basis of what I have said so far, we can see why the cases that have been the focus of attention in trolley problem discussions seem artificial and unrealistic. They are specifically constructed, like scientific experiments, to distinguish among and test theories and principles (e.g., consequentialist vs. nonconsequentialist theories) because one theory or principle would imply the permissibility of conduct that the other theory or principle would deny. Using our intuitive judgments about which implications for cases are correct helps us decide among, and also revise, theories and principles. (It would not help us with these goals to do as some recommend and spend less time thinking about unrealistic cases involving hard choices, such as letting five die or killing one, and more time making sure that in real life we always have other options available.)

In taking up at least part of the challenge of explaining what the nonconsequentialist side-constraint on harming amounts to, there are two general questions with which we shall deal in these lectures. First, there is the question of whether there is a moral difference between killing others and only letting them die, such that someone who would otherwise kill many people may permissibly kill fewer other people instead, but someone who would otherwise only let many people die may not kill fewer other people instead. A second question is whether there is a constraint on harming people for the sake of producing a greater good only when we come to harm them in some ways but not in other ways. In other words, is coming to harm them in some ways consistent with proper respect for persons but coming to harm them in other ways not?

These questions are analogous to those typically asked by detectives in mystery cases when someone has been killed, namely *who* done it and *how* was it done? Like prosecutors, we can also be concerned that the answers to these questions may bear on whether foul play has occurred.

This lecture will focus on the "who" question and Lecture II on the "how" question. In particular, the first part of this lecture will discuss various elements and proposed solutions to the trolley problem as I have so far characterized it. It will then consider an alternative view of what the trolley problem is. The second part will deal with some recent views of the philosopher Judith Thomson, expressed in her 2008 paper "Turning the Trolley,"[5] about how a moral distinction between killing and letting die may eliminate what she now thinks of as the trolley problem. The third part will consider a different argument for the conclusion that Thomson favors, but it ultimately attempts to resurrect the trolley problem and to help defend a position that Thomson herself once held in earlier work.

## 2.

A. Understood as the contrast between Transplant and Trolley Cases, many proposals have been offered to solve the trolley problem. One relies on a view known as the Doctrine of Double Effect (DDE), which implies that it is impermissible to kill in Transplant because the doctor *intends* the death of the single person as a means to saving the five. The DDE holds that it is wrong to intend an evil such as a person's death, even as a means to a greater good. In Foot's case, by contrast, the death of the one is only a foreseen side effect of turning the trolley and, according to the DDE, merely foreseen harms caused by using otherwise innocent and necessary means can be outweighed by producing a greater good. (A revision of the DDE would also rule out intending merely the involvement of the single person when it foreseeably leads to his death.[6])

B. Responding to this proposal, Foot argued that, intuitively, it is often wrong to use otherwise innocent, necessary means that will merely foreseeably cause someone's death (without even intending his involvement) in order to maximize lives saved. For example, she said, it seems impermissible for a doctor to use a gas that will save five patients if it is foreseen that the gas will kill one immovable bystander as a mere side effect (the Gas Case). Similarly, it seems to me impermissible to set off a bomb that will stop the trolley from hitting the five when a piece of the bomb will kill a bystander as a side effect. (This is the Bomb Trolley Case as illustrated in diagram 3.) Furthermore, it has been argued by some that, contrary to the DDE, intending a harm cannot itself make an act impermissible though it can affect the moral worth of the act.[7] Here is an example involving a trolley: the driver could permissibly turn the trolley from five people even if he only did so because he intended to kill the one person on the other track who is his enemy (Bad Man Trolley Case). Hence, it seems, the DDE fails to explain why killing is permissible in Foot's case but not in Transplant.

# 3.

A. Foot's own proposal is that the driver may redirect the trolley because he is choosing between a negative duty not to kill five people and a negative duty not to kill one person, and he should kill fewer rather than a greater number. By contrast, the doctor in Transplant is choosing between letting five die and killing one, and the negative duty not to kill takes precedence over the positive duty to aid. Hence, the distinction between negative and positive duties, in these cases represented by not killing and not letting die, is held to explain and justify the nonconsequentialist intuitive judgments in Foot's Trolley Case and in Transplant.

One possible objection to Foot's proposal is that it could be unclear whether the trolley driver is in the process of doing what will kill the five or, rather, is only in a position to let what will kill them—namely, the out-of-control trolley—occur. If the latter were true, he may become the killer of the five people in virtue of having first started the trolley and choosing to let it continue, but at the time of deciding whether to turn it perhaps he would only be letting the five die if he did not redirect. Judith Thomson agrees with Foot that the driver would be killing the five if he does not redirect. In her 2008 article, she imagines a case where a car driver "suddenly sees five people on the street ahead of him, but his brakes fail: he cannot stop his car, he can only continue onto the street ahead or steer to the right (killing one) or steer to the left (killing himself). If he doesn't steer to one or the other side, if he simply takes his hands off the wheel, he runs the five down and kills them. He cannot at all plausibly insist that he merely lets them die. So similarly for the trolley drivers."[8]

Hence, both Foot and Thomson see Foot's case as like one in which the driver is at a cross point and must decide whether to turn the trolley toward five or toward one. Let us assume that this is true in Foot's case, though we shall return to this issue in discussing other cases below.

B. Here is another objection to Foot's proposal that someone who would otherwise kill (not merely let die) a group of people may kill fewer other people. The objection is that her proposal would permit too much. To see this, suppose the driver could stop the trolley from hitting the five only by pressing a button that causes a device to topple a fat man standing on a bridge so that he falls in front of the trolley. His weight would stop the trolley though he would be killed by it. Call this the Driver Topple Case. (See diagram 4.) Intuitively, toppling the fat man seems as impermissible as killing in Transplant, even if toppling, like redirecting, would involve the driver's killing one rather than killing five by mechanical means. (My case involves use of a mechanical device because some have proposed that it is only the "up close and personal" pushing of the fat man that is impermissible. I disagree with this view.) Thomson introduced a case in which a *bystander*, not the driver, can stop the trolley only by pushing the fat man, and she concluded that his doing so was impermissible. (Call this the Bystander Topple Case.)[9] However, she did not consider whether the *driver* may push the fat man or topple him using a mechanical device when this is his only way to stop the trolley. In addition, as already suggested by diagram 3, I think the driver may not set a bomb to stop the trolley when a piece of the bomb would kill another person as a side effect. Furthermore, it seems to me that the driver may not even press a button to topple the fat man whose fall is needed to stop the trolley or set the bomb that will kill someone when he has another option of turning the trolley from the five people to a track where it will kill two other people. Call this the Driver Redirect or Topple Case.

Those who will otherwise impermissibly kill the five may not do just anything to minimize the number that they kill, even when doing so would be the strict alternative at a specific time to killing the five (or the strict alternative to killing two other people by redirecting the trolley). Suppose the driver's taking his hands off the steering mechanism would be his killing the five (as Thomson says), and his keeping his hands on it would involve his pressing the button that topples the fat man whose fall stops the trolley. Here, toppling the one to stop the trolley would be the alternative to one way of killing five, but it seems impermissible. Or suppose the driver's steering to the right would kill two people but pressing a button instead would topple the fat man whose fall would stop the trolley: each act would be an alternative to the other and to heading to the five people, but only steering to the right would be permissible. Foot's failure to consider the limits on what the driver may do is one problem with her analysis, I think.

Given the limits on the ways in which the driver may bring about others' deaths, some might think that the trolley problem is to explain why it is permissible to kill some people in some ways but not in other ways as the alternative to killing a greater number of different people, even if it is not permissible to kill someone as the alternative to merely letting others die.[10]

C. Another challenge to the adequacy of Foot's killing versus letting die explanation of the difference between Transplant and her Trolley Case is that it would permit too little, ruling out some permissible acts. This was the point of Thomson's brilliant Bystander Case, in which the driver is unable to do anything to stop the trolley but a bystander can press a switch and redirect the trolley.[11] (This case is the same as represented in diagram 2, except that a bystander, not a driver, would turn the trolley.) The bystander's doing so would involve his killing one rather than *letting five die.* If it is permissible for him to redirect the trolley, the distinction between otherwise killing and otherwise letting die will not explain why it is permissible for the driver to kill one in Foot's Trolley Case but impermissible for the doctor to kill one in Transplant when, like the bystander, the doctor too would otherwise let five die.[12] Possibly, the killing/letting die distinction could still explain why the driver who would otherwise kill the five might have a duty to kill fewer people in a permissible way while a bystander who would merely let five die has the option but not a duty to permissibly kill one other person. Now consider a case in which the driver himself would be choosing between killing one and letting five die. Suppose the driver faints after seeing that he is headed on a track toward the five people. In the absence of any hand on the wheel, the trolley is programmed to continue in the same way as it was being driven. The driver awakens in time to decide whether to let the trolley continue on or to redirect it. Arguably, at this point in time the driver does face a choice of letting the five die or killing one, even though letting die would result in his being the killer of the five in virtue of his past act of driving the trolley and his present one of letting the trolley continue on. (In Thomson's car-driving case, discussed earlier, the driver does not already have his hands off the wheel without having decided to remove them (e.g., he has not fainted). Perhaps this makes a difference between her case and mine with respect to whether the driver only lets die at a given time.) The same would be true if the driver is thrown from the trolley and so is not on the threatening entity, but is near a switch at the side of the road with which he could redirect the trolley. Call this the Bystanding Driver Two Options Case. I believe it is permissible for the driver to redirect the trolley in this case. If so, the fact that at a given time someone would be choosing to kill one person rather than to let five others die will not rule out killing.[13]

In many possible cases, it seems clear that sometimes an agent who starts a threat to some people and then separately does not save them from the threat because, for example, the only way to save them would require killing another person will have let the people die at the time he does not save them. This is so even though in virtue of this and his past act he will have killed the person.[14] Indeed, Thomson once discussed a version of Transplant like this.[15] She imagined that the five in Transplant suffered from organ failures caused by the very doctor who contemplates taking organs from his healthy patient to save his own victims. She concluded that, at the time when he would act, this culpable doctor faced a choice between killing one and letting the five die and that he had no more right than any other doctor to kill in Transplant even though he would become the killer of the five if he did not save them. Suppose that, unlike this culpable doctor, the driver in the Bystanding Driver Two Options Case is permitted to avoid having killed five by redirecting to one other person, even though he is not permitted to topple the fat man to stop the trolley any more than the culpable doctor may kill the one person to save his five victims. Then it might still be suggested that bystanders who will (as I shall say) *merely* let five die, and will not also thus become their killers, may not kill by redirecting the trolley. But, of course, it was the point of Thomson's original Bystander Case to argue against this last claim by suggesting that a mere bystander may also redirect the trolley. However, she also claimed that the mere bystander may not topple the fat man any more than the doctor in the original Transplant Case may kill one patient to save five. Table I.1 displays some of the distinctions we have been discussing:

*Table I.1* Some Distinctions

|  | *Redirect* | *Topple to Stop Trolley* |
|---|---|---|
| Kill vs. kill |  |  |
| Kill vs. mere bystander let die |  |  |
| Kill vs. killer let die |  |  |

In her 2008 article "Turning the Trolley," Thomson claims that the question of why a bystander may permissibly redirect the trolley rather than let five die but not topple the fat man to stop the trolley is (the whole of) the trolley problem.[16] She refers to the question of why a driver who is on the trolley driving it and would kill the five may redirect the trolley but the doctor may not kill in the original version of Transplant as "Mrs. Foot's problem." It may seem surprising that she says Mrs. Foot's problem is *not* the (or part of the) trolley problem, given that when Thomson introduced the title she applied it to Mrs. Foot's problem (as quoted in note 3). However, in a later article, she did switch her use of the title "Trolley Problem" so that it only applied to the contrast between the bystander turning the trolley and his toppling the fat man.[17]

It seems to me that the trolley problem should not be conceived as only the question of why a mere bystander may redirect the trolley but not topple the fat man to stop it. This is, in part, because the same problem of redirecting being permissible but toppling not being permissible arises, I claim, for the trolley driver. This is so whether he would otherwise kill the five people at the time or would let them die, as in the Bystanding Driver Two Options Case.

Both Thomson and Foot fail to consider what the driver may not do and what the bystanding driver may do. In addition, I believe that Foot's original problem is (as it was originally considered by Thomson to be) at least part of the trolley problem. It may just be best to call it and all the "cousin cases" of that original problem parts of the trolley problem.

D. The most striking claim offered by Thomson in her 2008 article is that she now believes that it is not permissible for a mere bystander to redirect the trolley. Indeed, in that article Thomson reversed herself, claiming that it is not any more permissible for the bystander to redirect the trolley toward the one than to topple the fat man to stop the trolley; and therefore, she, a founding mother of the trolley problem, believes there is no trolley problem (given her second view of what the problem is).[18] On these grounds, she further claims that her original Bystander Case cannot be used as an objection to Foot's proposal for distinguishing Foot's Trolley Case from Transplant—namely, that killing one is the permissible alternative to killing five but not to letting five die (and so the driver may redirect but the doctor may not kill). Indeed, she endorses Foot's proposal for distinguishing Foot's Trolley Case and Transplant. In the next part of the lecture, I wish to consider whether Thomson's reversal on the permissibility of a mere bystander redirecting the trolley is right (or whether we should defend something like Thomson's original position against her revised one).[19] However, it is first important to re-emphasize that if being in the position of letting five people die rather than killing another person rules out turning the trolley, then the bystanding driver will also not be permitted to turn the trolley. If, as I believe, he is permitted to do this, Foot's proposal might be minimally revised to allow this on the grounds that "one may not kill rather than merely let others die but one may kill rather than become the killer of others." But if a bystanding driver or even a regular driver is permitted to kill by redirecting, but still is not permitted to topple the fat man to stop the trolley killing the five, then at least one component of the broader trolley problem will remain—namely, about moral differences in how we come to kill someone.[20]

# 4.

Let us now put aside the Bystanding Driver Two Options Case and consider Thomson's 2008 discussion of her mere Bystander Case.

A. One of her arguments against the permissibility of a mere bystander redirecting is based on what she calls the Bystander's Three Options Case (diagram 5). By contrast to the ordinary Bystander's Two Options Case, in which the bystander has a choice between letting five die or redirecting the trolley to a track where one different person will be killed by it, in the Bystander's Three Options Case:

> The switch available to this bystander can be thrown in two ways. If he throws it to the right, then the trolley will turn onto the spur of track to the right, thereby killing one workman. If he throws it to the left, then the trolley will turn onto the spur of track to the left. The bystander himself stands on that left-hand spur of track, and will himself be killed if the trolley turns onto it. Or, of course, he can do nothing, letting five workmen die.[21]

(In diagram 5, "X" represents the bystander.) Concerning her Bystander's Three Options Case, Thomson first argues that the bystander may not redirect toward the right when he could redirect toward himself: "if A wants to do a certain good deed, and can pay what doing it would cost, then—other things equal—A may do that good deed only if A pays the cost himself."[22] Call this the Self-Cost Claim. Second, she argues that since the bystander is not morally required to sacrifice his life to save the five, doing so would be altruism (and supererogatory, I would add). Hence, given that he has permission only to harm himself to save the five when he can harm himself, and he does not want to and morally need not do so, he should let the five die. When in the Bystander's Two Options Case there is actually no option of turning the trolley on himself, Thomson says there is still "no way in which he can decently regard himself as entitled to make someone else pay" a cost that he would not pay if he could. Let us consider this first argument before presenting another one that she offers. In saying, in the second step of the argument, that the bystander need not sacrifice his life to save the five, Thomson is relying on another aspect of a nonconsequentialist ethical theory: that one has, in general, no duty to do what will bring about the greatest good at extreme cost to oneself, even if one would violate no side-constraints in doing so. I agree with this part of her argument. It helps us see that one could raise some of the same issues that Thomson raises by her Bystander's Three Options Case by using a two-options case. For suppose that if a bystander were to turn the trolley away from the five, it would break the bystander's back. From a nonconsequentialist point of view, this could be a justification for his not turning it, even though the five will die. Suppose that to avoid breaking his back, he permissibly would not turn it. How then, we might ask, can he decently turn the trolley in cases where it would not break his back but will kill one other person?

My first concern with Thomson's argument is that she moves from a three-options case to a conclusion about a two-options case. It might be said that one cannot, in general, move from a conclusion in a three-options case to one in a two-options case (and vice versa). For example, if we have three choices, among letting a murder occur or stopping it by killing the murderer or stopping it by shooting him in the leg, it is impermissible to kill him. However, this does not mean it is impermissible to kill him if that is one's only alternative to letting the murder occur. Here is a more complicated case involving moving from permissibility in a three-options case to impermissibility in a two-options case. I assume it is impermissible for the driver to topple a fat man to stop the trolley even when this will only paralyze him; he must let the trolley go to the five in this two-options case. Yet this is consistent with the permissibility of toppling the fat man in the following three-options case: If the driver turns the trolley away from the five, it will go up on a bridge and kill a fat man. If he instead topples the same fat man in front of the same trolley to stop it, the driver will only paralyze him. If he would otherwise permissibly turn the trolley and so kill the fat man, it becomes permissible, and even only permissible, for him in this three-options case to topple this fat man.[23] Yet the permissibility of toppling in the three-options case as a substitute for what would be a more harmful permissible option were it one's only option does not imply toppling is permissible in the two-options case.

However, in these cases, the third option—shooting the murderer in the leg or paralyzing the fat man—that either is not present or should not be taken in the two-options case would be taken in the three-options case. In Thomson's argument, the third option of the bystander sacrificing himself—which is missing in the two-options case—would permissibly *not* be taken. So it might be thought that if an option would permissibly not be taken even were it present, its absence in the two-options case could not affect what may be done, and so if it were impermissible to redirect to the bystander in the three-options case, it would be so in the two-options case.

But this is not so. For whether an option is permissible may depend on what the alternative is even if that alternative would not be taken. For example, there might be an interaction effect caused by the mere presence of the third option even if it is not taken, and this interaction effect might make the second option impermissible in the three-options case without its being impermissible when the third option is not present. In particular, making a choice between oneself and another might necessitate treating the other as one treats oneself, even if one need not treat him as one would treat oneself when there is no such choice to be made.[24] So someone might agree with Thomson that in the three-options case the bystander may not choose to sacrifice the other when he could sacrifice himself, or more weakly, that he must at least give himself and another equal chances of being sacrificed, and yet hold that he may turn the trolley on the one person in the ordinary two-options case.

In fact, I think that in the three-options case there is no special interaction effect between the second and third options, and the bystander need not refrain even in that case from imposing costs on another person that he could, but will not, impose on himself.

My second major concern with Thomson's argument is that in considering her Bystander's Three Options Case, Thomson first concludes that it is impermissible for the bystander to turn the trolley to the one person when he could turn it to himself instead. Only afterwards does she argue that it is permissible for the bystander not to turn it to himself to save the five.[25] Let us consider the first step on its own. Suppose, for argument's sake, that the bystander's turning the trolley toward the one person rather than toward himself would be indecent. This alone may not show that it is impermissible to so turn. For consider a case in which only a very small cost would be necessary to do the good deed of saving the five (e.g., throwing them one's spare life preserver) but the bystander is not willing to pay it. From what Thomson says, it seems to follow that it would be impermissible for him to make another person pay the very small cost in order to save the five (e.g., throw the other person's spare life preserver when that person also does not want to throw it). But even if it were indecent, it does not seem to be impermissible because refusing to pay the small cost is, presumably, wrong of each person given that five will otherwise die. (Thomson does not seem to object to imposing a cost on someone against his will if he would clearly have a moral duty to pay the cost himself.) Hence, the Self-Cost Claim does not seem to be true.[26] While I agree that the bystander's not giving up his life to save the five is not in itself impermissible, my point here is that, at the very least, one needs to first show that it is permissible for the bystander or the other person not to make a sacrifice to save the five before one argues for the impermissibility of the bystander's imposing the cost on another if he will not pay it himself. For if the cost is required of each, a person's failing to make the sacrifice may not show that it is impermissible for him to impose it on another. Indeed, a very strong general claim might be suggested:

*Strong Claim 1*

If it would be permissible to impose a cost on someone for some end were there no alternative, it need not become impermissible to do so merely because one does not impose the cost on someone else when one should.

(This claim is meant to apply whether the person on whom one should impose the cost is oneself or another person.) If this is so, then one cannot show that it is impermissible to impose a cost on another when it is either the only way or one of the ways to achieve a goal simply by showing that one would not impose it on oneself, even if one should impose it on oneself rather than on another. For example, suppose it is permissible to impose on rich people the small cost of saving many lives. However, one morally should impose the cost on the richest of the rich before one imposes it on the less rich. Even if it is morally wrong not to follow this order in deciding on whom to impose, this alone does not make it impermissible to impose the cost on the less rich person. For suppose that it would be a greater moral wrong for many people to die because of not imposing a small cost on a rich person rather than for a less rich person to be imposed on when a richer person should have been imposed on. Then the fact that we indecently or unfairly do not impose the cost on the right people does not show that it is impermissible to impose it on someone else.[27] (Notice that Strong Claim 1 does not deny that sometimes unfairness, which is an interaction effect between possible options, could be a more important consideration than what will happen if we do not do what would be permissible were no other option available. Hence, even if unfairness barred imposing on person A when we had the option to impose on person B, this would not imply that it is impermissible to impose on A when there is no possibility of imposing on B.) It may, of course, be impermissible to impose certain costs on others. My point is that it is not a sufficient argument for showing this that one will not or would not oneself pay the costs. (Below I will give another reason to believe this.) And if one had an independent argument for the permissibility of turning the trolley on someone, one should not assume that it is defeated by the fact that one would not turn the trolley on oneself even if failing to do so were wrong (which I do not think it is).

As background to my third major concern about Thomson's first argument, notice that Thomson's "indecency" argument (i.e., other things equal, there is no way one can decently regard oneself as entitled to make someone else pay a cost one would not pay if one could) may seem reminiscent of a type of argument presented by Gerald Cohen.[28] He suggested that if I do something wrong, I lack the standing to blame you for doing the same thing, even though you are wrong to do it and others besides me may be in a position to blame you. Of course, Thomson does not think that the bystander's failing to give up his life to save the five people would be wrong. It is just that her argument does not appeal to this at the beginning, as I have pointed out; rather, her argument draws a conclusion about what the bystander may not do to someone else just given his own unwillingness to make a sacrifice. This is what may make it seem like Cohen's argument. However, the most important way in which her argument is unlike his is that he is concerned with whether one has the standing to condemn someone's doing the same thing that one has done or is doing, or require that someone else *do* something when one is oneself refusing or has refused to do it, other things equal. This type of concern might imply that it is indecent or impermissible for the bystander to either condemn someone else for refusing *to volunteer his life* or *require him to volunteer his life* when the bystander is refusing or has refused or would refuse to volunteer his own life in the three-options case, other things being equal. By contrast, Thomson wishes to condemn as indecent and impermissible the bystander's *taking* someone's life without that person's consent when the bystander either will not or would not *volunteer* his own. But taking someone's life without his consent involves imposing a cost on another, and this is not the same as demanding that the other person impose the cost on himself altruistically when the bystander will not or would not impose the cost on himself altruistically. It may, of course, be impermissible to impose costs on others without their consent, but I do not think, contrary to Thomson, that a good argument for showing this is that one will not or would not oneself *volunteer* to pay the costs. One place in moral theory where this distinction between imposing a cost on another against his will and giving up something oneself comes to the fore is in Samuel Scheffler's discussion of the agent-centered prerogative not to pay certain costs to maximize the good.[29] Scheffler claimed that such a prerogative could be justified on grounds of protecting an agent's autonomy. However, he claimed that constraining agents from imposing costs on others that those others have a prerogative to refuse to pay on their own could not be justified on grounds of protecting autonomy. This is because constraints restrict an agent's autonomy and imposing costs on another does not restrict his autonomy by requiring him to act one way or another. Elsewhere I have argued in favor of constraints on imposing costs (or harms), negative rights not to have costs imposed without one's consent, and for the connection between constraints and prerogatives.[30] However, I think that sometimes it may be morally permissible to impose costs on others when no one would, or would be required to, impose them on himself (though it is permissible for him to impose them on himself).

Here are some examples. We may sometimes draft someone to be a soldier even if we (and also he) would not and need not volunteer for service (though perhaps only a government may do the drafting). I may permissibly present evidence leading to someone's conviction even if I would not and need not bear witness against myself (nor would he, or need he, bear witness against himself). I may permissibly compete with someone, causing him to lose his business so that I get funds for a cause, though I would not, and morally need not, close my own business to get funds for a cause. Suppose I am a morally innocent threat shot out of a cannon and hurtling toward a victim who will be killed if I fall on him. I do not think I would, or would have a duty to, kill myself to stop my impact. Yet if, as I am hurtling toward my victim, I see another such innocent threat hurtling toward killing another victim, I as a bystander am permitted, I believe, to kill him if this is necessary to stop his fall. Indeed, suppose I am one of two morally innocent threats hurtling toward a victim who will be killed only if both of us fall on him. I think it would be permissible for me to kill the other innocent threat to break his fall even though I would not, and am not obligated to, kill myself.[31] Getting closer to the trolley problem, I may put a shield around the five people protecting them from the trolley, knowing that when the trolley hits the shield it will be deflected to one other person, even if I would not and morally need not put a shield around the five when I know the trolley will be deflected to me. (Notice that in the draft case, resistance by the person imposed on is not (ordinarily) permissible. In the other cases, I think the fact that I may permissibly impose costs on another does not imply that the other may not resist the costs being imposed, at least in certain ways. So the person threatened by the trolley after it is deflected off the shield may permissibly send it back if he can.)

Hence, it is possible that a bystander's *not being willing to* redirect the trolley toward himself only implies that it is "indecent" of him to require someone else to redirect the trolley toward *himself;* it need not imply that it is indecent for him to redirect the trolley to someone else. Similarly, if it is *permissible* for the bystander not to give up his own life, he should recognize that the person on the other track also has the permission not to give up his own life. Further, if it is permissible for the bystander to impose the loss on the other person, he should recognize that it is also permissible for someone else to impose the loss on the bystander in order to save the five. This is the way in which impartiality is required of us. Similarly, if we all established a military draft, each is required to expose himself to the risk of being drafted, but this is consistent with no one having to volunteer for service.[32]

Certainly in cases of letting die, rather than killing or otherwise doing what harms someone, this difference between volunteering and imposing (in a broad sense) holds. Suppose that the only way for me to save five others from drowning is to let myself drown (by giving them a life preserver I need and could otherwise use). I could permissibly refuse to let myself drown and let the five drown instead. Yet it would also be permissible for me to let one *other* person drown, though he does not want me to, in order to save five others instead (by giving the five instead of the one a life preserver when I do not need it). I would permissibly impose a cost on that one by not aiding him that I would permissibly not impose on myself. This, of course, is a case of letting someone die, and Thomson believes (as do I) that there is a moral difference between killing someone and letting him die; but to show that a bystander may not redirect the trolley to the other person, more has to be said than that, other things equal, he should not make someone else pay a cost that he would not and need not pay himself. For this factor would also imply that he may not let the one die to instead save the five if he would not and morally need not let himself die in order to save the five. If one has an independent argument for the permissibility of letting someone die to save others, one cannot show that it is impermissible to do so merely because one would permissibly not let oneself die to save others.

B. Thomson's second argument for the impermissibility of the bystander turning the trolley explicitly does *not* depend on considering what the bystander would or would not do to himself.[33]

She notes that even if the bystander would be an altruist if he could, the one person he would kill if he redirected the trolley in a two-options case might not, and morally need not, consent to be an altruist. This, she thinks, makes the mere bystander doing what costs the other person his life impermissible. Whereas the first argument claims that one may not do to another without his consent what one morally need not and/or would not do to oneself, the second argument claims one may not do to another what he is not required to do to himself and would not consent to have done to him. If this argument were sufficient in itself to make turning impermissible, the fact that the first argument is problematic would not matter. So let us consider if it is sufficient. First, as was noted earlier, imposing a cost on someone is not the same as requiring him to act altruistically by either engaging in self-sacrifice or consenting to someone's imposing a cost on him. Furthermore, it is not generally impermissible to do something to save some people when it would lead to one other person suffering a loss he need not and permissibly does not consent to suffer. This is true in the case described earlier where we put a shield around the five people, knowing that it will deflect the trolley to the one; and in the case in which a bystander kills a morally innocent threat to prevent the threat killing his victim even though the innocent threat is not morally required to kill himself and does not consent to being killed. The cases mentioned earlier involving harmful competition and bearing witness against another also involve imposing costs on the other person he is not morally required to impose on himself and does not consent to suffer. Further, a person could permissibly not consent to give up his own life or a bystander's life-saving assistance so that the bystander may save five other people instead, and yet it would be permissible for the bystander to help the five and (in a broad sense) impose the loss on the one. If one has an independent argument for the permissibility of leaving someone to die, this argument is not defeated merely by showing that the person need not let himself die. (It is probably crucial to Thomson whether one would be killing rather than not aiding the one person, but I think that her argument is too broad to capture this distinction among cases.)[34]

Hence, for the various reasons I have given, I am not convinced of the truth of either Thomson's *ceteris paribus* claim (which is her Third Principle) that a bystander "A must not kill B to save five if he can instead kill himself to save the five," or of her claim that A must not kill B to save five others if B would permissibly not altruistically sacrifice himself.[35] However, it is important to emphasize that the permissibility of turning the trolley need not imply that the one person who would be hurt by it may not resist this even by turning back the trolley. This is consistent with his having no duty to be an altruist and also implies that it is permissible to resist (what one recognizes is) another agent's permissible act.

C. Now let us consider Thomson's argument for the view that the trolley driver is permitted and even required to redirect to the one person, even though that one does not and morally need not volunteer to be an altruist or consent to the imposition of the loss. (A sign that he need not consent, I believe, is that he may resist being killed even by sending the trolley back or toward the driver who sends it to him. Hence, he may permissibly resist the driver's act even if it is the driver's duty, and nothing about any duty the driver may have gives the one person a duty to consent to the imposition.) Thomson also thinks that the driver should redirect, even though he would not redirect the trolley in a way that will only kill himself to save the five when he has this third option. (Trolley Driver's Three Options Case, represented in diagram 6.) Thomson does think that the driver, unlike the bystander, probably has a duty to kill himself to save the five, though she says she leaves that question "open." This raises the possibility that she might think it permissible for the mere bystander to redirect the trolley when this will only kill the driver on the trolley.[36] The driver who will not kill himself or who has no option to do so is permitted to turn and even must turn toward the unwilling one, she says, because the driver would otherwise unjustly kill five who are also unwilling to be killed. By contrast, Thomson says, the mere bystander will have done no injustice if he leaves the five to die and this makes a significant difference to the permissibility of killing the one.

There are several things that concern me about this additional component of the argument relating to the driver. First, it is possible that a driver who will become the killer of five people because a trolley that he started will, owing to factors beyond his control, kill five people need not be required to deliberately do what will kill someone else even if this is by redirecting the trolley. Suppose the reason the trolley driver gave for letting the trolley go on to the five was that he could not deliberately do what will kill someone in order to stop the killing of five others when that will be due in large part to factors beyond his control. I doubt that we would say that this in itself involved his treating the five unjustly, just as we would not say this if he refused to topple the fat man to stop the trolley. (This argument would not apply if the trolley driver were a villain who had deliberately tried to kill the five.)

However, let us assume that the trolley driver would be unjust to the five both in killing them and if he does not turn the trolley in the ordinary two-options case. Thomson's first argument claimed that the mere bystander is permitted to not save the five when the cost to him of doing so would be very high—for example, his life. But what if the cost to the mere bystander personally is very small and furthermore he had promised to save the five? Then his not saving them may also involve some injustice to them. Presumably, in this case Thomson's view would be that it is impermissible for the bystander to turn the trolley since killing one person on the track is a more serious injustice than breaking a promise to save the five. My point is only that the supposed impermissibility of a mere bystander turning the trolley cannot depend on his committing no injustice if he does not turn. In some cases, if he does not turn, he might be failing to do something he ordinarily "must do," just as the driver would be failing to do something that he ordinarily "must do."

Of course, in arguing that the driver is permitted to redirect when the bystander is not, Thomson does not merely rely on the fact that the bystander's letting die involves no injustice whereas killing the five people is an injustice. She also relies on what she calls the Killing Five Vs. Killing One Principle, which specifically says that A must not kill five if he can kill one instead.[37] But this principle does not seem to be true.[38] For, as I noted earlier, even the driver with his hand on the wheel headed to the five may not set a bomb (with his other hand) that will stop the trolley but also directly kill one other person, and he may not topple the fat man from the bridge in order to stop the trolley from killing the five. (He may also not do these things to someone as the alternative to redirecting the trolley from the five toward killing two different people.) The fact that the driver will unjustly kill five people if he does not do what kills one other person, together with the Killing Five Vs. Killing One Principle, is not enough to free the driver to redirect to the other person if it does not free him to topple the fat man off the bridge or set the bomb as he is driving the trolley toward the five. Thomson says: "But his not steering to the right would itself be unjust, for his only alternative to steering to the right is killing five."[39] But if we could deduce the injustice of the driver's not turning the trolley from the fact that his only alternative is to kill five, we could also deduce the injustice of his not toppling the fat man from the fact that his only alternative is to kill five, but it is not unjust of the driver not to topple the fat man to stop the trolley.

In sum, as I have noted several times, Thomson in her 2008 article does not attend to what even the driver is not permitted to do. She also does not consider what the bystanding driver may do. This may be why she supports the Killing Five Vs. Killing One Principle. As I have already said, it may also be why she says that once we accept that the mere bystander may not redirect, the distinction between killing and letting die explains why the driver who would otherwise kill five may redirect the trolley but the doctor may not kill in Transplant, and the bystander who would merely let five die may not topple the fat man. But this explanation would not rule out the driver's toppling the fat man to stop the trolley when it is the only way to stop his driving into the five (or when it is a further alternative to turning the trolley away from the five and toward two other people). This explanation would also rule out the bystanding driver's killing one by redirecting the trolley rather than letting five die. Hence, it seems to me the explanation is not correct. Thomson is wedded to the idea that the driver must be permitted, and has a duty, to turn the trolley from five to one. Indeed, she is willing to conclude that her reasoning about the mere bystander is wrong if it leads to the view that the driver may not turn the trolley.[40] In the end, what we may find most surprising about Thomson's discussion is not that she argues that the mere bystander may not redirect the trolley, but that her arguments seem to imply that a driver who would otherwise kill five may, at the same time as an alternative, kill in any way at all fewer people in order to stop from killing the five.

It might be suggested that something else, either on its own or in addition to his strong duty not to commit an injustice and kill the five, explains the limited ways in which the driver may kill the one person to save the five (e.g., turning but not toppling). This additional factor could be that the driver's duty is to drive a trolley in the best possible way, so when not killing the five requires driving a trolley that kills one other person, he is permitted to kill. By contrast, toppling people or setting off bombs is not a duty of his, and in these respects he is not otherwise freer than a mere bystander. However, if the driver had to topple a rock or set off a bomb that would not hurt anyone, he would be obligated to do these things to save his five potential victims, even though he has no special responsibility for rocks or bombs. It is the permissibility of what he could do that determines his duty to do it rather than to kill the five, not his special duty for driving his trolley that determines permissibility.[41]

If the driver may do these other things besides drive the trolley to stop it from killing the five, then we cannot explain his not having permission to set off the bomb that will kill someone or topple the fat man to stop the trolley by his special responsibility for driving his trolley well. This again suggests that there is some difference in how an agent kills an innocent nonthreatening person that makes some killings to prevent five being killed permissible and other killings impermissible. A further hypothesis is that this difference marks a distinction between permissible and impermissible killings in general and so for a mere bystander, not just for the driver.[42] If this is so, that the killing would be done by someone who would otherwise kill a greater number of people rather than merely let them die would not be crucial for permissibility.

Indeed, one might be tempted by a strong general claim:

### Strong Claim 2

That one will otherwise unjustly kill innocents does not itself give one any *special* permission that others lack to kill other innocent nonthreatening people to prevent the first injustice.

(It might, however, give one excuses for killing impermissibly and obligations to kill, in ways permitted to everyone, to prevent oneself killing others. These excuses and obligations would not be had by mere bystanders.) Strong Claim 2 is consistent with the person who would otherwise unjustly kill innocents having other permissions that a mere bystander would lack. For example, he might have permission to sacrifice his wealth to save his potential victims even if this would seriously deprive his family. A bystander might not have such permission to do what seriously deprives his family to save the potential victims. The driver in the Trolley Case might also lack permission to go and save ten people he has promised to save rather than do what he can to save the five he would otherwise kill. By contrast, the mere bystander would have permission to go and save the ten others instead of the five. Strong Claim 2 would also have to be consistent with the fact that having to not kill people may give one a stronger reason for action than merely not letting them be killed by others, and that ordinarily having a stronger reason can make acts be permissible that are not permissible for weaker reasons. For example, it might be permissible for me to take your car without your permission if I have to get someone to the hospital but not if I only want to go for a drive. Suppose, however, that I do not have a duty to take someone to the hospital who needs to go but choose to do so anyway. I think it is as permissible for me to take the car as it is for a person who has this duty. It is that someone needs to be saved, not whether I have a duty to save him, that provides a reason that overrides the duty not to interfere with someone else's car. Someone's having a duty to save a person may be part of the stronger personal reason that the person has to act but it is not necessarily part of the stronger reason that overrides another's right to his car. (These are two different types of stronger reason.) This supports the permissibility of the mere bystander's turning the trolley if the driver may turn it, even if the bystander does not have an obligation to do so. That is, the driver has a stronger personal reason for taking advantage of the factors that may make turning permissible, but the factors that make it permissible are present for anyone.

However, here is a case that may be a counter-example to Strong Claim 2. Suppose a driver finds that his trolley will kill many people if it remains at a crossroad where he has driven it and he can redirect it to the left where it will kill Jim or to the right where it will kill Joe. Then he might toss a coin to decide which single person to kill. By contrast, if the trolley was already headed toward killing Joe on the right, it seems that a mere bystander should not toss a coin to decide whether to redirect it to kill Jim on the left. But is this really different from what someone who would otherwise kill may do? Consider whether a driver whose trolley is already headed toward killing Joe on the right may toss a coin to decide whether to redirect to Jim on the left any more than a mere bystander may. He may not be permitted to do this either, I think. Still, this is consistent with anyone who faces a choice between killing Jim or killing Joe *sometimes* (e.g., in the crossroad case) being permitted to kill Jim while someone who faces a choice between killing Jim or letting Joe die is not permitted to kill Jim. In the light of such possible same-number-of-people cases, Strong Claim 2 might have to be revised to the following:

*Strong Claim 3*

That one will otherwise unjustly kill a greater number of innocents does not itself give one any special permission that others lack to kill fewer innocent nonthreatening people to prevent the first injustice.

There might be indirect evidence that it is the general permissibility of killing only in certain ways that is at work in Trolley Cases, rather than that stronger reasons for not killing than for not letting die make killing permissible only for the driver. But the most direct route to showing that what is at issue in Trolley Cases is the general permissibility of killing only in certain ways is to give a good account of the moral differences between different ways of killing that would help explain why some ways are permitted to mere bystanders, as well as to potential killers. This is the question of *how* the trolley was turned rather than by *whom* it was turned. It is the question with which Thomson was at one time concerned when she said: "We ought to be looking within killings and savings for the ways in which the agents would be carrying them out."[43] I shall not discuss that question in this lecture, but will in Lecture II.

# 5.

I have considered Thomson's arguments for the conclusion that one may turn the trolley only if this is the alternative to one's killing people, not to one's letting them die. However, I believe the strongest argument for this conclusion may be one she does not give. Consider the following Bystander Saving-by-Letting-Die Case (diagram 7). Suppose the trolley is on its way to kill eight people. A mere bystander can either turn it away to the left, thereby killing one person on a side track, or turn it to the right, thereby blocking the pathway that he physically must and would shortly use to save five other people, for whose problems he is not responsible but whom no one else can save. In this case, he faces the choice of saving the eight by either killing one person or doing what (arguably) results in his letting five people die. I believe the bystander should do what blocks the pathway, and so do what (arguably) results in his letting five people die rather than in killing one. In this case, it seems, the bystander should not kill someone as the alternative to letting five die.[44] How, then, could it be permissible for the bystander to kill one person rather than let the five die in Thomson's original Bystander Case?

Indeed, what seems especially puzzling is that while the bystander should turn the trolley from the eight in a way that results in his letting the five die rather than in killing the one, if a trolley had been headed to killing the same five people when they were not soon to die anyway, then intuitively it would have been permissible for the bystander to turn it away from them so as to kill the one person. (See "hypothetical trolley" at bottom of diagram 7.) How can these judgments be consistent? How can it be both permissible to kill one rather than to let five die in the latter case and impermissible to kill one rather than to let five die in the Bystander Saving-by-Letting-Die Case?

There are several differences between the ordinary Trolley Case and the Bystander Saving-by-Letting-Die Case that might be thought to explain why the judgments are consistent. One is that when the eight are saved by doing what results in letting the five die, the redirected trolley interferes with some means (the pathway) needed to save the five; it does not threaten the five as it threatens the eight or as it would threaten the one. This would contrast with the regular Trolley Cases in which the trolley threatens the five, not just some means needed to save them. So we should consider another hypothetical two-options Trolley Case in which a trolley is headed to blocking the pathway that a bystander alone could and would use to save five people; it is not headed to the five themselves. In this case, may the bystander redirect the trolley when it will kill one other person instead? I do not think he may do this.[45] Most importantly, the driver of the trolley headed to block a pathway that he alone would use to save five (who were not threatened by him) should not turn the trolley toward killing one other person. Letting some die by allowing or even causing interference with, or destruction of, what is needed to save them (especially when one alone could provide or make use of these means and one is not interfering with others using them), at least intuitively, seems to have different moral significance from letting some die by not stopping what actually will cause their death (as when a trolley is coming at them).

This point is connected to another possible difference between the cases we are now discussing and the original Bystander Case. Namely, in the original Bystander Case, if the bystander turns the trolley from hitting five to hitting one, the one would die from what would have killed the five. By contrast, if he turns the trolley to the one so as to not block the pathway to the five's rescue, the one will not die of what would also have killed the five, as the five need to be rescued from an entirely different threat. However, I do not think this difference is morally crucial. Suppose that in the original Bystander Case, the trolley going toward the five would result in their death by causing a rockslide that killed them, whereas it would directly kill the one. This alone would not change the intuitive judgment that we should turn from the five to the one. Here, however, the second (rockslide) threat might be seen as an extension of the first. But in one version of what I call the Lazy Susan Case, where the trolley which cannot be redirected is headed to five who are seated on a large turntable, our turning the table so that the five are away from the trolley causes a rock slide that kills one person. (See diagram 8.) Here, the one would die of a different cause than would have killed the five (and it is not an extension of the original trolley threat). Yet, I believe, it is permissible to save the five. This supports the view that it is not merely because the one would die of a different cause than the five in the Bystander Saving-by-Letting-Die Case that we may not redirect to the one rather than to block the pathway to the five. Finally, notice that the five could be in need of assistance because before being sent to the eight, the same trolley injured the five who now need to be rescued. Then they would die of the same threat as would face the one, and yet the trolley should not be redirected from the eight to the one.

Notice, however, that if preserving means to save lives does not license killing as an alternative at a given time, this need not be based on a general view of the value of preserving such means by contrast to not killing someone. For it seems permissible to spend time and effort to avoid destroying means that can be used to save five people (even though doing this implies that we lose our only opportunity to save eight people from the trolley without harming anyone) when we can subsequently save the eight by redirecting a threat from them toward one other person. Indeed, we might go to merely rescue those means from being destroyed by natural causes, not avoiding our destroying them, though doing this implies that we also lose the opportunity to save the eight by means other than redirecting a threat to one other person. In these cases, we would not kill one person as a way to avoid interfering with means to save others' lives. Rather, by means that harm no one, we would not allow life-saving means to be destroyed and, as a consequence, we would later kill one by redirection (which seems to be a permissible means) to save eight. In cases where our only option of saving eight does not involve directly choosing between sending the trolley either to destroy the means of saving five or to killing one, it seems permissible not to give up on saving the means merely to be able to use a nonharmful rather than a harmful way of saving the eight.[46]

However, I do not think that pointing to a possible distinction between rescuing means and rescuing a greater number of people is a complete answer to issues raised by the Bystander Saving-by-Letting-Die Case. For it could be argued that it is a mistake to attach the title "Saving-by-Letting-Die" to the case (in diagram 7) at all. After all, we would not be letting the five die at the time when we redirect the trolley to block the path we need to save them. Do we even let them die later, when we lack the means to help them? For if there is later no way for us to help them, and thus we do not refrain from using means to help them, it does not seem right to say that we let them die at that later time. (Though it is true that in blocking the pathway, we do what will result in our being unable to save them.) Hence, there seems to be no time when we would let the five die if we redirected to the path. However, we can still imagine cases that better deserve the title of Bystander Saving-by-Letting-Die. Suppose a deadly car is headed toward killing the five people. If we turn the trolley away from the eight in the direction where it will kill one person, this will also trigger a device that stops the car from hitting the five people. If we turn the trolley away from the eight in the other direction, it stops almost immediately and hurts no one but nothing interferes with the car's hitting the five. (See diagram 9 for Bystander Saving-by-Letting Die (2).) I think the bystander should not do what kills the one; rather, he should save the eight by doing what involves letting the five die. What could distinguish this case from the ordinary Bystander Case? Again, there are several things that might be pointed to. My view is that the morally significant difference is, roughly, that in the ordinary Bystander Case the death of the one is a consequence of redirection when there is no other less harmful redirection possible. By contrast, in Bystander Saving-by-Letting-Die (2), the death of the one would be a consequence of what is really a mere means to saving the five because, even though redirection would also save eight, they could be saved by an alternative redirection that kills no one. Because there is an alternative way to save the eight, if we choose to turn toward the one person, doing what harms him when it also saves five will have the same moral significance as setting off the gas in Foot's case to save five when the gas kills one person as a side effect. Hence, for a nonconsequentialist, it is no wonder that we may not kill rather than let die in this case.[47]

A more difficult case with which to deal, I think, is a closer variant on the original Bystander Saving-by-Letting Die Case (shown in diagram 7). Consider the following case. Suppose the bystander has a choice of turning the trolley from the eight people either to the left, where it will kill one other person, or to the right, where it will disconnect the bystander's privately owned life-support machine that is already saving five people's lives. (See Bystander Saving-by-Letting Die (3), diagram 10, option A.) I believe that terminating one's ongoing life support of others in this way is a case of letting the five die, not of killing them. It seems, at least when it is optional for the bystander to be aiding the five, that he should turn the trolley to where it terminates his assistance to the five, rather than turn to where it will kill the one person.

If he should do this, it would be, at least in part, because the bystander has the permissible option to actively terminate life support he provides and allow the five to die. (I am ignoring the view that having started aiding some, one is committed to them in a way that one is not to those one is not already aiding and that is a definitive consideration.) But in the regular Bystander Case, he also has the permissible option to let the five die, so why is it not true, then also, that he should let the five die rather than kill the one? Could we account for a difference between these cases as follows? The trolley headed to five people in the ordinary Bystander

Case is threatening the lives of those who are not already receiving optional life support; they would lose life that they have a claim not to be interfered with by the trolley driver. So they would have a complaint if they were killed by the trolley driver. A trolley redirected by the bystander to the five on the bystander's life support will cause the five to lose lives they have no claim against the bystander that he not interfere with, when the way he interferes involves terminating his life support. So they would have no complaint if the trolley were redirected to them by the bystander. It is true in both this Bystander Saving-by-Letting-Die (3) and in the regular Bystander Case involving five threatened by the trolley that if the bystander turned the trolley to the one, he would provide life-saving aid to the five and not let them die. However, in the first case, he would save five who would have no complaint in being caused to die by the trolley, and in the second case he would save five who would have a complaint in being caused to die by the trolley.

It is true in both cases that if the bystander lets them die, the five would have no complaint against him in particular because he has no duty (and, in particular, no duty to them) to turn the trolley, even if it is permissible for him to do so. However, it seems that this is not what is morally decisive if it is permissible for the bystander to turn the trolley in the regular Bystander Case. What seems to be morally significant is simply whether the five have a complaint against the trolley's hitting them. If they do, the bystander may refuse to let them be hit. If they do not, he should not turn the trolley toward one person who has a claim not to be interfered with.[48] (This point could also be made by considering what the bystander should do if he faced the choice of turning the trolley from eight only to either five on his optionally provided life support or to five he is not supporting. (This is option B in diagram 10.) In this case, I think he should do what terminates his support rather than kill the five he is not supporting.[49]

By contrast, suppose the bystander faces a choice of saving the eight by redirecting either toward terminating his life support to the five or toward terminating his life support to one other person. (This is option C in diagram 10.) In this case, he may redirect to the one person instead of the five (but on my view this would involve letting the one person die, not killing him).

These points raised in connection with the bystander also apply to the trolley driver. For suppose the trolley driver were headed toward killing five people to whom he was optionally providing life support that they could get nowhere else. The trolley would disconnect them from that life support. I believe that he should not turn the trolley from the five toward killing one person to whom he is not optionally providing life support and who has a claim against him not to be killed. The trolley driver should let the five die rather than kill the one because, in this case, the five will have no complaint against the trolley driver if he ends the life support he is providing. If the trolley driver is unable to do anything, a bystander in this case should also let these five die rather than turn the trolley toward one. Furthermore, it may also be true that sometimes when the driver kills (rather than lets die by disconnecting life support he is providing), there will be no people who will have a complaint about what is happening. For suppose the driver is optionally providing the five with life support. They may have no complaint against him if the trolley directly hits them, rather than disconnecting their life support, for the driver will then be depriving them only of life he is providing to them by way of support he could permissibly discontinue. The five having no complaint may be sufficient grounds for the driver not redirecting the trolley to the one person.

It is important to recognize that these results do not imply that people on life support in general have a weaker right than others not to be killed, or in general have no right not to have their life support interfered with by others. For suppose that the five people in diagram 10 were on life support provided by someone other than the bystander or trolley driver. In such a case, a bystander who turned the trolley from the eight to these would not be letting die by terminating assistance he is providing; I think he would be killing the five by interfering with life support with which he has no right to interfere. The five (and/or those providing the assistance) would have a complaint against him. If so, this should show up in different judgments about the cases in diagram 10. For example, in option A, if the five are as immune from interruption of their life support by the bystander as the one is to being killed, and he may redirect away from the eight who have a complaint against the trolley driver, he would be permitted to redirect to the one person. Similarly, if the trolley driver is headed to five who are on someone else's life-support device, he may have as strong a reason to redirect to one person as if he is headed to five not on life support. This is because these are five who would have a complaint against his trolley's disconnecting their life support.

My tentative conclusion about the Bystander Saving-by-Letting-Die Cases is that even they do not show that a mere bystander may not turn the trolley away from killing the five toward killing one in the original Bystander Case. They just show that sometimes when one merely lets die, there will be no people who will have a complaint about what will happen to them, but that will not always be true when one lets die. However, some of these cases do suggest that whether a trolley may be turned could depend on who would turn it. This is because who threatens people with a trolley could affect whether those people have a complaint against being so threatened, a complaint that is needed to justify redirection. For example, the permissibility of turning could vary depending on whether someone who redirects is already involved in saving those who would be threatened by the trolley. On the other hand, who turns the trolley may not matter when it does not affect whether there is a complaint against being hit by the trolley.

Let me conclude this lecture with a final word about what the trolley problem is. If both the driver and the bystander are permitted to turn the trolley, but neither may topple the fat man or set off the bomb that would kill another person in order to stop the trolley, then the trolley problem is about why it is sometimes permissible to kill, even rather than let die, when we come to kill in some ways but not others. So understood, I think the trolley problem is a real problem that applies to cases not involving trolleys but with a similar structure, and solving it may require explaining the moral differences among different ways of coming to kill. If this is so, then a detective on the trolley problem mysteries cannot (usually) decide whether something wrong was done just by finding out who done it; further investigation would be needed.

## Notes

1. In 2010, I wrote a short entry on the trolley problem for the *International Encyclopedia of Ethics,* ed. Hugh LaFollette et al. (Oxford: Wiley-Blackwell, 2013). The entry was supposed to explain what the problem is, its origins and history, and some proposed solutions and other attempts to defuse the problem. In these lectures, I hope to explore some aspects of these topics at greater length.

2. "The Problem of Abortion and the Doctrine of the Double Effect," in Philippa Foot, *Virtues and Vices and Other Essays in Moral Philosophy* (Oxford: Blackwell, 1978), 19–32.

3. She said of the driver of the trolley (whom she named Edward) and the transplant surgeon (whom she named David): "Why is it that Edward may turn that trolley to save his five, but David may not cut up his healthy specimen to save his five? I like to call this the trolley problem, in honor of Mrs. Foot's example." Judith Jarvis Thomson, "Killing, Letting Die, and the Trolley Problem," *The Monist* 59 (1976): 204–217, 206. In her 1985 article, "The Trolley Problem," she changed her use of the title, applying it to a different set of cases. I shall return to this point later in the lecture.

4. This is one reason why Allen Wood's suggestions that trolley tracks are dangerous places and the one person might be liable to be hit because he is where he should not be is really beside the point and shows his failure to understand the import of the Trolley Cases. See his comment on Derek Parfit's

Tanner Lectures in Derek Parfit, *On What Matters* (New York: Oxford University Press, 2011), vol. 2, 66–82.

5. Judith Jarvis Thomson, "Turning the Trolley," *Philosophy & Public Affairs* 36 (2008): 359–374.

6. See Warren Quinn, "Actions, Intentions, and Consequences: The Doctrine of Double Effect," reprinted in his *Morality and Action* (Cambridge: Cambridge University Press, 1994).

7. See, for example, Judith Jarvis Thomson, "Physician-Assisted Suicide: Two Moral Arguments," *Ethics* 109 (1999): 497–518; T. M. Scanlon, *Moral Dimensions: Permissibility, Meaning, Blame* (Cambridge, MA: Harvard University Press, 2008).

8. Thomson, "Turning the Trolley," 369.

9. Thomson, "Killing, Letting Die, and the Trolley Problem."

10. It might be thought that Foot's proposal could also be faulted for implying that it would be permissible for a doctor to merely let a patient die in order to then acquire his organs for transplantation into the five, for then the doctor would be letting one die (not killing him) rather than letting five die. Foot discusses a case like this and says of the doctor's letting the patient die that "presumably we are inclined to see this as a violation of negative rather than positive duty." Foot, *Virtues and Vices*, 28. This does not seem true, however. If it is wrong that the doctor in this case lets one die in order to save the five, and yet he does not violate a negative duty in doing so, then, it may be said, it is not clear why the distinction between negative and positive duties and between killing and letting die is helpful in distinguishing between Transplant and Trolley. Still, it is possible that we may not violate a negative duty to fulfill a positive one even if we may not always fail in a positive duty to someone in order to fulfill a positive duty to more people, just as I argued in (3B) that we may not always kill fewer people to avoid killing more people.

11. Thomson introduced the Bystander at the Switch Case in her "The Trolley Problem," *Yale Law Journal* 94 (1985), 1397. She says (in n. 5) that a similar case is discussed in N. A. Davis, "The Priority of Avoiding Harm," in Bonnie Steinbock, ed., *Killing and Letting Die* (Englewood Cliffs, NJ: Prentice-Hall, 1980), 172, 194–195. However, in "Killing, Letting Die, and the Trolley Problem," Thomson also discussed a similar case in which the trolley driver dies and only a passenger on the trolley, who would not kill the five if he does nothing, can turn it away from the five.

12. Notice that the doctor in Transplant would not be permitted to kill the one even if she were trying to save the lives of five who would be victims of another person's killing them.

13. In yet another case, the driver may be a mere bystander even if he is *on* the trolley that he is driving toward the five. For suppose that the only way to stop his trolley from hitting the five is for the driver to redirect *another* out-of-control trolley that he is *not* driving and whose driver has died. That second trolley is headed toward killing four and can be redirected onto the track where it will interfere with his own trolley's hitting five, but it will also go on to kill another person (Driver's Other Trolley Case). In this case, the driver is a mere bystander with respect to the second trolley, but he faces a choice between (a) killing five and (b) either letting four die or redirecting the second trolley when this will kill someone but also save the five he threatens. It seems permissible for him to redirect the second trolley, though he then kills one rather than lets four die, all in order to avoid killing the original five. Furthermore, this seems true, even if it were physically possible for him to redirect his own trolley to where it will kill two different people, and even if it would remain impermissible for him to set the bomb that kills one person or to do what topples the fat man from the bridge as a means to stop his trolley.

14. I discussed cases like this in my "Constraints and You," a paper presented at the American Philosophical Association, Pacific Division, in 1983. It became a chapter in my *Morality, Mortality*, vol. 2 (New York: Oxford University Press, 1996). For a simpler example of letting one's victim die, suppose an agent gives someone a slow, deadly poison and then days later when he comes upon an antidote, he refuses to give it to his victim.

15. Thomson,"The Trolley Problem," 1399.

16. Thomson, "Turning the Trolley," 363.

17. She shifted her use of the title in her 1985 article "The Trolley Problem," where she first introduced the Bystander at the Switch Case. There she said: "What I shall be concerned with is a first cousin of Mrs. Foot's problem, viz.: Why is it that the bystander may turn his trolley, though the surgeon may not remove the young man's lungs, kidneys, and heart? Since *I* find it particularly puzzling that the bystander may turn his trolley, I am inclined to call this The Trolley Problem. Those who find it particularly puzzling that the surgeon may not operate are cordially invited to call it The Transplant Problem instead" (1401). As I noted in n. 11, in "Killing, Letting Die, and the Trolley Problem," she had already introduced a case in which she thought it was permissible for someone (a passenger) to turn the trolley and so kill one rather than let five die. Yet in that article, it was not to the contrast between that Passenger Case and Transplant (structurally similar to the case of the bystander toppling the fat man) that she applied the title "The Trolley Problem." That is why I say the switch in her use of the title begins in the 1985 article.

18. Thomson, "Turning the Trolley," 368.

19. There are reasons, aside from their inherent interest, for examining her arguments for the reversal. When a major figure whose past work on a problem has been admired and served as a basis for subsequent work by others changes her mind, one wants to be sure that the reversal is justified, especially since so many still believe there is a Trolley Problem and continue to produce work dealing with it. It is a happy fact that whether Thomson's reversal is shown to be justified or unjustified, Thomson—either Thomson 1 or Thomson 2—will be vindicated.

20. Such differences in how we may kill will also morally distinguish the version of Transplant in which the doctor would kill to save his own victims, from the Bystanding Driver Case in which the driver would redirect to save his own victims from the threat.

21. Thomson, "Turning the Trolley," 364. This case is like the Trilemma Case presented by Peter Unger in his book *Living High and Letting Die* (New York: Oxford University Press, 1996). (I discussed it in an examination of his book; see "Grouping and the Imposition of Loss," *Utilitas* 10 (1998): 292–319, reprinted in my *Intricate Ethics* (New York: Oxford University Press, 2007). In Unger's case, a trolley is headed toward six people and a bystander can redirect it toward three other people or toward the bystander himself. Note that Unger's case would involve killing three others if one does not kill oneself, Thomson's just one other. This may seem to make it harder to justify killing someone other than oneself in Unger's case. Unger's aims are to show that it is permissible for a bystander to turn from six to three, and that if he would do this, he should turn to one instead, even if he is the one. He believes that what he calls the Principle of Ethical Integrity requires us to be willing to do to ourselves what we would do to others. Some of the concerns I had about Unger's views will arise again in my discussion of Thomson, though her conclusions are very different from his.

22. Thomson, "Turning the Trolley," 365. The assumption is that using a random decision procedure to decide between killing oneself and another is also something one may not do in this case; one may not impose even a 50 percent chance of death on the other person. Unlike Unger, she argues that if you will not turn the trolley toward yourself, you may not turn it toward another. He argues that you should turn it toward yourself as much as to another, but he does not deny that if you do not turn it to yourself, you should turn it to the three.

23. I discussed cases like this as instances of what I call the Principle of Secondary Permissibility in *Morality, Mortality*, vol. 2, and in *Intricate Ethics*.

24. This example was suggested by Larry Temkin. I discussed other examples in my "Supererogation and Obligation," reprinted as chap. 15 in my *Morality, Mortality*, vol. 2. The general point is the denial of the principle of independence of irrelevant alternatives if "irrelevant" means "alternatives that would not be taken."

25. That is, she first argues for her "Third Principle: A must not kill B to save five if he can instead kill himself to save the five," and then claims her "Fourth Principle: A may let five die if the only permissible means he has of saving them is killing himself." Thomson, "Turning the Trolley," 365.

26. In this case, I give someone else's life preserver to the five. Hence, it is a case in which a cost imposed on someone else causes the five to be saved and so it is closer in causal structure to the Bystander Topple Case than to the Bystander's Two Options Case. In the latter, redirecting a threat away helps the five but as a side effect kills one person. This distinction bears on an analogous case that Thomson uses to try to support her claim that the bystander may not impose a cost on others that he would not impose on himself. She says, suppose I do not want to give my own money to Oxfam when I am able to. I am not permitted to steal someone else's money in order that Oxfam have money. Thomson, "Turning the Trolley," 365. One concern I have about this case is that it is closer in structure, and hence a more appropriate analogy, to the case of the bystander toppling the fat man, because in both cases a harm done to the one person is a means to saving the five, not a consequence of saving them. Here is a closer Oxfam analogy to redirecting the trolley. I want to help Oxfam by directing its funds to poor people; without directing the money, poor people will not be helped. If I direct in one way, saving one set of people, it will reduce the value of my investments; if I direct in another way, saving another set of people, it will reduce the value of someone else's investments to the same degree. Thomson may think that my choosing the latter way, other things equal, is impermissible. My only point is that doing this is different from doing what she imagines in her Oxfam case, and closer in causal structure to what is at stake in her Bystander's Three Options Case. Another concern I have with the Oxfam analogy is that it involves helping distant people very indirectly. By contrast, my Life Preserver Case is like the Bystander Case in that someone nearby needs help right away from only those present. These factors may bear on the permissibility of taking another person's resources to help.

27. Thomson herself uses an argument somewhat like this in discussing what the trolley driver should do. She says the driver should redirect the trolley away from the five in a way that results in his own death rather than

redirect in a way that kills one other person. But, she says, even if he would commit an injustice in not following this order, he should still redirect to one person rather than commit the injustice of killing five.

28. See G. A. Cohen, "Casting the First Stone: Who Can, and Who Can't, Condemn the Terrorists?" in his *Finding Oneself in the Other* (Princeton, NJ: Princeton University Press, 2012), 115–133.

29. See his *The Rejection of Consequentialism* (New York: Oxford University Press, 1982).

30. See, for example, my *Morality, Mortality*, vol. 2. Indeed, at one point in that discussion, I suggested that it was "contemptible" to impose costs on others that one would not pay oneself.

31. What if one thought that only in this last case am I not permitted to kill the other party (at least without giving him and myself an equal chance)? This would be some indication that we cannot extrapolate from a case where one actually has a choice between killing oneself or instead another to achieve the very same goal, to a conclusion about what one is permitted to do when one does not actually have such a choice (as in the case where one stops the fall of someone else onto a different potential victim whom one does not threaten).

32. The permissibility of, and being willing to, impose costs on others that one will not impose on oneself is sometimes referred to as the *self/other asymmetry*. I discuss it in connection with war, in "Failures of Just War Theory," reprinted in my *The Moral Target* (New York: Oxford University Press, 2012), where I consider that it may be permissible to impose costs on enemy civilians that one would not and morally need not impose on one's own civilians (or even tolerate being imposed on them by the enemy). I discuss the asymmetry in connection with permissible collateral harm to civilians, harm that could but will not be absorbed by military personnel, in "Killing in War: Traditional and Non-Traditional Views," also in *The Moral Target*.

33. See Thomson, "Turning the Trolley," 366–367.

34. Sometimes a person may be required to pay certain costs and yet it would be wrong for someone else to impose those costs on him. For example, if A owes B money that A is not repaying, it may still be wrong for C to take the money from A's account to give to B. Shelly Kagan suggested that this case alone shows that someone's permissibly imposing a cost and someone else's being required to pay it can go separate ways, so they might also go separate ways when one may impose costs on another but another is not required to pay them. I am not convinced by this argument because another interpretation is that if imposing is impermissible even when a cost is required, then imposing is likely to be impermissible when there is no requirement to pay.

35. I do recognize that the issues raised by these claims are very important, and related issues arise in many contexts. For example, as mentioned in n. 32, in wartime it is thought that in order to defend itself or another victim of aggression, a country may attack military facilities of the aggressor, despite a certain amount of even foreseen certain-to-occur collateral deaths of innocent civilians (even noncitizens) in the aggressor country. Military personnel are supposed to take certain "reasonable" risks rather than cause such harm, but they are not required to take an alternate route to achieve their mission when it is known that this will kill them. It is standardly thought to be permissible for them to create externalities (harm to others) rather than internalize the cost of their operations. The issues raised by Thomson's argument bear on the permissibility of such conduct as well.

36. Thomson, "Turning the Trolley," 371. This is because she thinks the driver probably has a duty to kill himself to stop the trolley, and she does not explicitly endorse the view that no one may impose costs on others even if these others have a duty to pay them. If so, this would imply that the bystander could permissibly turn the trolley away from the five in a way that kills the driver rather than the one other person on the track, though the driver was unwilling to do this. Suppose the driver's duty not to kill five implied that he, being a very fat driver, should throw himself in front of the trolley to stop it. Then the bystander might also be permitted to eject the driver in front of the trolley to stop it. Furthermore, suppose the driver had been thrown from the trolley so he could no longer drive it, and he landed so that he was the one on the track to which the bystander would have to redirect. Then Thomson's view might be consistent with the bystander's being permitted to redirect the trolley toward the driver if avoiding becoming the killer of five, as a result of a past act of driving, gave the driver the same duty of self-sacrifice as not killing while he is driving. For example, he might have a duty to redirect the trolley to himself had he landed on the track. (However, I think it is not clear that someone who is no longer part of a threatening entity owes his potential victims this when he is not culpable for the event that will kill them. For example, suppose the driver of the runaway car in Thomson's example were thrown from his car while it continued on toward killing the five and he was at the side of the road. Even if we could have shot him to stop the car when he was in it, may we shoot him when he is at the side of the road if this would stop the car? If not, perhaps he is also not more liable than any other person to having the car redirected to him by a bystander if this will save his victims. I briefly discuss a case of a driver at the side of a road—the

Sideline Case—in Chapter 1 of my *Ethics for Enemies* (New York: Oxford University Press, 2011).)

37. This principle may be meant to apply only if the five would be killed impermissibly.

38. And its untruth is not on account of Taurekian reasons, such as numbers of deaths do not count, that Thomson mentions but says she will ignore.

39. Thomson, "Turning the Trolley," 372.

40. Thomson, "Turning the Trolley," 368.

41. In this connection, we might also reconsider the Driver's Other Trolley Case (discussed in n. 13). The driver headed to the five can stop his trolley only by redirecting a second runaway trolley from four and toward one. In this case, the driver is not responsible for driving the second trolley in the best possible way. Yet, I suggest, it is permissible for him redirect it to stop his trolley. Indeed, it seems that he may redirect any non-trolley threat (e.g., a large rock) headed to a greater number of people away from them, though it will kill another person if the new position of the non-trolley threat can stop his trolley from hitting the five. Yet he has no special responsibility for positioning non-trolley threats per se.

42. Note that the difference in how any agent comes to kill need not be crucial for permissibility when the driver or bystander would do what kills himself. It need not be impermissible for the driver or bystander to throw himself from the bridge in front of the trolley or to set a bomb that will kill him to stop the trolley.

43. See Thomson, "The Trolley Problem," 1401.

44. Is this also true of a certain sort of driver? That is, suppose that he would kill the eight if he did not redirect the trolley, but would also become the killer of the five if he did not help them because it was he who set in motion what threatens them. Should he turn the trolley that he is driving away from the eight so that it kills one or so that it blocks the path he needs to save his other five victims? Does his special responsibility to aid his five victims make it permissible for him to kill one when a mere bystander to the deaths of the eight and the five should not? If it does, this might seem to be a counter-example to Strong Claim 3 (at least if it applies to those who would otherwise become killers through not aiding). However, in this case it is not his otherwise killing a greater number of people that alone would give him a unique right to kill. It is this in combination with his becoming the killer of the five others. Indeed, a bystander to the deaths of eight who would become the killer of the five if he did not aid them might also be permitted to turn to the one.

45. I first pointed this out in my *Morality, Mortality,* vol. 2. I argued that the value of the greater good of five saved (or the claims of the five to be saved) cannot be transmitted to the means for saving them so that it competes with someone else's life in deciding where to send the trolley. But this cannot be because the value of the greater good can never be transmitted to the means, since we should do what we must to keep the path clear to be able to use it to save five people rather than go to save one other person instead; that is, we may let the one die in order to spend our time saving the means that will be used to save the five. For more on this issue, see text that follows.

46. However, suppose the two cases could be combined—that is, when we faced the direct choice between killing one or saving the means to save five, we know that we would instead save the means (independently under threat) in a non-harmful way and then come back to save the eight by redirection to the one. In this case, the one person would die no matter what we do. Given that he will be no worse off if we just redirected to him rather than to the means, that redirection, which would have been impermissible were it our only option, becomes permissible if it would both save the eight and save the means from threats. Here it is a substitute for a different permissible act that would also lead to killing the one by redirection. This is an instance of what I call the Principle of Secondary Permissibility (discussed in my *Intricate Ethics,* among other places).

47. There would not be a comparable problem in the following case. Suppose we want to save the five from the car and discover that we can do this only if we turn a trolley from eight to one when there is no other way to save the eight from the trolley. This means of saving the five could be permissible if saving the five is another effect of an act whose bad effect of killing one is already justified as the effect of a permissible redirection. The permissible redirection does not become impermissible just because it has another good effect. Of course, it remains to show why redirecting is permissible. My only point now is that there are structural differences between Bystander Saving-by-Letting-Die (2) and other trolley cases that may justify distinguishing them morally, and that the last case involving the car headed to the five is no more problematic than an ordinary Trolley Case.

48. Notice that "have a complaint" should be interpreted more broadly than "would be treated unjustly by someone." For suppose it were a natural event, such as a very strong wind, that is moving the trolley toward five people in the original Bystander Case. If it is permissible for the bystander to turn the trolley in this case, it cannot be because the five have a complaint against anyone in particular that the trolley is headed toward them. We will have to allow that

they may have a complaint simply because there is no rightful treatment of them taking place. By contrast, rightful treatment of them can be taking place when someone disconnects them from his optionally provided life support.

49. However, none of this should imply that if a trolley were headed toward five whom the bystander is not already saving, it would make sense for him to save these five by redirecting the trolley to stop the life support he is already providing to the other five. Hence, it can be true that these two groups of five people have equal weight relative to each other considered on their own and yet they have different weights relative to the alternative of killing the one person on the left track.

# Lecture II

# How Was the Trolley Turned?

## F. M. KAMM

## 1.

Our primary aim in this lecture is to consider some positive proposals[1] that might explain why it is at least thought to be permissible to harm some people to save others in two basic Trolley Cases discussed in Lecture I, one involving a trolley driver as the agent and another a mere bystander. Recall the basic Trolley Case introduced by Philippa Foot (shown as Trolley Driver's Two Options Case, diagram 2; diagrams of the various cases discussed in Lecture I and Lecture II appear on pages 103–109). It involves a driver in a trolley whose brake does not work when the trolley is headed toward killing five people on the track.[2] The driver can only stop this by diverting to another track where the trolley will foreseeably kill one other person. For the driver, it is said, it is a choice between killing five and killing one, when all the people are assumed to be alike in morally relevant respects. The basic Bystander Case introduced by Judith Thomson involves the same trolley when the driver is unable to do anything but a mere bystander can divert the trolley, killing the single person on the side track. For the bystander, it is a choice between letting five die and killing one.

In Lecture I, I considered Thomson's most recent view that whether killing one person by turning the trolley is permissible depends on who turns the trolley. She thinks that the driver may permissibly turn the trolley because it is his only way of not committing the greater wrong of unjustly killing five people, but a bystander may not turn it because he will otherwise only let five people die and this is not unjust. I had two major concerns about this view. First, it does not explain why the driver may kill one person by turning the trolley but not by pressing a switch to topple a fat man from a bridge so that he lands in front of the trolley, when his weight would stop (or redirect) the trolley so that it does not kill the five (Driver Topple Case, diagram 4). Second, I was not convinced by her arguments that someone who would otherwise only let five people die is not permitted to do what someone who would otherwise kill five is permitted to do. However, I was willing to accept that a bystander, too, may not topple the fat man (in a case like the one in diagram 4) and also that only the person who would otherwise kill the five might be obligated to turn the trolley.

At the end of the first lecture, I suggested that if both the driver and the bystander are permitted to turn the trolley, but neither may do certain other things that would save the five and kill another person, then the trolley problem is about why it is sometimes permissible to kill innocent, nonthreatening people, even rather than let others die, when we come to kill in some ways but not others. In other words, a detective investigating the mysterious trolley problem who wants to know if the one person was killed permissibly should (usually) investigate how the person was killed (and also how the five were saved) rather than who did the killing.[3] I further said that we could see the trolley problem so understood as presenting a challenge to nonconsequentialists who reject the act-consequentialist view that we should always do what produces the best consequences. Nonconsequentialists, in some rough way, think that there is ordinarily what is called a side-constraint on harming an innocent, nonthreatening person to save five others, even if we assume that five being alive is a greater good and one being dead is a lesser evil. A side-constraint is not merely a factor that weighs against producing the greater good; it is supposedly a factor that has priority over producing the greater good. That is, we may produce the greater good only if doing so is consistent with respecting that constraint. One view is that side-constraints are individual rights, giving rise in others to correlative duties owed to the right-bearer, and that they reflect fundamental aspects of our conception of persons and their status. An example in which we are constrained from killing one to save five is the Transplant Case (diagram 1). If a doctor (or someone else) kills a single healthy person, she will be able to use his organs to save five fatally ill patients (for whose illness the single person is not responsible). Yet, intuitively, it is impermissible to kill the one person to save the five. The Transplant Case is presented as a counter-example to act-consequentialism. For nonconsequentialists, the challenge is to explain exactly what the side-constraint on harming amounts to, what its form is, if it does not exclude turning the trolley and thus killing one person to save five others.

I shall begin this second lecture by considering Thomson's proposal for why many people believe, mistakenly she thinks, that the bystander may turn the trolley, as her explanation focuses on the "how" question. I shall then consider an alternative proposal for why both the driver and the mere bystander may turn the trolley that focuses on different ways in which the trolley can come to be turned or otherwise stopped from killing the five. These different ways amount to both (a) different ways in which harm to some person or persons comes about; and (b) different ways in which the good of other persons not being harmed comes about. This proposal claims that if harm to some and prevention of harm to others come about in certain ways, it will seem (and perhaps actually be) permissible to turn the trolley. The proposal also attempts to characterize in a general way when it is and is not permissible to harm some to save others.

Though I will present some criticisms of this proposal, I will nevertheless consider how something like it relates to the moral distinction between killing and letting die, and then whether all elements of the proposal are required, given what others who would also kill rather than let die seem permitted to do. This will lead us to consider the role of partiality and impartiality in the decision to do what harms others. In conclusion, I will consider some cases that again raise the question of what the trolley problem is.

I should preface what is to come with a warning. Typically, people who work on the trolley problem employ the following methodology. They start off with some basic cases and suggest a principle to explain and perhaps justify intuitive judgments in those cases. But then other cases are imagined that show the proposed principle to be wrong or in need of revision. Perhaps a new principle is then suggested to explain and justify the judgments in the original cases plus the new ones. Then other cases may be raised that make problems for the new principle, and on and on. If a principle seems satisfactory in terms of cohering with intuitive judgments about cases, then the issue is to see if the principle reflects some morally significant underlying concepts or values.[4] In considering suggestions for a principle here, I will not be attempting to deal with all the many cases that have to be correctly accounted for. So any principle that seems to shed light on the basic cases may have to be, at the very least, modified. Here I just hope to show some directions that have been taken and some in which we might go. So while it may seem like we are considering many hypothetical cases, I assure you they will not be enough![5]

## 2.

Thomson concludes her 2008 article "Turning the Trolley" by offering an error theory for why it has been mistakenly thought that a mere bystander who would otherwise let five die is permitted to turn the trolley and kill one person. She believes that many people's judgments about the abhorrence (and hence, impermissibility) of killing varies with how "drastic an assault on the one the agent has to make."[6] This leads them to think, in her view mistakenly, that the bystander causing death by pushing the fat man is impermissible but the bystander causing death by turning a trolley is permissible because, in the latter case, "if he proceeds, he will bring about that more live by merely turning a trolley."[7] But if she were right about this, people should also think it is permissible to turn a trolley in the following Two Trolleys Case (diagram 11). Suppose one trolley is headed to the five people. We can redirect this trolley away from the five if we just turn a second trolley, running on a track where it would harm no one, into the first trolley. However, on its way to redirect the first trolley, the second trolley will kill another person as a mere side effect. I doubt that people would think that our saving more lives by "merely turning a trolley" makes turning the second trolley permissible. And if Thomson were right, should not people also think it is permissible for someone to topple the fat man in front of the trolley, not by pushing him over, but by merely turning a second trolley that goes up on the bridge and knocks him down? I doubt that people would think that "merely turning a trolley" in this case will make toppling the fat man permissible. Hence, an explanation of why people think turning the trolley in the standard Bystander Case seems morally permissible will have to point to some factor other than that it involves merely turning a trolley.

## 3.

Consider some alternative proposals to explain why people think (perhaps justifiably) that turning the trolley in both the Bystander Case and the Trolley Case is permissible. (Note that people may not be able to articulate these proposals, which nevertheless underlie their judgments.) One proposal is that if the one person is hit, he would stand in exactly the same relation to the same trolley threat that the five people would if they were hit. They would all come to be threatened by the same trolley going to them, either by its going to the five or to the one. This contrasts with what happens in the Two Trolleys Case, where the trolley that threatens the five is not the trolley that would threaten the one. (This is also true in the Bomb Trolley Case discussed in Lecture I, in which someone sets a bomb to move the trolley from the five people and the bomb kills the one other person, as represented in diagram 3.) Toppling a fat man from a bridge in front of the trolley so that his body stops (or redirects) it also involves something different happening to him from what would have happened to the five (i.e., they would have the trolley sent to them, whereas he would be sent to the trolley). Perhaps it is the potential victims standing in the same relation to the same threat that distinguishes the Bystander and Trolley Case morally from other cases of killing to save others?[8]

I think that one problem with this proposal is that it is too narrow, in the sense that these Trolley Cases may be one type of a more general class of cases in which the permissibility of harming can be explained in essentially the same way. We might come to see this by considering another aspect of turning the trolley in the basic cases: the good of five being saved seems to be the mere noncausal flip side of removing what threatens them (the trolley). That is, in the circumstances of these cases, where there are no other threats to them, the five people being saved is simply the trolley's moving away. The relation between the trolley moving away and the five being saved is not a causal relation but, rather, seems to be a constitutive relation.

By contrast, in the Two Trolleys Case, the second trolley, which is not a threat to the five, would cause the first trolley's moving away from the five, and the first trolley's moving away would have the noncausal, constitutive relation to the five being saved. In the basic Trolley Case, the means (namely, turning the trolley) that has the constitutive relation to the five being alive is what will directly cause the lesser harm to the one person on the other track, because the trolley that is moving away will hit the one. This way in which the means of saving the five comes to harm some and help others is causally different from the way in which the second trolley in the Two Trolleys Case would come to harm some and help others: that second trolley, whose movement does not have the noncausal, constitutive relation to the five being free of a threat and being saved, both causes the first trolley to move away and directly harms one other person. Perhaps it is impermissible to use means that have such a mere causal, rather than a noncausal or constitutive, relation to removing a threat and saving the five when those means will also directly harm someone else. (This may be related to what was said in Lecture I, in discussing the Bystander Saving-by-Letting-Die Cases. Both in those cases and in the Two Trolleys Case, being able to use means (the pathway or the second trolley) that can cause people to be saved does not have the same privileged position relative to causing harm to others that people actually being saved from threats has.) When the fat man is toppled so that he stops the trolley on its original route to the five people, his being in harm's way is, and is brought about by, a mere causal means to producing the greater good of five saved. So the harm to him is also not produced by means that have a noncausal relation to stopping the trolley threat and to the greater good; rather, his being hit causes the threat to stop and thereby causes the greater good. The noncausal, constitutive relation of the trolley's moving away to saving the five in the Bystander Case and the Trolley Case makes the cases very close to one in which the five being saved itself leads to harm to another person. For example, in Lecture I we supposed that we could not redirect the trolley away from the five, but we could move them away from the trolley by turning a swivel table—a large lazy Susan—on which they are seated. Their being in the safe location causes rocks in the area to fall, killing another person (diagram 8). In Lazy Susan II their being in the safe location causes another person, near the side of the lazy Susan, to be pushed into the trolley. In these cases, the five being moved away from the trolley has a noncausal, constitutive relation to their being safe from the trolley that threatened them and, in the context where this is the only threat, to their being saved. In the Lazy Susan Case, their being moved away causes another entity, rocks independently in the environment, to become a threat to someone else. (In the basic Trolley Case, by contrast, moving away an entity independently in the environment (i.e., the trolley), thereby causing it to become a threat to someone else, has a noncausal, constitutive relation to the five's being safe from that entity. This is possible because the trolley threatens the five originally, unlike the rocks in the Lazy Susan Case, which do not threaten the five.)

Suppose we think that moving the five away from the trolley in the Lazy Susan Cases is permissible for essentially the same reason that turning the trolley from the five in the Trolley Case is permissible. Then it would not be crucial to the permissibility of turning the trolley that we are not pushing another person into the trolley as we do that in Lazy Susan II. Nor would it be crucial that we are redistributing the same threat that already faced the five to another and that the other will stand in the same relation to the same threat that the five did. After all, in the Lazy Susan Case, it is rocks that are moved by the five being safe that threaten the one person, not the trolley that was headed to the five.[9]

In all these cases in which I have said that turning the trolley has as its noncausal flip side the five being free of that threat and being saved, it is strictly true that the flip side is only the first instant of their being unthreatened.[10] This is a component of whatever period of life is sufficient to make it the case that their being alive is a greater good relative to the death of one other person. (This component also helps cause the future instants of life that make up the future lives of these people. However, it is not a mere cause of the future life; it is also a component of that life.) We should not turn the trolley killing one person if the five would live for only one instant, but only if we have good reason to believe they will go on living long enough. Similarly, in cases where I have said that five being saved causes the death of the one person, it is strictly only the first instant of their being free of what threatened them that causes the one's death, as when the lazy Susan lands them where their weight causes rocks to fall on another person. This first instant of their being safe is a component, as well as a cause, of what we should reasonably expect will be a period of life for the five people long enough to be a greater good relative to the lesser evil of one person's dying.

An important aspect of the discussion so far bears mentioning. Foot drew her major contrast between the impermissibility of the doctor's killing in Transplant and the permissibility of the driver's killing in the Trolley Case. Similarly, most have emphasized the distinction between turning the trolley and pushing the fat man to stop the trolley, which is (as Thomson pointed out) the version of the Trolley Case that is like Transplant with respect to how the one person will be treated. However, in my own past work on the trolley problem, I emphasized a different contrast based on another of Foot's cases (which I mentioned in Lecture I), the Gas Case.[11] In arguing against the Doctrine of Double Effect (DDE) as an explanation of why the trolley may be turned, she noted that a doctor may not use a gas needed in surgery to save five people when it will foreseeably cause a bystander to die. This is so even though his death (or mere involvement) is not intended or causally useful to save the five, unlike getting organs in Transplant. I argued that given what was true in the Gas Case, it was crucial to explain why turning the trolley is permissible even though it, too, is a means to saving the five that we foresee will kill one person, whose being hit is not intended or causally useful to save the five. That is why I constructed the Bomb Trolley Case in Lecture I, which is like the Gas Case in that it is impermissible to use the bomb that will stop the trolley from hitting the five even though the bomb will kill one other person, harm to whom is a mere side effect not needed to save the five. This is also true of the second trolley in the Two Trolleys Case.

One problem with Foot's discussion may be that while she considered cases in which (1) harm is intended and is a means to helping others (Transplant) and (2) harm is a side effect of a mere causal means to helping others (Gas), she did not consider (3) cases in which harm is a side effect of others already being saved (Lazy Susan) and (4) cases in which harm is a side effect of means that have a noncausal, constitutive relation to the good they produce (Trolley). It is the latter two types of cases I focused on. She also did not recognize that mere causal means to saving the five (like the gas) might be used if it killed someone indirectly by, in particular, affecting some entity independently in the environment that would kill another person. For example, suppose the gas we introduce that is needed to help save the five in Foot's case is itself harmless to everyone. However, spraying it changes air currents so that some fatal germs that had previously been closeted now move to one person, killing him. Even if we knew this would happen, it seems permissible to use the gas to save five. Similarly, suppose the second trolley sent in to move the first one in the Two Trolleys Case did not kill a bystander. However, its movement caused rocks independently in the environment to fall, killing someone. Then perhaps it would be permissible to send in that second trolley to save the five.[12]

We could summarize as follows some of these views about permissibly and impermissibly seriously harming innocent non-threatening people to save others: Actions are *permissible* if greater good or a component of it (or means having these as a noncausal flip side) leads to lesser harm even directly. Actions are *impermissible* if mere means that produce greater good (like the bomb or second trolley) cause lesser harm at least directly, and actions are *impermissible* if mere means cause lesser harms (such as toppling people in front of a trolley) that are mere means to producing greater goods. (That an act is permissible does not imply that those who would be harmed by it may not also permissibly resist it and its effects.[13]) This is a rough description of one version of what I have called the *Principle of Permissible Harm* (PPH).[14] It might be described as a "downstreamish" principle in that it implies that the lesser, direct harms may permissibly be causally downstream of the greater good, components of it, or means having these as their noncausal flip side.

I say this PPH is a "downstreamish" view rather than a "downstream" view because, in certain other cases, removing the trolley threat that would kill the five people will result in harm to the one person that itself plays a further necessary causal role "upstream" to the greater good, either sustaining a component of the greater good by deflecting threats to it or helping to produce the greater good. The most famous example of this sort is the brilliant Loop Case introduced by Judith Thomson.[15] In this case, if the trolley is redirected, it would loop back to kill the five were it not that its hitting the one person on the track stops it. Here one person's being hit is a necessary causal means to the five being saved as much as in a Topple Case (involving either a driver or bystander doing the toppling). Yet the PPH might imply that turning the trolley is permissible because, unlike what is true in a Topple Case, the one's being hit is caused by the turning of the trolley threat that has a component of the greater good as its flip side. That is, we turn the trolley because this is a way to stop the trolley from killing the five in its initial direction. If we just consider what this leaves us with, abstracting from any new threats created by what we do in redirecting, we see (what I have called) the "structural equivalent" of the greater good—that is, the five are free of all threats they faced independently of our redirecting. This is a particular type of component of the greater good that would be the greater good if only it were not undermined by the new threat of the looping trolley created by our redirection. We turn the trolley because (or on condition that) it will hit the one person, for this will prevent the component from being undermined; the component will be sustained and become the greater good. But according to the PPH, we should not do anything (like giving the trolley an extra push not needed to get it away from the five) in order that it hit the one, for this would do something that did not have any component of the greater good as its noncausal flip side. The extra push would be a mere means to the one being hit, like toppling the man in a Topple Case.[16]

This discussion of the Loop Case is intended to show that, according to the PPH, it is important how we bring about the harm that will have a necessary causal role in saving the five. But it also shows that it is important what the harm is causally necessary to bring about. To make this point clearer, consider what I call the Tractor Case.[17] The five toward whom the trolley is headed also have a deadly tractor headed toward them. If we turn the trolley away, it will hit one person whose being hit will stop the tractor. Is it permissible to turn the trolley in the Tractor Case, as it is in the Loop Case? In the Loop Case, the threat to the five of the trolley coming back to hit them is itself produced by the redirection, and so abstracting from this new threat, we have the structural equivalent of the greater good as a flip side of redirection. It needs to be sustained and will be sustained by the hit produced by the same redirection. In the Tractor Case, the one person's being hit interferes with a threat to the five that exists independently of what we do to save them. So when we turn away the trolley and abstract from the further effects of what we do, it seems that we do not yet have the structural equivalent, or any component, of the greater good as a noncausal flip side for the five are still under a fatal tractor threat. The fact that the tractor threat exists independently of what we do to remove the initial threat of the trolley means that we need to *produce* another outcome—the removal of the tractor—when we redirect, rather than just *sustain* the structural equivalent of the greater good that we have already produced; and the harm to the person needed to produce this outcome is not caused by means that already have a component of the greater good as a noncausal flip side. So this productive harm is not downstream from a component of the good. The possible difference in the permissibility of redirecting in the Loop and Tractor Cases suggests that, in considering the permissibility of actions that will harm people, we should consider both how the lesser harm comes about and what the lesser harm is needed to bring about (and that these can be related).

The PPH is one version of an approach that focuses on different ways of bringing about goods and harms, as well as different causal or noncausal, constitutive relations between goods, harms, and means of producing them. An additional possible hypothesis is that supervening upon these differences are different relations between the people harmed and those saved from harm. In particular, one suggestion is that the permissible ways to harm some to save others involve some people being substituted for others (when this is done in certain ways) with regard to being harmed, whereas the impermissible ways to harm involve some people being subordinated to others, either by coming in certain ways to be used for others (as in toppling someone to stop the trolley in a Topple Case) or by direct harm to them being considered less important relative to the use of certain means (such as sending in the second trolley) when these means are causally useful for others. Harming by substitution could be permissible even if harming by subordination were impermissible.[18] Ultimately, identifying certain relations between people as permissible and impermissible could reflect a certain conception of persons and their status. It is not the point of this lecture to investigate these deeper possible meanings of the PPH I have described, but it is useful to keep in mind that finding the deeper meaning of any PPH (this or another) is both important to a complete understanding and justification of action in the Trolley Cases and to showing how the trolley problem is connected to our conception of persons and their status.

There are also problems with this proposed PPH, I believe.[19] Like earlier proposals, the problems stem from generalizing from too narrow a set of cases. Turning the trolley seems to be permissible in cases that do not satisfy the conditions of the PPH. Consider Tractor Case II, which is like the original Tractor Case except that the person's being hit on the side track has no causal role in stopping the tractor. Rather, the tractor is stopped by a switch that is pressed by the trolley as it is turned away from the five. In this case, no more than in the original Tractor Case, does the moving away of the trolley have the greater good or a component of it as its noncausal flip side, since the five are still under the threat of a deadly tractor before the switch is pressed. Yet it seems permissible to turn the trolley away though it kills one person, given that the tractor threat will be taken care of by innocent means of the trolley pressing a switch. In this case, it seems correct to say that the turning trolley has a causal, not a noncausal constitutive relation to the greater good or a component of it. More generally, there may be many cases in which turning the trolley is permissible and yet it only removes one threat that would impede the greater good. Other innocent means, even independent of turning the trolley, are needed to deal with other threats and thus produce the greater good. (Similarly there may be many cases in which the five moving away from the trolley, as in the Lazy Susan Cases, does not have a component of the greater good as its flip side because the five people are still subject to another fatal threat, and yet their moving away is permissible given that innocent means will deal with the other threats.[20])

Nevertheless, there is still a distinction between (i) the one person being hit by a mere causal means to removing a threat, such as the second trolley; and (ii) the one person being hit by the moving away of a threat to the five (or the moving away of the five from a threat) that would impede the greater good. The trolley turning in Tractor Case II may have a causal relation to the greater good, but it also has a noncausal, constitutive relation to the five being free of a threat that would impede the greater good, and so it is not a *mere* causal means to the greater good, like the second trolley in the Two Trolleys Case.

Hence, the two Tractor Cases and the Loop Case suggest that explaining why it is permissible to turn the trolley may rely on (i) its being a threat that is removed which kills one person, and (ii) how removal helps bring about the greater good (e.g., as in Tractor Case II and in the Loop Case versus in the original Tractor Case). It seems that when the one person being hit by redirection is a causal means to *producing* a greater good, but not when the harm caused by redirection is a mere side effect or needed to sustain what we have produced, the harm should have been caused by means that have a noncausal, constitutive relation to a component of the greater good and so be downstream from it.

Another possible problem with the initial proposal for a PPH is related to the version of the Bystander Saving-by-Letting-Die Case (diagram 10), in which someone would have to turn a trolley toward interfering with ongoing life support that he is optionally providing to the five people, rather than toward one other person to whom he is not providing such aid. It seems to me that the greater good is the five surviving, yet it was suggested in Lecture I that either the driver or a bystander should redirect the trolley in a way that terminates his aid rather than redirect to kill someone not receiving such aid. If this is correct, then the proposed PPH is too broad. I suggested that, in this case, the five would have no right *not* to have the person providing their life support terminate aid to them, and so the five would have no complaint if he directed the trolley to end the life support he was providing. By contrast, the one person would have a complaint in being hit. Hence, it is important that the greater good be a state whose not coming about someone would have a complaint against; not just any greater good will override the complaint of the person to whom the trolley is redirected. In the basic Trolley Case, the five would have a complaint if they were hit by the trolley driver, and this is one reason why the bystander and the driver may help them.

## 4.

Despite the problems with the initially proposed PPH, for purposes of illustration let us consider how such a type of proposal—one that focuses on relations between harms and goods and between potential victims and those who would be saved—connects with the question of whether a driver who would otherwise kill the five may turn the trolley, but a mere bystander who would let them die may not. Doing this may help illustrate a way nonconsequentialists could insist on the moral distinction between killing and letting die without also claiming that the distinction helps draw a line between what the driver and the bystander are permitted to do (at least in many cases).

A. First consider what I will call the *Agent-Victim Killing/Letting-Die Distinction*. Some nonconsequentialists think that we as agents must make greater efforts to avoid killing someone than to avoid merely letting someone die, because of differences in what we would do to the victim. I have argued that this is true at least when killing involves depriving someone of life that he would continue to have at that time independently of the agent's provision (e.g., he would go on living if the agent and his life-support devices did not exist, holding all else constant). When we let die, by contrast, someone loses life he would not continue to have at that time independently of the agent's provision (e.g., he would die if the agent and his life-support devices did not exist, holding all else constant). (Sometimes when an agent kills someone, the person killed also will not lose life he would have continued to have independently of the agent's provision. For example, this is so if we shoot someone to whom we are providing life support. In this case, there may not be a big moral difference between an agent's killing someone and his letting someone die by terminating life-sustaining aid in more ordinary ways; both may be equally permissible or impermissible. But this is because a property that is conceptually distinctive of letting die—i.e., someone losing out only on life the agent would be providing—occurs in this particular killing case.)

Hence, that one agent must choose between letting five die or killing another person, whereas another agent must choose between killing five or killing another person usually says something about what those victims will lose out on because of what the agent does and what those agents' relations are to the people whose lives are at stake. But some of those who focus on the Agent-Victim Killing/Letting-Die Distinction are saying that not only is there a moral difference in what an agent does to someone in killing him or letting him die, but also that what an agent may permissibly do (and so what relation he may have) to other people in order to avoid the relation of killing someone is different from what he may do (and so what relation he may have) to other people in order to avoid the relation of letting someone die.

However, there is a second type of relation, which holds *among the people whose lives are at stake,* rather than between those people and the agents who would affect them; and a question is whether the relation between these people is also sensitive to the distinction between killing and letting die. I shall call this the *InterVictim Killing/Letting-Die Distinction,* where the victims I have in mind are those who were originally threatened and those who would die if we saved those originally threatened. What relations hold between these people may depend on what an agent does to the people. But it is possible that at least certain relations *between the people* whose lives are at stake will be the same, whether those relations come about because of what is done by an agent like the trolley driver (who would kill some rather than others) or by an agent like the mere bystander (who would kill some rather than let others die). For example, suppose the driver of the out-of-control trolley is, as Foot and Thomson see it, in the process of killing the five. In this case, he is in the process of making them worse off, depriving them of lives they would have had independently of his provision at the time. If he redirects the trolley, he will be making someone else worse off in the same way. This is the Agent-Victim description. Put in InterVictim terms, the one person will be killed and, therefore, be made worse off as the alternative to others being killed and made worse off. This InterVictim description could be true whether it is the driver who turns the trolley or a mere bystander who turns it. Even though, as an agent, the mere bystander would let the five die and so not benefit them rather than make them worse off, the five would still be killed by the trolley and be made worse off.

Suppose, by contrast, that we thought of the five as already worse off than they had been in virtue of the threat to them, so that in turning the trolley, the driver would be improving their condition, albeit by doing what makes one other person worse off. Considered from the InterVictim perspective, the five would be improved by the trolley's being turned away and that turning makes the one person worse off. This could be true as well if the mere bystander turned the trolley. The fact that the driver bears an agent relationship to the five that is different from that of the mere bystander does need not mean that in these respects the individuals whose lives are at stake have different relations to each other depending on which agent acts. The same descriptions could be true of them whichever agent acts.

A further example may help to reinforce the distinction between the agent's relation to a state of affairs (at least put in terms of killing or letting die) and the InterVictim character of the state of affairs. Suppose a trolley driver faces a choice among: (a) killing the five, (b) turning the trolley away from the five onto a track that runs on a bridge so that two other people get toppled from the bridge, or (c) pressing a switch that moves one fat man off a bridge so that he stops the trolley headed to the same five people. (The InterVictim and Agent-Victim choices are represented in diagram 12.) Those who emphasize the Killing/Letting-Die Distinction may see the possible Agent-Victim relations here as killing five or killing two or killing one, in which case the one should be killed. However, the InterVictim relation between those whose lives are at stake will be very different depending on what is done. In option (b), two people will be killed as a consequence of removing a threat to five. In option (c), one person will be killed as a result of toppling him to stop the trolley's going to the five. These different InterVictim relations are a function of how the people come to be killed and their role in producing the greater good. In one option, two people are killed as a consequence of the removal of the threat to others; in the second, one person is killed as a consequence of a mere means (such as a switch) used to move him, so that he is a mere means to remove the threat to others. This could make it permissible to kill the two people, but not permissible even for the driver to kill the one other person. We must consider the relations between the people whose lives are at stake that would come about as a consequence of what is done.

Another way to make this point clearer is to consider the following variant on our case. The trolley driver has the option of turning the trolley away from the five either toward (b) toppling two people as a consequence or (d) toward toppling a fat man standing on a bridge whose fall will interfere with a *different* trolley headed to five *other* people. In this case, it is permissible to do what topples the fat man. His relation to the original five whose not being killed (supposedly) justifies the redirection that kills him is the same as when his being harmed is the consequence of turning the trolley away with no further good effects for others. Once causing his death is justified by its being the consequence of redirecting a threat from the first set of five, it does not become unjustified merely because it is causally useful to save the other five people. If the bystander instead of the driver faces the choice among letting five die or (b), (c), or (d), it could be that the same InterVictim facts that make (b) in one case and (d) in the other permissible for the driver also make them permissible for the bystander.

The rough proposal for a Principle of Permissible Harm that I described earlier identifies such relations between potential victims. For example, in some cases the person killed dies as a result of the greater number being saved (as when we move the five on the lazy Susan and their being in a safe area causes rocks to kill someone else). Here, (the first instant of) the greater good leads to lesser harm and then, the proposal suggests, the InterVictim relation is substitution with respect to being threatened and is permissible. In the Two Trolleys Case, the person is killed by a mere means to what would causally produce the greater good, and then his relation to those saved, the proposal suggests, is subordinating and not permissible.

It may be that the driver is permitted to kill fewer people by turning the trolley only because the InterVictim relation that would be created between the potential victims makes it permissible for him to act. And if the InterVictim relations are the same when the mere bystander turns the trolley, it may be as permissible for him to act even if, unlike the driver, he has no duty to act because as an agent he would only be letting five die. Suppose there is something about the InterVictim relation between the one and the five that makes it impermissible for the mere bystander to bring it about. When the one person should not be made to stand in that relation to the five just so that the bystander can avoid the relation to the five of letting them die, it is not clear why the one may be made to stand in that relation to the five just so that the driver can avoid the relation to the five of killing them.

Of course, if the relation between potential victims would be different depending on what an agent does, one could also say that the Agent-Victim relation is different in virtue of this. Namely, if the agent does one thing, the agent makes a victim stand in one relation to another potential victim; if the agent does another thing, he makes a victim stand in a different relation to another potential victim. However, this further description of the Agent-Victim relation is dependent in the first instance on the potential victims' relations to each other, and it is the InterVictim relations that are significant for the permissibility or impermissibility of the Agent-Victim relations.[21]

B. Suppose the relations between the potential victims determined whether it is permissible or not to kill some to save others. How would this affect the nonconsequentialist claim that there is a stronger duty not to kill than not to let die? It would not affect one implication of this claim—namely, that those who would kill the five have a duty, and should pay great personal costs, to not kill them, while those who would only let the five die (including let them be killed) may have no duty, and morally need not pay great personal costs, to save them. Furthermore, it need not affect the claim that there are side-constraints, such as its being impermissible for the driver or bystander to topple the one person in the topple cases. However, if relations between victims determined the permissibility of killing them, then the duty not to kill would not, in general, take precedence over a duty (should it exist) or desire not to let more people die.

This would be one instance in which what is, in general, stringent by the measure of there being a duty to do it, or having to pay a lot to do it, need not take precedence over what is weaker by those same measures. Here is another such case: I may be morally required to pay a lot of money to keep a contractual promise in business, but not similarly required to pay as much to save the life of someone drowning. And yet if I have a choice between doing an optional, even costly, rescue of the drowning person or else fulfilling the contractual duty, it is permissible for me to do the rescue.[22]

## 5.

Needless to say, many may not accept my proposal for a Principle of Permissible Harm, even amended, in relation to the Trolley Cases and to the question of killing versus letting die as I have described them. Hence, I wish to pursue yet another approach to establishing the relation between how a killing occurs and the permissibility of killing, whether the alternative is killing others or letting them die. It begins by considering some other people besides the mere bystander who would also only let die if they did not kill. The aim is to see how much is thought to be permissible for these people, and how the line between what is thought to be permissible and impermissible might be drawn.

Among those who would only let die if they did not do what kills another are the five dying of organ failure in the Transplant Case and the five to whom the trolley is headed in the Trolley Case. If the five were able to but did not kill someone else to save themselves, they would let themselves die. Let us begin with the five in Transplant. Even though their own lives are at stake, I believe it would be impermissible for them to kill one person for the organs they need in the way the killing comes about in the Transplant Case. I believe it would also be impermissible for them to release a gas that they need to cure themselves if the gas will, as a side effect, kill someone else as in the Gas Case.

However, suppose that the five could successfully treat their medical problem by means that harm no one. Then they will begin to breathe normally and their expanding chests will move some fatal germs in the atmosphere (not in their lungs) that would otherwise have been safely at rest. The germs will reach one other person and kill him (Breathe/Germs Case, diagram 13). Is it impermissible for the five to successfully treat themselves when they know all this will happen? Must they let themselves die instead? I think it is permissible for them to bring about their normal state even though their normal breathing will then turn an entity independently in the environment (the germs) into a fatal threat to others. I emphasize that this permissibility is not merely a matter of their being excused in acting wrongfully because they are in extreme circumstances; rather, they do not act wrongfully at all. Notice that in this case, unlike in the Trolley Case, the five are faced with one threat (organ failure) and their breathing normally causes another threat (moving germs). Even though they create a new threat to others rather than redirect an existing threat from themselves,

I think their action is permissible. In addition, as I noted earlier, if they need to release a gas to cure themselves and this gas in itself is harmless, it seems they may use it even if the gas being in the atmosphere changes air currents and so fatal germs, existing independently in the environment, move to kill one person.

Now suppose that what interferes with the organs of the five and their normal breathing is a heavy weight that is on them. If by some great effort they could breathe normally just once, their chest expansion would push away this heavy weight. However, it would then roll off to kill one other person (Breathe/Weight Case, diagram 14). Once rid of the weight, the five's organs and breathing would recover. (Their breathing normally, which moves the weight, is not the first result of the direct threat having been removed, as in the previous case. However, it is a component of their continuing to live for a longer time.) In this case, we have an entity present in the environment, independent of the actions of the five, that will either threaten them or harm the one. I think it would be permissible for the five to breathe normally in this case, thus removing the threat from themselves, though it will kill another.

What if the five know that once the weight is upon them there will be nothing they can do to save themselves? Suppose that they set up a defensive shield against it (perhaps only shielding themselves with their hands). They do this knowing that the approaching weight will also be repelled by the shield and will kill one other person instead (Shield/Weight Case, diagram 15). A shield is a device that does not itself lead to harm to others independent of something else interacting with it (by contrast to a dangerous gas). For moral purposes, the five using a shield seems close to maintaining their normal state. It would only produce harm to others if an entity independently in the environment interacts with what maintains their normal state, similar to when their normal breathing would itself push an oncoming weight away. It seems to me that the five shielding themselves is permissible despite its harmful effect on another person.

If the five may move the weight by breathing normally or as a consequence of shielding themselves from it, the question that remains is whether they may simply move the weight away—for example, with their hands—in order to breathe normally and not die, though the weight will then kill one other person (Move Weight Case, diagram 16).

## 6.

In the Trolley Cases, the same issues just described in variants of Transplant could arise for the five if they do not let themselves die, though this will result in the death of one other person. (Hence, some of the diagrams used for the variants on Transplant can do double duty for the cases I will now discuss.) Even though their lives are at stake, the five toward whom the trolley goes are not, I believe, permitted to use a device to topple the fat man in front of the trolley, nor may they use a bomb that will stop the trolley but kill someone else. However, suppose the trolley is coming down a track toward one person, the five are between it and him, and their being hit will save him. It is permissible for them to run away or duck even if the one person is killed instead, because they are thus terminating protection that they are not required to provide him. (Duck Trolley Case, diagram 17.)

What if, in another case, the five are alone on the track and the trolley is preprogrammed so that if they move away from it, it will start up in another direction, hitting one other person? They are permitted to move away, I believe. Alternatively, what if the five move away from the trolley and wind up in a safe area, and their being in this area causes some rocks to fall that kill another person (Move to Safety Case, diagram 18)? I believe it would be permissible for them to escape the trolley in this case, too. And if their merely breathing normally caused the trolley to move away from them toward another, I believe they may breathe. These cases fall into the class of the first part of the good of the five being alive causing an entity—either the trolley that threatened them or rocks—to become a threat to another person.[23]

If the trolley is headed only to the five, they may also, I think, shield themselves from it even if its interacting with the shield will cause the trolley to be deflected toward another person. Here it is not a component of the greater good itself that leads to the lesser harm but a device that maintains the good, without causing harm to others independently of the trolley interacting with it.[24]

The question remains whether those who can do all these things rather than let themselves die, even when what they do kills one other person, may simply move the trolley away from themselves so that they are safe. This is like the question, asked earlier, whether the five on whose organs a weight is pressed may just remove the weight when it will then roll onto someone else.

What could morally distinguish what it is agreed the five may permissibly do from turning the trolley? Here is a proposal: If they push the threat away (or press a switch that does so), the five would get rid of the threat by actively and deliberately doing something to *it*, just as they would do in setting a bomb that kills someone. But suppose that if the five push the trolley away, it will come to rest away from anyone or any potentially threatening entity. However, it has been preprogrammed by others to start up again toward another person. Or suppose that if the five actively push the trolley away, it will come to rest away from anyone but something in the lay of the land causes it to move off again toward another person. Are these not counter-examples to the proposal in question because here, too, the five push the threat away but their actions seem to be permissible?

Perhaps pushing the trolley away could consistently be thought permissible in these cases even by those who think it wrong for the five to turn the trolley on tracks going toward the one person. This might be because without the preprogramming done by others in the first case, and an intervening condition in the land in the second case, pushing the trolley away would not hurt anyone. Hence, it might be said, it is not the pushing away of the trolley that *alone* causes the one person to be killed, though it is as certain that he will be killed if the trolley is pushed away as in the original Trolley Case. By contrast, it might be said, in a physical situation like that in the original Trolley Case, the five turning the ordinary trolley away is impermissible because doing this is sufficiently causally responsible for the other person's being killed, without an intervening condition or prior programming being causally important.

In response to this emendation of the original proposal (p. 81), some of those who think that the five potential victims may permissibly turn the ordinary trolley away when it goes on tracks toward someone else might construe what the five do as simply turning a threat away, with every further bad effect being attributable to the presence of trolley tracks. This would make the case be in morally significant ways like the case in which the trolley moves off again because of the lay of the land. I think it is unlikely that this could be a correct explanation of the permissibility of turning the trolley, in part because it would distinguish permissible cases from ones in which the five moving a threat away directly puts the trolley onto someone else. I do not think that such a distinction should be drawn.

To sum up the last part of this discussion, we have considered a proposal that actively and deliberately doing something to the threat itself (perhaps by pressing a switch), when this is sufficiently causally responsible for the one being harmed, is morally no different from setting the bomb that kills a bystander, and so they both differ from permissible ways of the five dealing with the trolley threat. My fundamental concern with this proposal is that it draws no moral distinction between actively and deliberately doing something to an entity that is a threat to the five and to an entity (like the bomb) that is not. The former can constitute the five's being free of a threat; the latter does not. The alternative view is that the five's removing a threat to themselves is in itself as permissible as their breathing normally or moving to safety when this results in their being free of a threat. If the five's breathing normally and coming to be in a safe area are permissible though they cause an entity in the environment to harm someone else, then it seems their moving the trolley threat away should be permissible even when this causes it, an entity in the environment, to be a threat to someone else.

## 7.

Before we consider what implications, if any, cases where the threatened people need not let themselves die may have for mere bystander (or driver) cases, let us consider some other potential victims who face a choice between letting themselves die or killing others. Suppose *one* person has multiple organ failure that is causing his death. He is not permitted to simply kill five people to get their organs or to use a gas to save himself that will kill five. But suppose the one person was able to cure his organ failure by innocent means so that he could breathe and his chest expanded properly. Does the fact that this would move germs in the atmosphere to *five* other people mean that it is not permissible for him to cure himself? Intuitively, I think not. Suppose a weight pressing on him is causing his problems. If he could breathe normally once, and this moved the weight away, is he permitted to do this if the weight will roll onto five others, killing them? I think he is. These conclusions would be consistent with the nonconsequentialist view that sometimes it is permissible to do acts that do not produce the best consequences; it all depends on the nature of the acts.

Suppose the trolley is originally headed to *one* person and the question is what he may permissibly do to save himself, even though it results in five people dying instead. He may not, I believe, topple five fat men in front of the trolley to stop its hitting him, and he may not use a bomb to stop the trolley when it will kill five people as a side effect. However, there seem to be other things he would be permitted to do. Suppose the trolley is headed to him as he stands on the track in front of the five people. It would be permissible—not merely wrong and excusable—for him to duck or run away, knowing the trolley would then go on to kill the five. From a nonconsequentialist perspective, he has no obligation to stay put merely to provide protection that will produce a greater good. When I originally introduced the nonconsequentialist view, I contrasted it with act-consequentialism on the issue of side-constraints that prohibit us from always doing what can produce the greater good. But nonconsequentialists are also commonly contrasted with act-consequentialists on the issue of persons having no general duty to promote the greater good at great personal cost, even when doing so would violate no side-constraint. Hence, someone is not always morally required to act for the impartial greater good, but may have what is known as a personal prerogative to act from his partial point of view.

It also seems to me that the one person is permitted to shield himself from the trolley even though the trolley's hitting the shield will deflect it toward five people. May he move to safe ground when he knows that his being there will cause rocks independently in the environment to fall on and kill five people? I believe it is permissible for him to move.

So far, surprisingly, it seems that the one person may permissibly do a lot of what the five are permitted to do rather than let himself die. This is so even though his actions cannot be permissible because greater good or a component of it (or means having these as its flip side) may cause lesser harm, since his being saved is a *lesser* good and the five being harmed is a *greater* harm. Of course, there must still be some important good at stake for the one to justify his doing various things that will foreseeably harm people. But the focus here is totally on the type of action he takes—how he brings about a good, how he harms, and how the good and the harms are related—rather than on what is at stake, namely greater good coming about at the cost of lesser harm. In addition, the question arises for the one as for the five whether, given all he is permitted to do, he may simply push the trolley away from himself, when it will then go toward the five.

This discussion of the single person suggests that any possible Principle of Permissible Harm should be seen as having two parts: (1) a part that distinguishes different ways of bringing about harm to innocents, and (2) another part that applies these distinctions when it is a question of greater good being produced at the cost of lesser harms. Its first part would seem to still govern the behavior of the single individual acting on his own behalf even when its second part does not apply.

## 8.

We have been discussing a case in which one person is originally threatened by the trolley. But one person may also face the question of whether to let himself die rather than to kill when the trolley is redirected from five people toward him by the driver, by a mere bystander, or by the five. May this person to whom a trolley is redirected permissibly resist the assault on himself by simply turning the trolley back whence it came?[25] Call this the Sending-Back Case. It might at first be thought that the single person's permission to do this would be an indication that the trolley had been impermissibly redirected. However, if the single person had permission to send the trolley back even in cases in which the driver redirects it, would we think it showed that even the driver may not redirect the trolley? I suggest instead that the one has permission to resist in this way what is a permissible act of redirection. Even those who argue for the permissibility of imposing costs on someone despite his personal prerogative not to volunteer them need not argue that it is impermissible for someone to resist the costs being imposed on him. (Similarly, the five may permissibly resist the one redirecting to them the trolley originally headed to him, and this would not show that his redirection was impermissible.) Even if he has no right that the trolley not be redirected toward him, when this is done, his general right not to be harmed is infringed, and this could result in his being wronged in the course of a permissible act. This would be one of many cases (such as have been discussed in wartime contexts) in which those who would suffer harm collaterally by permissible acts may prevent this harm by harming those who acted permissibly (for example, soldiers who would bomb military facilities while satisfying *jus in bello* conditions on action).

However, the permissibility of one person's sending back the trolley is not likely to be very helpful in deciding what one person who was originally threatened with the trolley may do. This is because sending back the trolley would cause the five originally benefited by the redirection to lose that benefit, leaving them no worse off than they were originally. It might also involve harming those who turned the trolley (e.g., a bystander who turned the trolley) and who infringed the one person's right not to be harmed. None of this would be true of persons harmed by redirecting the trolley away from the one person if it originally threatened him.

In sending the trolley back or using the shield, the one person would be resisting what from an impartial perspective is a better state of the world by returning things to the way they were for the five. However, as already noted, he might not be limited to returning things to the way they were. For sending the trolley back could also threaten, for the very first time, several bystander agents or the driver who had permissibly redirected the trolley. The one person's sending back the trolley would still be permissible, I think. That even multiple agents who redirected permissibly would be susceptible to being permissibly threatened in this way by one person to save himself raises several issues. First, given that a bystander's acting permissibly (or in the case of the driver, perhaps, dutifully) does not make him immune to defensive acts by others, is it also permissible for the person to whom the trolley would be redirected to defend himself by directly interfering with the permissible act of the person who would redirect? For example, is his killing the actual or potential redirector in some way other than by reredirecting permissible for defensive purposes? Second, a bystanding agent's liability to being harmed by the one person's resistance in this way might (in part) explain why it is only permissible, not obligatory, for the bystander to turn the trolley. For such an act opens him up to permissibly being harmed (at least in certain ways) by a self-defending victim. (Will this fail to explain why a bystander is not obligated to redirect the trolley when it is known that there is no risk to him of the trolley's being sent back? Perhaps the mere fact that he would be doing an act to which such a response would be permitted is enough to make his act nonobligatory?) Suppose the trolley driver has a duty to accept personal losses to save the five, as Thomson argues. Then the possibility of the driver's being hit by the return of the trolley would not imply that *he* had no duty to redirect. Third, suppose the five people themselves redirect the trolley away from harming them, toward the one other person. Then they might become liable to a self-defending or self-protecting victim, making them even worse off than they originally would have been (e.g., dying more painfully). They, like the bystander agent, become liable to being made worse off than they would otherwise have been in virtue of their agency even if they act permissibly. This is a stronger conclusion than that they may be harmed up to the point of losing the benefit they got from redirection.

## 9.

Are there implications *from* what the five and the one to whom the trolley is originally headed are permitted to do rather than let themselves die *for* what a mere bystander is permitted to do rather than let others die? Why should we think there are any implications? In thinking about what it is permissible for the one or the five to do, we have not relied on any view that implies that people who are themselves threatened may do just anything they need to do to save themselves. Hence, our conclusions about the one and the five may generalize to the bystander who would kill rather than let die. However, suppose the bystander was permitted to do for the one or the five what it is agreed they could permissibly do to save themselves, and suppose also, for argument's sake, that the five and the one were permitted to turn the trolley from themselves though it would kill some innocent(s). Then it would turn out that the mere bystander might be permitted not only to turn the trolley from five to one but also to turn it from one to five. This seems like a rather shocking conclusion to reach.

But it need not be so shocking if the bystander is a "mere bystander" only in the sense that he will not kill anyone if he does not redirect the trolley. He might still be a close friend of the one person or be his bodyguard. Then it might not be surprising that the bystander is permitted either to help the one person act permissibly or to do in his stead what it would be permissible for the one person to do. From a nonconsequentialist perspective, a bystander is not always morally required to act impartially, but may have a personal prerogative to act from a partial point of view.

However, what about the bystander who has no good reason not to be impartial between the one and the five, when from an impartial perspective it is better if five survive than if one does? Suppose the trolley is headed for the five, but the one is in front of them and his being hit will stop the trolley. Suppose he is unable to duck or run away, as he is permitted to do, but a bystander could easily move him off the track, though he could not move the five. This would save the one person but result in the five being hit. It would be impermissible for a bystander to move an inanimate object that blocked the path of the trolley to the five. Yet I think even an impartial bystander may and should help the one escape.[26] One way of explaining why it can be permissible to save the one person and let the five be killed is that if there were nothing to be gained by the one person being hit, the bystander should certainly save him, and the fact that other people would benefit from the one person's being hit (given that he has no duty to help them in this way) is not a sufficient reason for him to be left in that situation. It is true that helping the one would result in the five's facing a threat from which they had previously been protected. But it would do so by removing the person who protects them when the reason to help him is not defeated by his usefulness in protecting them.[27]

All this is consistent with its being right for an impartial bystander who cannot help everyone to remove the five from the track if he can, leaving the one to be hit by the trolley. In this case, he saves a greater number of people by means that do not require that the one be hit, though the one will foreseeably be hit because he is not saved.[28] Removing the one person who would shield the five is also consistent with its being impermissible for an impartial bystander to remove the only person toward whom the trolley is headed when his being in a safe location will cause rocks to fall, killing five others. In this case, the bystander should refuse to offer the easy assistance he should ordinarily give to the one person, because he avoids creating a threat to a greater number of people who were not already being protected from the threat by the one person. Giving the one person a shield that would also deflect the trolley toward five others whom the one person does not already protect also should not be done. This is because it will help cause a threat to a greater number of previously unthreatened people, and not by removing protection already provided to them by the one person.[29]

Furthermore, an impartial bystander removing the one, and so preventing him from stopping the trolley headed to the five when the five cannot be removed, is at least consistent with turning the trolley away from the five though it hits the one. Indeed, suppose the impartial bystander had moved the one person away from the trolley to the only safe location possible, expecting the five to be hit by the trolley. Then he newly discovers that he could redirect the trolley away from the five but only in the direction where the one had been moved for safety. It would be consistent for him to do this, for here the one's death would be the result of getting the trolley away from the five, not the result of omitting to help the one merely because he can be useful in protecting the five from the trolley.[30]

The point is that the impartial nonconsequentialist bystander should favor keeping the greater number of people alive, but only by means that do not treat other people improperly and create improper relations between the one and the five. Earlier (p. 85), it was suggested that any Principle of Permissible Harm should be seen as having two parts, one that distinguishes different ways of harming innocents and a second that applies these distinctions only when it is a question of greater good being produced at the cost of lesser harm. Therefore, it seems that if there is a correct PPH, *in its entirety* it would only govern the acts of impartial agents. (Note that a PPH does not directly speak to the question of not aiding, only of harming. So it does not account for some of what I have said about an impartial agent's rescuing the one person or instead rescuing the five people.[31]) The impartial nonconsequentialist bystander may do a great deal more of what the five are permitted to do to help themselves than what the one is permitted to do to help himself. For example, the impartial bystander is permitted to move the five to safety and also to shield them, even if their being on safe ground causes rocks to kill the one and the shield deflects the trolley to one. But, as I said, he should not shield the one (who does not provide protection against the trolley to the five) or move him to safe ground if doing either will kill five people. The question remains, as it did in our earlier discussions of the five and the one: if the impartial bystander is permitted to cause the death of the one person in these ways rather than let five die, why not by turning the trolley?

Table II.1 provides a template for some distinctions covered in this discussion as they pertain to the trolley problem. I will not fill in the answers.

*Table II.1*

| | Agents | | | |
|---|---|---|---|---|
| | *5* | *1* | *Partial* | *Impartial* |
| | *themselves* | *himself* | *Bystander* | *Bystander* |
| Means | | | | |
| (1) Remove person(s) | | | | |
| (a) stop protecting others | | | | |
| (b) cause threat to others | | | | |
| (2) Shield person(s) | | | | |
| (3) Redirect threat | | | | |

## 10.

We have been considering whether there is greater moral diffi-culty in justifying killing by turning the trolley when the alter-native is that one would otherwise let people die rather than kill them. Would any supposed difficulty go away for someone who would otherwise let people die when he need not kill, but only do what enables someone else to kill? Suppose the driver in the trolley is going uncontrollably toward hitting the five people. He does not want to kill them, but he cannot stop the trolley and he cannot redirect it toward another track where his enemy, whom he would kill if he could, is located. A mere bystander is able to redirect the trolley with the driver on it away from the five toward the other track, and once the trolley is on that track, the driver alone can control whether it stops or whether he drives it into that one person. The bystander knows the driver will drive it into his enemy. In this case, if the bystander turns the trolley, he does not kill the one person but he will have enabled a deliberate murder to take place. I do not think this makes it impermissible for the bystander to turn the trolley, given that five people will be saved and it is the driver's choice, not the bystander's, to kill the one.

This is one of a set of cases in which someone does not redirect a mechanical threatening entity with no will of its own (as in the Trolley Case) but, rather, redirects a threatening agent who can still make some choices. Often when people try to show that the trolley problem has real-world instances, they do not point to cases in which nonagents, such as flood waters or unmanned missiles, are out of control and need to be redirected in order to reduce deaths. They point to cases in which a still-responsible person, who can and should be making correct choices but is not doing so, can have his more harmful actions prevented by our intervening in ways that lead him to choose to cause less harm. For example, an enemy pilot is on his way to bomb a large city and our government could redirect him to where he could bomb only a small town. In this case, the pilot not only will have a choice when he is over the small town whether to kill or not but also (unlike the driver in our earlier example) is in control of whether to kill when he is still headed to the large city. This sort of case involves the government's doing what enables a deliberate killing of fewer people even before everything has been done by the pilot, still capable of choice, to create the larger threat. While the latter condition may seem to give the government greater opportunity to stop his threat, it does mean that the government is enabling a threat to others when the coming to pass of the larger threat is not yet out of the hands of the other agent.[32] (Notice that there does not seem to be any comparable moral problem in intervening with such a still-responsible agent to reduce the harm he would do to the *same set of people* rather than redirecting him to others. For example, it would be permissible, I believe, to enable him to kill only some [randomly selected members] of the group all of whose members he could otherwise have chosen to kill.)

Another type of case would involve the government's redirecting a pilot who is in control and headed to bombing a large city so that his plane heads to a small town instead, where he will lose control, crash and cause less harm. Here it seems the government would kill fewer people rather than just enable the pilot to do so, but the government does also redirect before the threat the pilot would present to the large city is beyond his control.

All I will say here about cases of this type is that they may raise moral issues that are different from those raised by cases involving out-of-control devices. Insofar as we are concerned with what the trolley problem is, I think they should not be used as examples of the trolley problem. However, they are related to the trolley problem and are worthy of much further study because cases of their type are common in real life.

Table II.2 presents four combinations of factors related to control by the trolley driver in different types of cases (and subcases) involving the choice between five being killed and one being killed. "D" is the driver of a trolley. The standard trolley problem involves the driver's only having control to turn from the five.

*Table II.2* Some Distinctions

|  | D can still control toward 5* | D can not still control toward 5** |
|---|---|---|
| D can still control toward 1*** | a | b |
| D cannot still control toward 1 **** | c | d |

* Subclassifications: (i) Can control when on track to five people; (ii) can control only by turning to track with one person.

** (i) Cannot control when on track to five; (ii) cannot control by turning to track with one. In standard Trolley Case, only (i) is true.

*** (i) Can control while on track to one; (ii) can control only by turning to track with five. (Note: Possible that cannot turn from five to one but can turn from one to five.)

**** (i) Cannot control while on track to one; (ii) cannot control by turning to track with five. Standard Trolley Case is silent about (ii).

## Notes

1. These are in addition to ones already considered in Lecture I.

2. All diagrams should be understood to allow a trolley, represented by a horizontal line, to be moved back from where it is and onto a different track.

3. See Lecture I Section 5 for some cases where who turns the trolley could matter and why.

4. This description of method follows the one in my *Intricate Ethics* 5 (New York: Oxford University Press, 2007).

5. For a more detailed but still incomplete discussion, see my *Intricate Ethics*, of which part of section 3 in this lecture is a brief synopsis.

6. Judith Jarvis Thomson, "Turning the Trolley," *Philosophy & Public Affairs* 36 (2008): 374.

7. Thomson, "Turning the Trolley."

8. We have already briefly considered a proposal like this in Lecture I (pp. 40–41). The current discussion will expand on objections to it. T. M. Scanlon has suggested that it is significant that in the Trolley Case the same right (not to be hit by a trolley) is threatened in the five and the one. By contrast, the fat man would have a different right threatened (not to be manhandled into harm's way) than is threatened in the five. See his "Some Intricacies," *Philosophy and Phenomenological Research* 80 (2010): 694–701. I discuss his proposals in "Substitution, Subordination, and Responsibility: Response to Scanlon, McMahan, and Rosen," *Philosophy and Phenomenological Research* 80 (2010): 702–722. But if we turn the second trolley in the Two Trolleys Case, the one person would also have his right not to be hit by a trolley threatened and yet this does not make hitting him to save the five permissible. This led me to consider a proposal that focuses on being in the same relation to the *same* threat.

9. However, we could also imagine a case in which the five being away from the trolley is what causes that very trolley to threaten someone else. For example, we could imagine that their being in safe territory causes a shift in the land that causes the trolley to be redirected toward one. Presumably it would be permissible to save the five even though this will happen.

10. I made this point in *Intricate Ethics* in response to comments by Derek Parfit.

11. For example, in F. M. Kamm, "Harming Some to Save Others," *Philosophical Studies* 57 (1989): 227–260, in *Morality, Mortality*, vol. 2 (New York: Oxford University Press, 1996), and in *Intricate Ethics*.

12. In *Intricate Ethics*, in discussing harm that is a side effect of a mere means, I emphasize the difference between what we introduce into an environment having harmful properties (such as the gas in Foot's Gas Case) and its triggering harm by entities independently in the environment. Alexander Friedman (in his doctoral dissertation "Minimizing Harm: Three Problems in Moral Theory," unpublished), argues that there is no difference between Foot's Gas Case and the removal of the trolley. Since Thomson claims in her 2008 article that Friedman "showed clearly, that none of the most interesting solutions [to the trolley problem] worked" ("Turning the Trolley," 363), I think it is worth considering whether his view is correct that there is no moral difference between turning the trolley and using the gas (or setting the bomb).

One of Friedman's arguments is as follows: Using the gas to save five when the gas will kill one is wrong. Suppose we have multiple options for how to save five from a trolley headed to them. One of the options involves turning the trolley from them when it will then kill one person; all the other options involve using means to move the trolley that have the side effect of killing the same one person. Friedman believes, and I agree, that in this case it makes no difference whether one turns the trolley or uses one of the other options. However, he also believes that what he calls the Firm Borderline Principle (FBP) is true. This principle says (roughly) that if act B is not permissible when it is the only act we can do, but act A is permissible when it is the only act we can do, then if we have an option in one case of doing either one, we should choose A or do nothing. This principle implies that if turning the trolley is permissible on its own, then in his multiple-options case it should be morally preferable to do it. He thinks that if, intuitively, it does not matter morally which we do in his multiple-options case, and if B on its own is wrong to do, then A must also be wrong on its own. Hence, turning the trolley when it is the only option must be just as wrong as using any of the other means he mentions when they are the only option.

I think this argument is not correct. The problem is that the FBP is not correct. An act that may be impermissible when it is one's only option can become morally equivalent or preferable in a multiple-options case to another act that would be permissible were it one's only option. For example, I believe (1) it is impermissible to move a person into a path of the trolley (as in the Driver or Bystander Topple Cases) when this is our only option even if this will only paralyze his legs, but (2) it is permissible to turn the trolley when this is our only option even if this will kill the same person. However, in a case where we can do either to that same person, given that being paralyzed is less bad for someone than death, it becomes permissible to do the less harmful act that would not be permissible on its own as the alternative to doing the more harmful act. The different ways in which we would cause harm to someone that can be constraints on action when an act is our only option become morally less significant when an equal or greater harm will occur to that same person if we do what would be permissible were it our only option. Indeed, the less harmful act that would be wrong were it one's only option can even become the only permissible act when it is a substitute for another act that was permissible on its own and would otherwise be done. (I have referred to this as the Principle of Secondary Permissibility and discuss it in *Morality, Mortality*, vol. 2, and in *Intricate Ethics*.) Hence, in Friedman's case, a way of killing someone that would be impermissible were it one's only option can become permissible when it is a substitute for our otherwise killing the same person in a permissible way. I conclude that Friedman's argument does not show that if using the gas when it is one's only option is impermissible, turning the trolley when it is one's only option is also impermissible. (A similar problematic move may be present in Derek Parfit's claim (in conversation) that since many would prefer to die as a means to the good of others rather than as a mere side effect, it can be as permissible to kill someone as a mere means when this is one's only option as to kill him collaterally when this is one's only option. It can be true that when one will be killed as a side effect anyway, one would prefer that one's death occur as a mere means to someone else's good, and so it is permissible to kill a person as a mere means instead of as a side effect in this case. But this does not show that it is permissible to kill someone as a mere means when this is one's only option even if it is permissible to kill someone as a side effect when this is one's only option.)

13. I noted this in Lecture I and will discuss it further in this lecture.

14. This formulation of the PPH speaks of whether in fact there are certain causal relations. But I believe the PPH should actually be formulated with a modal condition. That is, we should be concerned with whether, for example, a harm is *necessary* to produce an end or whether our act makes it the case that it is *possible* to produce an end without a harm if the harm (that actually produces the greater good) would not occur. I discuss this in *Intricate Ethics*.

15. Judith Jarvis Thomson, "The Trolley Problem," *Yale Law Journal* 94 (1985): 1402.

16. The one person's being hit is a necessary causal means to saving the five, but unlike standard cases in which we intend to bring about means to our end, in this case we take advantage of the causal role of a side effect (the one's being hit) of what we do (turn the trolley). It is said that a rational agent must intend

the means to his end, but this need not be so when the means will come about as a side effect of what we have some other reason to do (turn the trolley away from one of its threatening positions).

Here is a wartime analogy. We bomb a munitions plant whose blowing up kills a few children as a foreseen side effect. We do not intend their deaths. However, there would be no point in our bombing mission if they did not die, as it is only because they die that their parents are grieving and cannot quickly rebuild the factory. In this case, we do what destroys munitions only on condition of the causal role of a foreseen bad side effect, but it would be wrong to do anything besides what is necessary to bomb the plant in order to bring about the deaths of the children as a means to their parents' grief. I call this the Munitions Grief Case. It is neither a case of mere collateral (useless) harm nor a case of deliberately killing innocents to cause grief. For more on this, see chap. 4 of my *Intricate Ethics*.

17. Which I discuss on page 137 of *Intricate Ethics*, among other places.

18. I should emphasize that the relation of substitution between people that seems to bode well for permissibility is between those harmed and those saved from harm, not between various candidates who might be substituted for those originally threatened with harm. For example, suppose we could choose between either (a) sending the trolley from the five to where it will kill Joe or (b) setting a bomb that will stop the trolley and also kill Jill. What is important according to the proposed PPH is not that using the means that will kill Jill is the strict alternative (or flip side) of using the means that will kill Joe. What matters is in what relation—perhaps substitution or subordination—Joe or Jill would stand to the original five if those means of saving the five are used. If Jill would stand in a subordinated relation, whereas Joe would stand in a substituted relation, this might be a morally significant difference. I have argued elsewhere that one problem with Peter Unger's discussion of the trolley cases in his *Living High and Letting Die* (New York: Oxford University Press, 1996) is that he treats a substitution relation between potential victims who could be harmed to save others as having the same moral significance as the substitution relation between those others who would be saved and those who would be harmed instead. For example, he emphasizes the choice between pushing one person into a trolley or alternatively turning a trolley away though it will harm one other person. His "method of multiple options" relies on substitution among potential victims who are possible alternative victims to the original threatened parties, but this is not the morally relevant form of substitution, I think. I discuss his views in detail in my *Intricate Ethics*, chap. 6.

19. I noted some of them in *Intricate Ethics* and draw upon that discussion in what follows.

20. Among such cases that I discussed in *Intricate Ethics* was one in which the five threatened by the trolley are dying of organ failure. Suppose that we can go on to save them with perfectly legitimate organ transplants if we first save them from the trolley. Then turning away the trolley seems permissible even if, given that the five are still under a deadly threat when the trolley is away from them, its being away has no component of the greater good as a noncausal flip side. Furthermore, we could combine the Loop Case and the Tractor Case II. The one person being hit is causally necessary to prevent the trolley's looping and the looping will be stopped even before the trolley presses on the switch that will stop the tractor. It seems permissible to turn the trolley here (but not to give the extra push just so that the one is hit). Hence, even when the person being hit is causally necessary to *sustain* the removal of the trolley, the hit need not be caused by means that have a noncausal relation to a component of the greater good.

21. While I described these relations between potential victims in earlier work, and characterized them as possibly involving substitution or subordination relations in *Intricate Ethics*, I did not previously try to make clear my view on how these relations bear on the distinction between killing and letting die, which I here try to do. However, the distinction I am drawing between emphasizing Agent-Victim relations and emphasizing InterVictim relations is reminiscent of a contrast I drew in my earlier work on what is called the Paradox of Deontology in, for example, *Morality, Mortality,* vol. 2. There I distinguished between an Agent-Centered (or -Focused) and a Victim-Centered (or -Focused) account of the source of some side-constraints on action. In the paradox, the question is why one may not kill one person as a means to save five other people from being similarly killed to save others. Some have claimed that if one were concerned with the rights of victims, one would minimize rights violations. Others have tried to explain the constraint on killing the one person by focusing on the relation that the agent would have to the potential victims: he would be killing the one but only letting the five die. Yet others tried to explain it by focusing on the relation between agents: one agent would be killing one victim to prevent another agent from killing five, but an agent is responsible primarily for her own killings. One problem with the last proposal is that the same agent who would kill the one could also be responsible for killing the five (e.g., because he set a bomb to kill them that will soon go off and his killing the one will stop this), yet this would not make it permissible for him to kill the one person.

By contrast to these approaches to the paradox, my approach to explaining the constraint was Victim-Focused: each person that an agent would attempt to kill has a right not to be killed that is a barrier to his being killed. If it were permissible to kill the one to save the five, this would mean that all people (including the five) have a weaker right not to be killed than they would have if this killing were impermissible. The status of each person in terms of his inviolability would be lower. If we are not permitted to kill the one to save the five, what will happen is that the five will be killed and have their right not to be killed violated, but it remains true of them that they have a highly inviolable status. This is because status is about what it is permissible to do to people, not what happens to them, and it remains impermissible to kill them even if they are killed. The reason an agent should not kill the one is, fundamentally, because of the status and right of the potential victim the agent comes up against, not because the agent would be killing the one when he would otherwise only be letting five die. In the current discussion, the emphasis is on permissible and impermissible relations between those saved and those harmed that gives rise to only certain forms of inviolability and only rights not to be killed in certain ways, but this could similarly be construed as a truth about each person's status such that standing in certain relations to others is ruled out by that status. I am grateful to Johann Frick for pointing out to me the continuity between my earlier work and the present discussion with respect to adopting a Victim-Focused rather than an Agent-Focused approach.

22. In previous work on this issue (in "Supererogation and Obligation," reprinted in *Morality, Mortality*, vol. 2), I described how supererogation may take precedence over a duty, and the seeming intransitivity involved in this phenomenon. That is, while performing the strong duty takes precedence over not paying large personal costs and not paying the large personal costs may take precedence over performing a rescue, it is not true that performing the strong duty takes precedence over performing the rescue.

23. However, it is worth noting that some of these cases involve not merely the five being safe but their moving to an area where they are safe. Can one change one's location to help oneself when being in that (unoccupied, unowned) location has bad effects on others in the way described? Is this so different from moving one's chest from one location to another by breathing, rather than holding it in, when this has bad effects on others (as described in a variant on the Transplant Case)?

24. In the cases I have mentioned, some entity is made into a threat to someone else in virtue of the five being saved or protected. But it might also be that the five themselves are turned into threats to others. For example, their being

safe involves their landing on someone who already occupies safe territory. Or they might move to safety by turning themselves away from the trolley on the lazy Susan, which hits another person in the process. I shall not here commit as to whether these acts are also permissible. However, if the initial component of the greater good causing lesser evil were the correct explanation of why some acts are permissible, the explanation would imply the permissibility of these acts as well.

25. I raised this issue in *Intricate Ethics* and in Lecture I.

26. This is what I said in previous work about helping the one escape in the Loop Case, where the one being hit would be useful in a somewhat different way. See, for example, the discussion in *Intricate Ethics*.

27. A somewhat similar issue would arise in a variant of Transplant in which someone's dying from a disease would make his organs available to save five others. If a medicine that can cure the one person (but not the five) became available, we, as impartial but nonconsequentialist agents, should not refrain from giving it to him simply because his dying is necessary to save the five. In this medical case, an impartial bystander should let five die rather than let one die.

However, this case differs from helping the one off the track in the following way. In the medical case, the five are already threatened independently of what we do. Helping the one person does not result in the five's facing a threat they did not already face. In the imagined trolley case in which the one person stands between the trolley and the five so that its hitting him would stop it, helping the one would make the five face a threat from which they had previously been protected.

28. Suppose the bystander should and will remove the five though the one will be left to die. However, the harm to the five in being removed would be greater than if they were left behind the one on the track so that he shields them. Given that the one will die either way, not moving the five or the one (because the one shields the five) can become permissible (perhaps the only permissible course). This is another example of the Principle of Secondary Permissibility (first mentioned in n. 12, according to which an act that would be impermissible (e.g., not removing the one person) if it were one's only option can become permissible (and even the only permissible act) as a substitute for another permissible act that is not less harmful to the person who will be harmed).

29. Suppose the one person stands between the oncoming trolley and the five and his being hit would protect them. If he is given a shield, it would deflect the trolley onto another track that loops back to the same five. In this

case, the redirection would cause the death of people who would only be alive because the one person would have continued to protect them if he did not use his shield. I think this may make providing the shield permissible. I suspect that this case is in principle no different from the case in which the one person would be removed from the track. It may also be true that if an impartial bystander should remove the one person from the track in the Loop Case, then that impartial bystander should also provide the one person with a shield even if this deflects the trolley to a second looping track that leads to the five. Its being right to use these means to protect the one person though they interfere with saving the five may seem to imply that it is impermissible to turn the trolley in the Loop Case. But this is not so, for it being right to use these protective means does not imply that we may not turn the trolley threat and take advantage of the usefulness of the side effect of the one being hit, when we do not refrain from using any separate available ways to prevent that hit. For related discussion, see *Intricate Ethics*, chap. 4, and "Nuclear Deterrence and Reliance on Harm to Noncombatants," in my *The Moral Target: Aiming at Right Conduct in War and Other Conflicts* (New York: Oxford University Press, 2012).

30. If the impartial bystander had foreseen in advance that he would kill the one by redirecting the trolley to save the five, he could permissibly instead have left the one in front of the five on the track to die. For then, leaving him makes no difference to the well-being of the one person because he would otherwise lose his life anyway. This is another instance of the Principle of Secondary Permissibility.

31. Here is a particular instance of how not aiding does not seem to abide by a principle comparable to the PPH I have described (on pp. 66–67). Suppose the bystander needs to use a certain complicated device in order to remove the five from trolley tracks, and simply because he is employing these means he cannot go to save one person who will be hit by the trolley first. Then it is using certain mere means to saving the five that leads to his letting the one die. It is permissible for him to do this even if, according to a PPH, he may not use mere means to save the five that will directly kill the one person (like the bomb). But note that letting someone die because one is occupied with mere means to helping the five involves some other entity (e.g., trolley independently in the environment) killing the one person. Previously we noted that it is possible that mere causal means may be used to save the five when their use causes some other entity (e.g., germs independently in the environment) to kill the one. This points to an underlying similarity between not aiding and some ways of harming.

32. In my "Responsibility and Collaboration" (reprinted in revised form in *Intricate Ethics*), I suggested there might be a moral difference in one agent's causing a lesser harm before rather than after another agent has done all he can do to produce a greater harm. This issue was also present in cases of Nazis being redirected from killing a larger number of people when it was known that if redirected they would instead decide to kill a smaller number of other people. (The latter case also raises the issue of collaboration with the Nazis by those who attempted to minimize deaths among Jews. Collaboration involves jointly decided upon action by those who do the redirecting with those who are redirected. This issue does not arise in the standard trolley cases.) I discuss the Nazis case in "Harming Some to Save Others from the Nazis," reprinted in *The Moral Target*. It is not clear whether the differences between standard trolley cases (involving out-of-control devices) and these other cases (involving in-control agents) make a moral difference—for better or worse—but it is something to think about.

# Diagrams

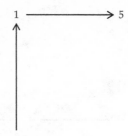

*Diagram 1:* Transplant Case
Kill one person for organs to save five.

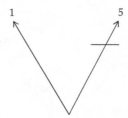

*Diagram 2:* Trolley Driver's Two Options Case
Driver can kill five or turn trolley to kill one. (The trolley is represented here and below by the short horizontal line.)

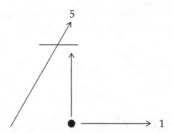

*Diagram 3:* Bomb Trolley Case
Someone can set off bomb to stop trolley from killing five, bomb kills one.

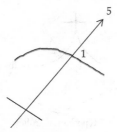

*Diagram 4:* Driver Topple Case
Driver can kill five or topple fat man in front of trolley, killing him to save five

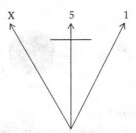

*Diagram 5:* Bystander's Three Options Case
Bystander (X) can let five die, or turn trolley to kill one, or turn trolley to self.

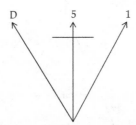

*Diagram 6:* Trolley Driver's Three Options Case
Driver can kill five, or turn trolley to kill one, or turn trolley to self.

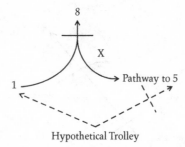

Hypothetical Trolley

*Diagram 7:* Bystander Saving-by-Letting-Die Case
Bystander (X) can let eight die or turn trolley to one or to block path needed to save five

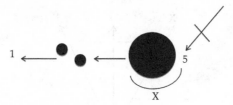

*Diagram 8:* Lazy Susan Case
Bystander (X) can let five die or turn lazy Susan; five moved away and rockslide caused that kills one.

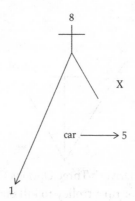

*Diagram 9* Bystander Saving-by-Letting-Die Case (2)
Bystander (X) can let eight die or turn trolley to one also stopping car from hitting five or turn trolley to empty track

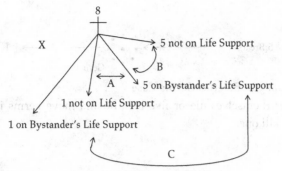

*Diagram 10* Bystander Saving-by-Letting-Die Case (3)
Bystander (X) can let eight die or turn trolley to fewer either on or not on his life support

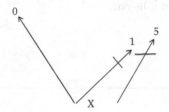

*Diagram 11* Two Trolleys Case
Bystander (X) can let five die or turn second trolley to stop first; second trolley will kill one.

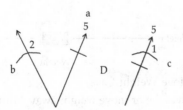

*Diagram 12:* Inter-Victim/Agent-Victim Choices
(a) Driver can let five die or (b) turn trolley that saves five and topples two, or (c) topple one to stop trolley and save five.

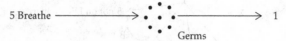

*Diagram 13:* Breathe/Germs Case
Five let themselves die or five breathe and move germs in area; germs kill one.

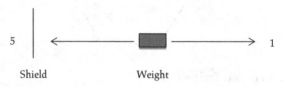

*Diagram 14:* Breathe/Weight Case
Five let themselves die from weight or five breathe and move weight from them; weight kills one.

*Diagram 15:* Shield/Weight Case
Five let themselves die or shield themselves and weight moves off of five's shield, killing one.

*Diagram 16:* Move Weight Case
Five let themselves die or move weight away, killing one.

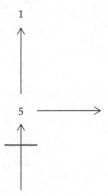

*Diagram 17:* Duck Trolley Case
Five let themselves die or move away and one is hit by trolley.

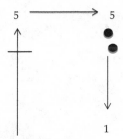

*Diagram 18:* Move to Safety Case
Five let themselves die or move to a safe area, causing rockslide that kills one.

# Comments

# Kamm on the Trolley Problems

## JUDITH JARVIS THOMSON

## 1.

Kamm's lectures seem to me to bring home that we should remind ourselves of what the trolley problems are.

In her article, "The Problem of Abortion and the Doctrine of the Double Effect," Philippa Foot drew attention to some objections to that doctrine.[1] She then said that many people think we have to take it seriously despite the objections, on the ground that we don't seem to have any other way of explaining why morality delivers what appear to be conflicting directives in cases that are the same in certain morally important respects. Thus, for example, the surgeon surely may not kill the one in:

*Transplant*

> A great transplant surgeon can save the lives of five of his patients by cutting up a healthy person and installing the person's heart, lungs, and kidneys in the five.

But the driver surely may kill the one in:

*Driver*

> The driver of an out-of-control tram—"trolley" in American English—will run down and kill five track workmen unless he

steers the tram off the straight track onto a branch of track to the right. Unfortunately, there is one track workman on the right-hand track whom the driver will run down and kill if he turns onto it.

Indeed, Foot says, "the driver should steer for the less occupied track."[2] How can it be that the surgeon may not kill the one though the driver may? For what the agents do if they kill the one is in the following morally important respect the same: the outcome of their killing the one is that one dies instead of five.[3]

I bypass the way in which it is thought that appeal to the doctrine of double effect would enable us to explain this difference. What is of particular interest in Foot's article is the explanation that she herself offered. She drew attention to some other cases that are, intuitively, relevantly similar to Transplant and Driver, and suggested that the wanted explanation lies in the distinction between negative duties and positive duties—and the use she made of that idea strongly suggested that she had in mind the following:

*Worseness Thesis*

Though (1) killing five is worse than killing one, (2) killing one is worse than letting five die.

How exactly does that bear on the two agents? She is standardly interpreted as taking it to yield, and thereby explain, the following generalization:

*Choice Generalization*

Though (1') if A must choose between killing five and killing one, then he may kill the one, (2') if B must choose between killing one and letting five die, then he may not kill the one—he must let the five die.

It follows from clause (1') that the driver may kill the one, and from clause (2') that the surgeon may not. Thus, the Worseness Thesis explains why the following is the case: though the driver may kill the one, the surgeon may not.

Those ideas are very attractive. So Foot's explanation of the difference between Transplant and Driver was very attractive.

Alas, something got in the way of it. In an article that responded to Foot's, I drew attention to a case that made trouble for it; in a later article, I drew attention to a case that made trouble for it in the same way but perhaps more clearly:

### Bystander

An out-of-control trolley will run into and kill five track workmen unless a switch is thrown, which will turn the trolley onto a branch of track to the right. Fortunately, there is a bystander standing next to the switch, and he can throw it. Unfortunately, there is one track workman on the right-hand track, and if the bystander throws the switch, he will thereby kill the one.[4]

Clause (2') of the Choice Generalization yields that the bystander may not kill the one. He therefore must not throw the switch. However, most people say that while it is very unfortunate that the bystander will kill the one if he throws the switch, it is nevertheless permissible for him to throw it. But then clause (2') of the Choice Generalization is false, and thus the Choice Generalization is itself false. And then it won't do to explain why the surgeon may not kill the one by appeal to the Worseness Thesis on the ground that it yields and thereby explains the Choice Generalization.

So we are back where we started.

In the earlier of the two articles of mine that I mentioned, I said that I liked to call the following "the trolley problem" in honor of Foot's case of the driver: why may the driver kill the one whereas the surgeon may not? Call that "driver baptism." In the later of the two articles that I mentioned, I said I find the following problem particularly puzzling, and I am therefore inclined to call it "the trolley problem": why may the bystander kill the one whereas the surgeon may not? Call this "bystander baptism." Those two problems are not the same. The one Foot set herself to solve was the trolley problem (driver baptism). The trolley problem (bystander baptism) arose only because, given that the bystander may kill the one, Foot's solution to the trolley problem (driver baptism) is not satisfactory. I regret having muddied the water by giving the same name to both problems.

Fortunately, that water-muddying doesn't seem to have done any harm. The two problems are intimately connected, and contributors to the philosophical literature describe themselves as concerned with the trolley problem whichever problem they are primarily concerned with. (Most of them have been primarily concerned with the trolley problem (bystander baptism).) A reminder of the differences between the two problems nevertheless seemed to me to be called for—for clarity about their significance in moral theory, and about what they require of moral theorists.

## 2.

Referring to the trolley problem (driver baptism), Kamm says: "this suggestion about what the trolley problem is should not be understood so narrowly that the Problem concerns only these two cases [Transplant and Driver] rather than all cases that are structurally similar" (p. 12). And at the end of her first lecture she says that the trolley problem is "about why it is sometimes permissible to kill, even rather than let die, when we come to kill in some ways but not others" (p. 47). I take her to mean: the trolley problem is about when it is permissible to kill and when not, and why. How did that happen? How did the particular problem "Why is it that though the driver may kill the one, the surgeon may not?" get to *be* the general problem "When is it permissible to kill and when not, and why?"[5]

I take this to be an important question. Before turning to it, however, we must stop to take note of a disagreement.

## 3.

Kamm believes that the bystander may kill the one, and therefore that the correct solution to the trolley problem (bystander baptism) must yield that he may. Many people share the belief that he may, and I certainly held that belief at the time of writing the second of the two articles I mentioned. But some years later I came to believe it a mistake, and I argued that it is in a third article.[6] I therefore now conclude that there isn't really any such thing as the trolley problem (bystander baptism). Kamm disagrees, and devotes a considerable part of her first lecture to a great scatter of arguments to the effect that I am mistaken.

In very brief, I said the following. Call the lone workman Workman. Suppose it seems that the bystander has three options: he can throw the switch so that it kills Workman (thereby saving the five), he can throw it so that it kills himself (thereby saving the five), or he can do neither (allowing the five to die). If that is the case, then he may not throw the switch so that it kills Workman, because neither he nor Workman is required to pay the cost of saving the five, and therefore if he wants the cost paid, he must pay it himself. I stress: if he doesn't want to pay it himself, and therefore won't, then he must let it go unpaid. Suppose, however, that it turns out after all that the bystander has only the two options described in Bystander. All the same, he may not throw the switch so that it kills Workman because neither he nor Workman is required to pay the cost of saving the five, and therefore, since he can't pay the cost himself (whether or not he would like to), he must let the five die.

Kamm's "first concern" is that "one cannot, in general, move from a conclusion in a three-options case to one in a two-options case" (p. 23). I didn't rely on any general thesis to the effect that one can. Indeed, I supplied the three-options case primarily in order to bring out more vividly the consideration that makes it impermissible for the bystander to kill Workman in the two-options case—namely, that neither the bystander nor Workman is required to pay the cost of saving the five.

Kamm's "second major concern" is about the order in which I argued for the premises on which I rely: I should have argued for them in a different order. I bypass this objection.

What Kamm calls her "third major concern" is a variety of different objections. She begins with what she calls "background," and I am not clear where the background ends and the foreground begins. But perhaps the foreground begins with her drawing attention to Scheffler's claim that, as she puts it, "constraining agents from imposing costs on others that those others have a prerogative to refuse to pay on their own could not be justified on grounds of protecting autonomy" (p. 28). For perhaps Kamm here implies that since (i) constraining agents from imposing those costs is justified only if it is justified by appeal to autonomy, and (ii) Scheffler is right in claiming that it isn't justified by appeal to autonomy, I am mistaken in thinking that we may not impose those costs. I leave open that Scheffler is right; that is, I bypass the question why we should believe (ii). I don't bypass the question why we should believe (i). I claimed that if a person is not morally required to pay a cost, and neither are we required to pay it, then other things being equal, it is not open to us to impose the cost on him. What exactly does Kamm think shows that that won't do?

She says: "I think that sometimes it may be morally permissible to impose costs on others when no one would, or would be required to, impose them on himself . . ." (p. 28). And she gives some examples. The first few are obviously irrelevant. I take space to describe only two. She says: "We may sometimes draft someone to be a soldier even if we (and also he) would not and need not volunteer . . ." (p. 28). Who's that "we"? It is at most governments who may draft people—indeed, it is only governments that so much as *can* draft them—and what governments may do to people is not the same as what people may do to people. Again, she says: "I may permissibly compete with someone, causing him to lose his business so that I get funds for a cause, though I would not, and morally need not, close my own business to get funds for a cause" (p. 29). People who engage in business under our legal system are rightly understood to consent to the risk that others will compete with them and cause them to lose their businesses.

Kamm herself agrees that those cases, and some others that she describes, are some distance from the target case. So she says:

> Getting closer to the trolley problem, I may put a shield around the five people protecting them from the trolley, knowing that when the trolley hits the shield around the five it will be deflected to one other person, even if I would not and morally need not put a shield around the five when I know the trolley will be deflected to me. (p. 29)

Really? This case got Kamm too close to the trolley problem, for what difference could it be thought to make that a person deflects the trolley by putting a shield around the five instead of by throwing a switch? Her declaring that she may put a shield around the five is dialectically as effective as her simply declaring that the bystander may throw the switch would have been.

Finally (I *think* this completes Kamm's third major concern), she says:

> Suppose that the only way for me to save five others from drowning is to let myself drown (by giving them a life preserver I need and could otherwise use). I could permissibly refuse to let myself drown and let the five drown instead. Yet it would also be permissible for me to let one *other* person drown, though he does not want me to, in order to save five others instead (by giving the five instead of the one a life preserver when I do not need it). (p. 30)

Two cases are described here. In (i), I must choose between giving five my life preserver, in which case they will live but I will drown, and keeping my life preserver, in which case the five will drown but I will live. Other things being equal, I certainly may choose to keep my life preserver. In (ii), I must choose between giving five my life preserver, in which case they will live but one person other than myself will drown, and giving that one person my life preserver, in which case the five will drown but the one person other than myself will live. Other things being equal, I may certainly choose to give my life preserver to the five. So? Why are we to attend to these two cases?

Kamm says: "[In (ii),] I would permissibly impose a cost on that one by not aiding him that I would permissibly not impose on myself [in (i)]" (p. 30). But I don't *impose* a cost on the one if I choose to give my life preserver to the five in (ii): what I do is to refrain from preventing his suffering a cost. Just as I don't *impose* a cost on the five if I choose to keep my life preserver in (i): what I do is to refrain from preventing their suffering a cost. Indeed, Kamm herself says that (ii), "of course, is a case of letting someone die, and Thomson believes (as do I) that there is a moral difference between killing someone and letting him die ..." (p. 30). So to repeat: why are we to attend to these two cases?

She goes on:

> [B]ut to show that a bystander may not redirect the trolley to the other person, more has to be said than that, other things equal, he should not make someone else pay a cost that he would not and need not pay himself. For this factor would also imply that he may not let the one die to instead save the five if he would not and morally need not let himself die in order to save the five. If one has an independent argument for the permissibility of letting someone die to save others, one cannot show that it is impermissible to do so merely because one would permissibly not let oneself die to save others. (p. 30)

I see no reason at all to believe that the sentence beginning "For this factor would also imply" is true. Does Kamm here forget that she just granted that there is a moral difference between killing someone and letting someone die? I take it to be clear that the moral difference between killing and letting die *is* the more that has to be said. It *is* what makes it the case that I may refrain from saving one person in order to save five though I would not refrain from saving myself in order to save the five, whereas I may not *kill* the one in order to save five if I would not kill myself in order to save the five. If Kamm thinks that the moral difference between killing and letting die doesn't make that the case, then I find it hard to see what she can plausibly think it does make the case. I add, finally, about the concluding sentence of that passage: the best I can make of it is that it merely repeats the point of the sentence that precedes it.

So much—so far as I can see—for cases (i) and (ii).

Kamm goes on in the remainder of her first lecture to produce many arguments against things I said about Bystander; many are just repetitions of arguments that I have already summarized, and the rest, so far as I can see, are irrelevant to whether the bystander may kill the one.

In sum, I find nothing at all in Kamm's first lecture that counts against my argument to the effect that the bystander may not kill the one.

But there is a second lecture, so let us turn to it.

# 4.

Kamm says at the outset of her second lecture that its primary aim is to consider some proposals about "why it is at least thought" that both the driver and the bystander may kill the one. If there is an explanation of why both may kill the one, then it follows that both *may* kill the one, and it therefore follows that the bystander may kill the one.

The proposal she invites us to take seriously is that both the driver and the bystander may kill the one because their saving the five would be "the mere noncausal flip side of removing what threatens them (the trolley)" (p. 62). What *does* Kamm mean? She goes on: "That is, in the circumstances of these cases, where there are no other threats to them, the five people being saved is simply the trolley's moving away. The relation between the trolley moving away and the five being saved is not a causal relation but, rather, seems to be a constitutive relation" (p. 62). I therefore take it that she means the following by X's being "the mere noncausal flip side" of Y: X's being identical with Y. And I therefore take it that the proposal we are to take seriously is: the driver and bystander may kill the one because their acts of saving the five would *be* their acts of removing the trolley.

The ontology of action is disputed territory in metaphysics, and it isn't a good idea to wander around in it in the dark. I know of two theories of action that yield that Kamm is right to say that the driver's and bystander's saving the five would *be* their removing the trolley; the other theories of action that I know of yield that she is not right.[7]

Let us bypass that source of trouble. Let us arbitrarily assume that one of the two theories that yield Kamm's identity claim is correct. According to those theories, her identity claim is true since if the driver and bystander remove their trolleys, (i) they will save the five by removing the trolley, and (ii) the time of the end-point of their removing the trolley is the time of the onset of the five's being safe from death by the trolley.[8]

On that assumption, Kamm's proposal really does yield that the driver and bystander may kill the one. See the Addendum on the Loop (p. 128) for discussion of another case for which Kamm's proposal yields that the agent may kill the one. Thus, so far, so good for her purposes.

But no further. In a certain possible case—we might as well call it Bat—we can save the five by removing the trolley, but we can remove the trolley only by hitting it with a heavy bystander. If we remove the trolley, (i) we will save the five by removing it, and (ii) the time of the end-point of our removing the trolley is the time of the onset of the five's being safe from death by the trolley. Therefore, the proposal that Kamm would have us take seriously yields that we may kill the one in Bat.[9] It hardly needs saying that that won't do.

So the proposal has to be drastically amended, or some new theory of the ontology of action invented, if the proposal is to serve Kamm's purposes. Similarly for the very complicated, obscure generalization she went on to construct from the proposal.

Kamm herself turns out to be dissatisfied by that complicated, obscure generalization, for reasons I am not at all clear about. She suggests that it won't do because it issues "from generalizing from too narrow a set of cases. Turning the trolley seems to be permissible in cases that do not satisfy" the generalization's conditions (pp. 69–70). She describes several cases that she says don't satisfy the generalization's conditions, but I have been unable to see why she says that they don't—partly, no doubt, because I don't understand the generalization, though partly also because the cases themselves are hard to get one's mind around. In the case Kamm calls the Tractor Case, "The five toward whom the trolley is headed also have a deadly tractor headed toward them. If we turn the trolley away it will hit one person whose being hit will stop the tractor" (p. 68). I *think* Kamm holds that turning the trolley is permissible according to the generalization, and should be, though I really can't be sure. In any case, she holds that our turning the trolley is not permissible according to the generalization in what she calls Tractor Case II, "which is like the original Tractor Case except that the person's being hit on the side track has no causal role in stopping the tractor. Rather, the tractor is stopped by a switch that is pressed by the trolley as it is turned away from the five" (p. 70). Yet she says that our turning the trolley in this case "seems permissible."

*Many* other hypothetical cases follow in Kamm's second lecture, many even more ornate. "Suppose a trolley driver faces a choice among: (a) killing the five, (b) turning the trolley away from the five onto a track that runs on a bridge so that two other people get toppled from the bridge, or (c) pressing a switch that moves one fat man off a bridge so that he stops the trolley headed to the same five people" (p. 74). And many more ornate than that. Why is our attention drawn to such cases? I will return to that question in the following section.

But first: may the bystander kill the one? I found nothing in Kamm's first lecture that counts against my argument to the effect that he may not. The proposal in her second lecture would, if correct, yield that he may, but it isn't correct. And I find no further arguments in Kamm's second lecture to the effect that he may.

## 5.

In section 4, we looked at a disagreement: Kamm thinks the bystander may turn the trolley whereas I now think he may not. Let us return now to the problem that Philippa Foot set before us: namely, the trolley problem (driver baptism). As I said, Kamm tells us that that problem really is the problem "When is it permissible to kill and when not, and why?" And I asked: how did the particular problem "Why is it that though the driver may kill the one, the surgeon may not?" get to *be* the general problem "When is it permissible to kill and when not, and why?"

The answer is that it can't have, so it didn't. We do best to take Kamm to mean not that the particular problem is the general problem, but that solving the particular problem requires solving the general problem. So although her second lecture begins with a proposal about the driver and bystander in particular—that is, the proposal we looked at in the preceding section—it rapidly turns to trying to solve the general problem.

More precisely, her second lecture rapidly turns to beginning to try to get ready to try to solve the general problem. Early in her second lecture, Kamm describes the enterprise she thinks called for. Start with some hypothetical cases whose agents, we believe, may kill a person, and some hypothetical cases whose agents, we believe, may not kill a person, and then try to find a generalization that yields those outcomes. Then see if the generalization you've found needs revision in virtue of there being further hypothetical cases whose agents, we believe, may, and hypothetical cases whose agents, we believe, may not, kill a person; and if the generalization does need revision, try to find a revised generalization. And so on and on and on, hypothetical case after hypothetical case. She says: if we reach a generalization that seems satisfactory "in terms of cohering with intuitive judgments about cases," then we should see if it "reflects some morally significant underlying concepts or values" (p. 60). But she tells us that she won't reach that point in what follows, for she won't be trying to survey all the many hypothetical cases our beliefs about which have to be accommodated. So she says about what follows in her second lecture: "while it may seem like we are considering many hypothetical cases, I assure you they will not be enough!" (p. 60).

And so that is what happens in her second lecture: we drift along, from hypothetical case to hypothetical case, some extremely complicated. Kamm draws connections and points to differences among her beliefs about them, and she makes interesting suggestions from time to time; but no suggestion is followed up very far, and nothing is explained, before something else occurs to her and off we go in another direction. Moreover, there is no summary at the end, so we don't know how much progress Kamm herself thinks she has made in her two lectures in the search for the generalization that she says we need.[10]

Why does Kamm think that philosophy requires our engaging in that enterprise? She isn't the only one who thinks that *kind* of enterprise is required. Compare the markedly less rich, though itself quite deadly, generating of hypothetical cases that went on in the literature on the Gettier problem.

It certainly doesn't go on in the great works we study in learning how to do philosophy. What the authors of those works were at pains to do is to find *theories*. Moral theories in the case of those who find morality interesting but puzzling: it is precisely what the morally significant underlying concepts and values *are* that they try to discover. And none of them seems to have thought that, in order to find out what they are, they must first find generalizations of the kind Kamm is in search of.

Were they just mistaken? *Is* there good reason for thinking that one can't explain why the driver may kill the one whereas the surgeon may not unless we already know when anyone, however situated, may or may not kill a person?

By way of illustration of what can be done under the name "moral theory" by focusing on the question why the driver may kill the one whereas the surgeon may not, we might usefully take a second look at Philippa Foot's article.

By way of reminder, Foot proposed that explanation of the fact that, though the driver may kill the one, the surgeon may not, lies in the distinction between negative and positive duties—and the use she made of that idea strongly suggested that she had in mind the following:

*Worseness Thesis*

Though (1) killing five is worse than killing one, (2) killing one is worse than letting five die.

I said that she is standardly interpreted as taking it to yield, and thereby explain, the following generalization:

*Choice Generalization*

Though (1') if A must choose between killing five and killing one, then he may kill the one, (2') if B must choose between killing one and letting five die, then he may not kill the one—he must let the five die.

But that is only one way (an overly simple way) of interpreting the Worseness Thesis. Anyone who interprets it in that way takes it to tell us about the relative values of acts of certain kinds—takes it, in short, to be about killings and lettings die. We may instead take it to tell us about killing and letting die. Thus, we may instead take it to say:

*Worseness\* Thesis*

Though (1\*) an act's being a killing of five counts in favor of its being impermissible more strongly than an act's being a killing of one counts in favor of its being impermissible, (2\*) an act's being a killing of one counts in favor of its being impermissible more strongly than an act's being a letting five die counts in favor of its being impermissible.

(That "counting in favor of an act's being impermissible" is what moral theorists ascribe when they say, as they so often do, not "he acted wrongly" but, rather, "other things being equal, he acted wrongly," attributing the burden of proof that he didn't act wrongly to anyone who thinks that he didn't.) This thesis is weaker than the Choice Generalization in one way: its truth is entirely compatible with there being situations in which we may kill five rather than kill one, and situations in which we may kill one rather than let five die.[11] Yet it is stronger than the Choice Generalization in another way: it yields information about why it matters whether an act is a killing of five or one, and why it matters whether an act is a killing of one or a letting five die. Not being a consequentialist, I claim that both clauses supply us with information, and not merely the first. I add that there isn't anything in either of Kamm's lectures that sheds any doubt on it.

The chief advantage of the Worseness\* Thesis for our purposes is that it makes clear what needs explaining. *Why* does an act's being a killing of five conduce more strongly against performing it than an act's being a killing of one conduces against performing it? *Why* does an act's being a killing of one conduce more strongly against performing it than an act's being a letting five die conduces against performing it? (What exactly might Foot's talk of negative and positive duties be thought to come to and rest on?) What is needed in order to answer those questions isn't dozens of hypothetical killings and lettings die, but a moral theory.

A moral theory whose answers to those questions thereby also explain why some features of some killings and lettings die conduce more strongly than others to impermissibility and how strongly they do. One way in which we are helped to see what those answers are is to focus on Driver and Transplant. *Why* is it that nothing we have been told about in being told about the driver conflicts with the conclusion that he may kill the one, and nothing we have been told about in being told about the surgeon conflicts with the conclusion that he may not? It is these cases that *themselves* need attention, not the indefinitely many other possible cases in which one person kills another.

My own impression is that there is a theory that looks as if it could have been tailor-made to yield answers to those questions and their ilk, namely the theory of rights. But that is a topic for another occasion. What matters now is only that it *is* moral theory that moral philosophy requires of us.

## Addendum on the Loop

In the seminar following the sessions at which Kamm gave her lectures in Berkeley, I drew attention to the following variant on Bystander:

*Loop*

The city has added a loop of track to the tracks in Bystander, which connects the right-hand track with the straight track in such a way that if nobody were on the right-hand track, then the bystander's turning the trolley would cause it to circle round and hit the five from the rear, killing them. Things being as they are, if the bystander throws the switch, then the trolley will be blocked by the (very heavy) one on the right-hand track, but will kill him. If the bystander doesn't throw the switch, the trolley will be blocked by the five, but will kill them.[12]

I called it a variant on Bystander because I had meant—and it is standardly assumed by people who hear of Bystander that I meant—that the tracks in Bystander are *not* connected by a loop of track. Like many other people, at that time I believed:

(1) The bystander may throw the switch in Bystander.

It wasn't a surprise that many people feel reluctant to accept:

(2) The bystander may throw the switch in Loop.

For wouldn't the bystander be *using* the one to save the five by blocking the trolley? Compare the surgeon, who (plainly unacceptably) uses the one to save the five.[13] But I claimed that "we cannot really suppose that the presence or absence of that extra bit of track makes a major moral difference" as to what the bystander may do, and thus that we should accept

(3) If you believe (1), then good sense requires you to believe (2).

So discomfort or no, good sense requires us to believe (2). Kamm herself believes (1) and (2), and the question I raised at the seminar was how she is to obtain both (1) and (2), given that the proposal she invited us to take seriously—which we looked at in section 4 of this comment—yields that the bystander may save the five in Bystander, but does not yield that the bystander may save the five in Loop. I didn't understand the reply she made at the seminar, and I find even less clear what she means by the remarks she inserted about Loop into her second lecture.

But my question at the seminar issued from a mistake on my part. I hadn't realized at the time of the seminar that both of the theories of action that I mentioned in section 4 yield that the bystander's saving the five in Loop would *be* his removing the trolley. (Just as the bystander's saving the five in Bystander would *be* his removing the trolley.) Both theories yield that identity because if the bystander saves the five in Loop, (i) he saves the five by removing the trolley, and (ii) the time of the end-point of his removing the trolley is the time of the onset of the five's being safe from death by the trolley. (Note that (ii) is true in Loop because, given that there is a heavy man on the right-hand track, the five are safe once the trolley is turned. That is because even though the heavy man hasn't yet been hit by the trolley, once it has been turned, he will be hit by it.)

However, my main reason for this addendum is (3). I no longer think (1) is true and, *a fortiori*, I no longer think (2) is true, but I still think it plain that (3) is true. I was therefore much surprised to find at the seminar that many people disagreed. So herewith two reasons for accepting (3):

(a) Suppose a Good Samaritan believes that although (1) is true, (2) is not. And suppose, first, that he now knows he is either the bystander in Bystander or the bystander in Loop, but doesn't know which. Thus, he knows that if he turns the trolley, then he thereby kills the one, whichever case he is the bystander in. But he should hesitate to turn the trolley because, if he is the bystander in Bystander, then his turning the trolley and thereby killing the one would be all right, whereas if he is the bystander in Loop, then his turning the trolley and thereby killing the one would be all wrong.

He should think that if there's time, he had better phone City Hall to find out whether he is or isn't on a loop-connected track.

That strikes me as a thoroughly odd idea. It is the odder the larger the loop is in Loop. Suppose the loop in Loop is twenty miles long. The possibility of a loop connection twenty miles away—which would mark the Good Samaritan as the bystander in Loop rather than as the bystander in Bystander—should make the difference as to whether the Good Samaritan's turning the trolley, and thereby killing the one, would be all right or all wrong?

(b) Moreover, suppose that he is not the only one who doesn't know whether he is the bystander in Bystander or the bystander in Loop: suppose nobody knows. And indeed, suppose he knows that nobody knows. Then he also knows that it wouldn't be any use for him to phone City Hall to find out because the mayor himself doesn't know.

How can that be? Suppose the workmen are currently finishing the work on the loop connection, but haven't yet completed it. Suppose also that the projected loop connection is twenty miles away, and that it would take the trolley forty minutes to get to it if the Good Samaritan turned the trolley onto the right-hand track and there were no heavy man in the way. Suppose, finally, that it hasn't yet been decided whether the work is to be finished in thirty-nine minutes or spread out to fill forty-one minutes: the mayor and the union representatives haven't yet come to agreement. Knowing all this, the Good Samaritan hesitates, miserably. For if they decide to, and therefore will, spread out the work to fill forty-one minutes, then he is the bystander in Bystander, and therefore may now turn the trolley and thereby kill the one; but if they decide to, and therefore will, finish the work in thirty-nine minutes, then he is the bystander in Loop, and therefore may not now turn the trolley and thereby kill the one.

And there's more for the Good Samaritan to worry about, for mightn't they change their minds after they have made their decision? Suppose they decide and thus announce that they will spread out the work to forty-one minutes; then, after he has already turned the trolley and thereby killed the one, thinking it all right for him to do so, they decide—perhaps for a good reason—to speed up the work to thirty-nine minutes instead, and do so, thereby making it have been all wrong for him to turn the trolley and thereby kill the one. Or suppose they decide and thus announce that they will speed up the work to thirty-nine minutes, and then, after the Good Samaritan has refrained from turning the trolley, so that the five die, thinking it would be all wrong for him to turn the trolley, they decide—perhaps for good reason—to slow down the work to forty-one minutes instead, thereby making him have lost an opportunity to save five lives it would have been all right for him to save.

Poor Good Samaritan. His goodness of heart calls for admiration, but not his goodness of head.

## Notes

1. Philippa Foot, "The Problem of Abortion and the Doctrine of the Double Effect," *Oxford Review* 5 (1967), reprinted in Philippa Foot, *Virtues and Vices and Other Essays in Moral Philosophy* (Oxford: Blackwell, 1978), 19–32.

2. Foot, *Virtues and Vices*, 23.

3. Foot actually began by contrasting with Driver a case in which a judge can save five hostages from a mob by framing an innocent person and having him executed, Transplant appearing only later in her article. I replaced the judge with the surgeon in my summary here, since Transplant figures far more prominently in the literature on the trolley problem. An equally prominent contrast with Driver is the case often called Fat Man, in which an agent can save five people by toppling a fat man off a footbridge into the path of a trolley that threatens the five; this case appeared in my "Killing, Letting Die, and the Trolley Problem," *The Monist* 59 (1976): 204–217.

4. The earlier article was "Killing, Letting Die, and the Trolley Problem." The later article was "The Trolley Problem," *Yale Law Journal* 94 (1985): 1395–1415. In the earlier article I had invited readers to imagine that the trolley's driver died of shock and a passenger can turn the trolley onto the

other track. Some people find it clearer that a bystander has nothing to do with the trolley's threat to the five than that a passenger does—hence Bystander.

5. There are passages that suggest that Kamm thinks the trolley problem is more general still, namely "When is it permissible to harm and when not, and why?" I ignore this further spread.

6. See Judith Jarvis Thomson, "Turning the Trolley," *Philosophy & Public Affairs* 36 (2008): 359–374. A graduate student, Alex Friedman, had argued in his thesis that despite the great ingenuity that so many people have brought to bear on it, nobody has succeeded in solving the trolley problem (bystander baptism), and he said that maybe the reason why nobody has succeeded in solving it is that the belief that generated it is a mistake—the belief, in particular, that the bystander may kill the one. In "Turning the Trolley," I argue that that belief *is* a mistake.

7. For one theory that yields Kamm's identity claim, see G. E. M. Anscombe, *Intention* (Oxford: Blackwell, 1959); and Donald Davidson, "The Logical Form of Action Sentences," reprinted in his *Essays on Actions and Events* (Oxford: Oxford University Press, 1980). For another theory that yields Kamm's identity claim, see Judith Jarvis Thomson, *Acts and Other Events* (Ithaca, NY: Cornell University Press, 1977). For a theory according to which Kamm's identity claim is false, see Alvin I. Goldman, *A Theory of Human Action* (Englewood Cliffs, NJ: Prentice-Hall, 1970). See also Jonathan Bennett, *Events and Their Names* (Indianapolis, IN: Hackett, 1988).

8. According to the theory found in the works by Anscombe and Davidson, clause (ii) is irrelevant; according to the theory found in the work by Thomson, clause (ii) is not irrelevant. But both theories yield that the identity claim is true if (i) and (ii) are both true.

9. Moreover, the proposal that Kamm would have us take seriously also yields that we may kill the one in her complicated Two Trolleys Case. (In that case, we can save five who are threatened by trolley 1: we can save them by removing trolley 1, which threatens them. But we can remove trolley 1 only by turning trolley 2 into it, killing one person as a side effect.) Kamm thinks, surely rightly, that we may not save the five in that case, and tells us that the proposal does not yield that we may. Not so. Given that one or other of the two theories of action is true, the proposal does, in fact, yield that we may.

10. I say there is no summary at the end, though there is a short table that Kamm says "presents four combinations of factors related to control by the trolley driver in different types of cases (and subcases) involving the choice between five being killed and one being killed." I regret having to say that I found it unintelligible.

11. I am sure that Foot didn't herself really intend for us to accept the Worseness Thesis on the understanding of it according to which it entails the Choice Generalization. For example, she says, in summarizing at the end: "I have not, of course, argued that there are no other principles. . . . It may also make a difference whether the person about to suffer is one thought of as uninvolved in the threatened disaster, and whether it is his presence that constitutes the threat to the others." Foot, *Virtues and Vices*, 29.

12. I offered this "loop variant" in "The Trolley Problem," 1402.

13. It was, in fact, my aim in constructing Loop to point to the fact that given we believe (1), good sense requires us to believe (2), and therefore that the trolley problem (driver baptism) can't be solved by appeal to the fact that the surgeon uses his one whereas the driver does not.

# Trolleys and Permissible Harm

## Thomas Hurka

I'd like to start by quoting a letter that appeared in *The Globe and Mail* a few years ago, after that newspaper had run a book review that mentioned the trolley problem:

> The ethical dilemmas involving a runaway trolley illustrate the uninformed situations that cause people's eyes to glaze over in philosophy class. Trolleys and trains are unlikely to run away because they're equipped with a "dead man's pedal" that applies the brakes if the driver is incapacitated.
>
> The potential rescuer would not have the choice of "throwing the switch" because track switches are locked to prevent vandalism. And the rescuer's response would depend on the speed of the trolley. If the speed were less than 15 kilometers an hour, the rescuer could jump onto the trolley, sound the bell and save all five lives. If the speed were less than 30 km/h, then the rescuer (with a switch lock key) could throw the switch and kill only the one person on the branch line.
>
> If the trolley were moving faster than 30 km/h, throwing the switch would cause it to derail, which would injure or kill the passengers but save the workers on the tracks. So the better choice is to allow the occupied trolley to run through on the main track and, regrettably, kill the five workers.
>
> —*Derek Wilson, former CN Rail transportation engineer and project manager, Port Moody, B.C.*

At the risk of annoying any retired rail engineers who may be reading, I'll take the opportunity afforded me by Frances Kamm's stimulating Tanner Lectures to say something philosophical about trolleys.

Kamm's widely recognized brilliance as a moral philosopher has two sides. She's an incisive critic of other moral views, pointing out implications their proponents didn't realize they have and challenging them with arresting counter-examples. But she's also a creative philosopher who's proposed many novel moral principles and ideas. Her critical side is to the fore in her first Tanner Lecture and her constructive side in her second. I'll focus on a positive claim about the trolley problem from her second lecture. This will involve my trying to play the role of critic.

The trolley problem asks why it's impermissible to save five people by throwing a fat man in front of a trolley but permissible to save them by diverting the trolley to another track where it will likewise kill one person. This is a problem because the natural explanation of why it's wrong to throw the fat man—that then you actively do something that causes his death rather than merely allow him to die—implies that it would also be wrong to divert the trolley, which isn't what most of us intuitively believe. And while the doctrine of double effect seems to yield the right results here, Kamm thinks it has counterintuitive implications in other cases and should therefore be rejected. Hence her proposal, both in earlier writings and in the first part of her second lecture, of a novel Principle of Permissible Harm that she says avoids these pitfalls.

Like the view that distinguishes doing from allowing, Kamm's principle looks at the causal process that produces the death of the one rather than at any facts about your mental state. But, unlike that view, it doesn't consider how *you* relate to his death. Instead, it focuses on a causal distinction that arises later in the causal process, after you act. That's one reason for calling it a "downstream" principle: its vital distinction occurs after or downstream from you.

What is this distinction? Both when you throw the fat man and when you divert the trolley your act produces an evil, namely, one person's death, but it also produces a greater good, which Kamm describes as "the five being saved." I think this is an ambiguous description, and will return to this issue later; for now, I'll accept the description. What her Principle of Permissible Harm says is that it matters how the lesser evil is caused. If this evil results from a causal means to the greater good, then the act producing the greater good is impermissible. That's why throwing the fat man is wrong. He'll be killed by his body's colliding with the trolley, which is a causal means to stopping the trolley and thereby saving the five. But an act that produces the same evil may not be impermissible if the evil results from the greater good itself or from something that's not a causal means to it but instead has the greater good as what Kamm calls its "noncausal flip side," so the two are in effect the same thing. That's why, according to her, diverting the trolley is permissible. Here what saves the five is the trolley's moving away down the other track, and that's not a causal means to their being saved but the same thing under a different description. As she puts it, "the five being saved is simply the trolley's moving away" (p. 62). In both the Fat Man and Diversion (which Kamm also calls the Trolley Driver's Two Options) Cases you actively do something, and your act leads, by a series of intermediate steps, to a good and also to an evil—namely, the death of the one. In the first case the evil results from one of the intermediate steps, which is why throwing the fat man is wrong. But in the second case it results from the good itself or from something effectively equivalent to it, which makes diverting the trolley permissible.

As so applied, the Principle of Permissible Harm seems to yield the right result in the trolley cases. But it has what I think are highly counterintuitive implications in other cases and is therefore open to the same kind of objection Kamm makes to the doctrine of double effect. A case of this type first occurred to me while I was thinking about the ethics of war, so let me start with it.

There's a munitions factory that's a legitimate military target and that we want to bomb, but that has civilians living near it who'll be killed by our attack. Most moral views say that if the number of civilians who'll be killed is not disproportionate to the factory's military importance, the bombing is permitted. But Kamm's Principle of Permissible Harm says that whether that's so depends on how the civilians will be killed. If they'll be killed by a flying piece of the bomb, the bombing is morally impermissible. That's because the good our act can achieve is the destruction of the factory, the bomb's exploding is a causal means to that, and causing even a lesser evil by a means to a greater good is forbidden. But if the civilians will be killed by a flying piece of factory, the bombing is permitted. The factory's exploding isn't a causal means to the destruction of the factory; it's effectively the same thing, or has the destruction of the factory as its noncausal flip side. So the principle that allows the diverting of the trolley also allows bombings in which civilians are killed by flying pieces of factory but doesn't allow bombings in which the same civilians are killed by flying pieces of bomb.

I find this implication very hard to accept. Whatever the morality of collateral harm in war ultimately says, I don't think anything in it can turn on whether civilians are killed by one kind of flying object rather than by another. Nor do I think the world's militaries have a strong duty to develop weapons that will kill civilians only indirectly, by what they make explode, rather than by their own explosive force. Even if Kamm's principle yields attractive results in the trolley cases, it seems extremely implausible here.

I presented this case to her at a workshop on the ethics of war some years ago, and in reply she gave me a winning smile and said, "They all laughed at Christopher Columbus." She was acknowledging that her principle has the implication I pointed out and saying that, however surprising the implication may be, we should accept it. And she's continued to acknowledge that it follows from her principle. In her recent *Ethics for Enemies* book she says that, if we applied the principle in war, "it might be permissible to drop bombs on a military factory if the side-effect deaths of civilians were caused by the destruction of the factory itself but not if they were caused by the bombs."[1]

But accepting the implication would be a strange thing for her of all people to do. Her primary method in moral theory has been what she calls the "method of cases." It establishes moral principles by appealing to our intuitive judgments, but the primary intuitions concern particular examples. We don't first decide that certain principles are correct and then settle cases by applying the principles to them. We first consult our intuitions about cases and accept principles only if they match those intuitions.

She'll therefore sometimes reject an attractive-sounding principle because it conflicts with just one or a few particular judgments. In an earlier paper, Judith Jarvis Thomson proposed that it's less morally objectionable to redirect an existing threat, as you do when you divert the trolley, than to create a new threat, as when you throw the fat man.[2] Kamm has rejected this proposal because it yields what she thinks is the wrong result in the Lazy Susan Case described in her second lecture, where rotating a lazy Susan with five people on it to remove them from the path of a trolley causes a rockslide that kills another person. Even though the rockslide is a new threat, she thinks rotating the lazy Susan is permitted.

On a scale of "ingenuity in philosophical examples," I'd say this Lazy Susan Case comes pretty high up—I certainly couldn't have invented it myself. But precisely for that reason, I find it less than completely decisive. Even if, once I've understood how it works, I share Kamm's intuition that rotating the lazy Susan is permitted, I'm not very confident about that intuition just because the example is so far from reality.

But my factory bombing case comes much lower on the scale. In recent years there have been thousands of bombings of military targets in which thousands of civilians have been killed, some directly by the bombs and some indirectly by their effects—for example, by the collapse of a targeted building. Yet no one has thought that in these real-life cases Kamm's distinction makes a moral difference. In *Ethics for Enemies* she notes that her distinction isn't recognized in standard just-war theory, but I don't think that's only because the theory's framers didn't think of it. I'm pretty sure that if they had thought of it, they would have given it no weight and would have been very confident in doing so. However much force the Lazy Susan Case has against Thomson's proposal about redirecting threats, I think the factory bombing case has more force against Kamm's Principle of Permissible Harm.

It may be relevant, however, that the case occurs in war, and this suggests a possible response for her. In *Ethics for Enemies* she suggests that war may be a special context that alters the morality of harming in certain ways, so perhaps a principle that yields the right results in trolley cases isn't properly applicable in war, in which case a counter-example set in war doesn't tell against its use elsewhere. And her book sets her Principle of Permissible Harm aside for just this reason when discussing issues about war.[3]

I don't myself believe that war is a special context. Like others such as Jeff McMahan, I think the morality of war is just an extension of the everyday morality of self- and other-defense. And even if war is a special context, we'd need a specific argument why one of its effects is to make a Principle of Permissible Harm that's otherwise applicable no longer so, and it's hard to see how that argument could go. Finally, war can presumably be a special context only for those involved in it, as soldiers or at least as citizens of a warring nation. But imagine that our enemy has located its munitions factory on its border with a neutral country, so the civilians who'll be killed are neutrals. Our duties to them surely haven't changed, yet I still think it makes no difference whether they're killed by a flying piece of bomb or a flying piece of factory.[4]

Moreover, parallel cases can be constructed outside war and even involving a trolley. Imagine that an out-of-control trolley is hurtling toward me and four other people and, if we do nothing, will kill us. We can't divert the trolley, but we have a bomb we can throw to stop it. There's no one on the trolley, but there's a bystander next to the track who'll be killed if we throw the bomb. May we do so?

People may disagree about this case. I think Thomson will say we may not throw the bomb; we're not permitted to kill the bystander but must instead let the trolley kill us. My own view is that we may throw the bomb, and not just because there are five of us. Even if I were alone on the track I'd be permitted to throw the bomb because, in circumstances like these, each person is permitted to care somewhat more about his own good. So I think we may act.

But Kamm's Principle of Permissible Harm implies that whether or not we may throw the bomb depends on how the bystander will be killed. If she'll be killed by a piece of bomb, we're not permitted to save our lives because then her death will result from a causal means to the stopping of the trolley. But if she'll be killed by a piece of trolley, we are permitted because the trolley's exploding just *is* its stopping or has its stopping as its noncausal flip side. Kamm implicitly acknowledged this in her first lecture. The case I've just described is close to her Bomb Trolley Case, and about it she said, "it seems to me impermissible to set off a bomb that will stop the trolley from hitting the five when a piece of the bomb will kill a bystander as a side effect" (p. 15; also pp. 16–17). Why the reference here to a piece of the bomb killing the bystander? Why not just say you may not set off the bomb? I think Kamm was recognizing that, given her principle, using a bomb to stop the trolley isn't wrong if the bystander will be killed by a flying piece of trolley.

So her Bomb Trolley Case is exactly analogous to my factory case, and my intuition about it is exactly the same. Just as it makes no difference in the wartime case whether the civilians will be killed by a piece of bomb or a piece of factory, so it makes no difference in the trolley case whether the bystander will be killed by a piece of bomb or a piece of trolley. I don't say this just because I think throwing the bomb is permissible. I suspect that Thomson, if she thinks throwing the bomb is impermissible, will agree that it doesn't matter whether the bystander is killed by one flying object rather than another. And if that's right, then it's not true that Kamm's Principle of Permissible Harm has counterintuitive implications only in wartime, when it might be argued that it doesn't apply; it also has them in cases involving trolleys. Though it may fit our intuitions about the two cases in the original trolley problem, it doesn't fit our intuitions in other cases and therefore fails in the same way as does the doctrine of double effect.

So far I've followed Kamm's "method of cases" and criticized her Principle of Permissible Harm for failing to match some particular intuitions. But I don't think that's the only method we should use in moral theory. Like Shelly Kagan, I think our moral principles should not only match our particular judgments but also be intuitively appealing in themselves; in fact, they must be appealing in themselves if they're to *explain* the particular judgments. Here I see a further difficulty for Kamm's Principle of Permissible Harm as she applies it: the downstream causal distinction it draws doesn't seem in itself morally significant.

The traditional deontological principles concern your relation to an evil: they say it's more objectionable to cause than to allow an evil or to intend than merely to foresee it. And the relevant evils are ones that matter in themselves, so they involve either the existence of an intrinsic evil, such as a victim's pain when you torture him, or the destruction of an intrinsic good, as when you kill him. Kamm's principle likewise concerns the causing of evils that matter in themselves, such as the death of the one in the trolley cases. And I think her principle will be most plausible if the goods it permits the evils to follow from likewise matter in themselves—for example, by being states that are intrinsically good. If being caused by a good is so important, shouldn't the good in question itself be one that's important?

This condition is satisfied in a case from later in Kamm's second lecture, where five people who cure themselves from a fatal condition then breathe normally and their expanding chests move some fatal germs in the atmosphere that kill another person (p. 78). Here the death of the one results from the five's being alive, which matters morally in itself. But the condition isn't satisfied in other cases, most obviously in my factory bombing case.

In that case Kamm's principle takes the relevant greater good to be the factory's being destroyed, but that's not something of intrinsic moral significance. The world isn't any better just because a factory no longer exists. Instead, the factory's destruction matters only as a means—more specifically, as a means to the ultimate goods in the war's just cause, such as ending an unjust aggression or preventing a genocide. It's because and only because it will further a good like this that the destruction is worth pursuing. In fact, we can describe a sequence of means leading to this ultimate good, including the plane's taking off, the pilot's pressing the button that releases the bomb, the bomb's exploding, the factory's being destroyed, and then whatever further means to our end the factory's destruction allows. Perhaps there are a hundred means in this sequence, with the bomb's exploding being number 37 and the factory's being destroyed number 38. What Kamm's principle does, when applied to this case, is to say that an act that kills civilians in pursuit of the ultimate good is permissible if the deaths result from means 38 but not if they result from means 37 or earlier. Why is that reasonable? Why say causation by one means to an end is permissible but causation by another means to the very same end is not? And why make the cut exactly between numbers 37 and 38? Why not between 36 and 37, so the bombing is forbidden if the civilians' deaths are caused directly by the pilot's pushing the button but not if they're caused by the "good" of his bomb's exploding? Or why not make the cut after 38? It seems that selecting any means in a sequence of a hundred and labeling it a morally significant "good" is arbitrary and unmotivated.

It may be replied that this again shows why my bombing case isn't relevant to Kamm's principle. Just because the case doesn't involve a good of the right, intrinsically mattering kind, it's not one to which the principle applies. But this reply only makes the principle look worse. If the factory's destruction is just a causal means to the truly relevant good, then bombing the factory is wrong by Kamm's lights, both when the civilians are killed by a piece of bomb and when they're killed by a piece of factory. In fact, killing civilians is then permitted only when it results from the final achievement of the war's just cause, which means it's never permitted while the war is in progress. I take it that's not an implication Kamm wants her principle to have.

The same difficulty arises in the trolley cases, which brings me back to the question of what the greater good in those cases is. Kamm, recall, describes the good in the Fat Man and Diversion Cases as "the five being saved." But what exactly does that mean, and is it something that matters morally in itself or only as a means?

Different readings of the phrase are possible, but at one point Kamm equates the five being saved with "the five being alive" (p. 62; also pp. 64, 81), and if this was the greater good it would be something that matters in itself. But we need to ask *when* the five would be alive, or, if your intervention causes them to be alive, *when* it causes them to be alive. To sharpen the issue, imagine that the trolley will reach the divide in the track at 8:00 and that if you don't divert it, it will then travel for ten minutes down its original track until it reaches and kills the five at 8:10. Given these facts, the greater good you achieve by diverting the trolley can't be their being alive at 8:01, 8:04, or 8:07, since even if you don't divert the trolley they'll be alive at those times. It must be their being alive at 8:10 and after. But I don't see how their being alive at 8:10 can just "be" the trolley's moving away, or be something the trolley's moving away has as its noncausal flip side. Two outcomes related in that intimate way must surely be contemporaneous, or happen at the same time. But the trolley's moving away happens at 8:00 and the five's being alive at 8:10 happens at 8:10, and nothing that happens at 8:00 can be identical to or constituted by something that happens at 8:10. The trolley's moving away at 8:00 must therefore be a causal means to the five's being alive at 8:10; and then, given this reading of "the five being saved," Kamm's principle doesn't permit you to divert the trolley. What causes the death of the one—namely, the trolley's moving away—isn't the greater good or something constitutively related to it, but a causal means to it. And the principle forbids acts in which the lesser evil results from a causal means.

A different reading of "the five being saved" equates it with the five's being saved from the threat of the trolley, or being out of danger from the trolley, and Kamm sometimes talks in this way too (pp. 64, 75). Now this good *is* plausibly seen as effectively equivalent to the trolley's moving away, or as something the trolley's moving away has as its noncausal flip side; certainly the five's being saved from the threat of the trolley happens at the same time as the trolley moves away, namely at 8:00. But on this reading the greater good isn't something that matters morally in itself; on the contrary, it matters only as a means. To see this, imagine that, no matter what you do with the trolley, a rockslide will come and kill the five at 8:10. Here saving the five from the threat of the trolley is pointless and diverting the trolley would be wrong, because it would needlessly kill the one. That the five are saved from the trolley matters only if it causes them to be alive at 8:10, and the same is true of their being free from any other threat, or indeed from threats in general: all of these matter only as means to something like their being alive. That means the situation given this reading is just like that with means 37 and 38 in the factory case. Imagine that to divert the trolley you have to pull a long handle, one so long that pulling it will knock a thin man off a bridge and kill him. Here Kamm would say that divert-ing the trolley is wrong because the thin man's death will result from a handle-pulling that's just a means. But if the five's being saved from the threat of the trolley is likewise just a means to what really matters, why think a death resulting from it or from something effectively equivalent to it is any different? What jus-tifies giving different means to the same end such different moral status?

There are, then, two readings of Kamm's phrase for the greater good, "the five being saved." On one reading, this good matters morally in itself, but the trolley's moving away is only a causal means to it and her principle forbids diverting the trolley. On the other reading, the trolley's moving away isn't a causal means, but the so-called greater good doesn't matter in itself and is itself only a means to what does. On this reading, the principle can only permit diverting the trolley by drawing an arbitrary distinction between different means to the same end. On neither reading is it true both that the Principle of Permissible Harm yields the results Kamm wants in the Diversion Case *and* that the principle is intuitively appealing in itself.

I've criticized Kamm's Principle of Permissible Harm both because it has counterintuitive implications in the factory and trol-ley bombing cases and because it's not intrinsically appealing. The two criticisms are connected. The problem in the bombing cases is that the principle attaches moral significance to something that doesn't have it—namely, the difference between one flying object and another. The reason why the principle isn't appealing is that it makes an arbitrary distinction between items in a sequence of means. And that's precisely what it does in the bombing cases: make an arbitrary distinction between flying objects that are means to the same good end.

But I don't want only to criticize Kamm, and will conclude with some more positive comments on her principle and the ideas behind it.

My second criticism concerned cases where what Kamm calls the "greater good" is just a means to what really matters, and it therefore doesn't apply to applications of the principle where that isn't the case. I already mentioned one of these: where five people cure themselves of a lethal condition but their breathing moves some deadly germs that kill another person. In this case, the death of the one results from something—the five's being alive—that does matter morally in itself. Moreover, the claim that in this case the five's curing themselves is permissible even though it will kill the one seems to me right, and Kamm's principle may be the explanation why. I have nothing against the principle's use in these cases.

In addition, there are cases where an analogous though not identical principle, one that draws a similar downstream causal distinction, does seem morally relevant. Let me describe two of them, from the morality of war.

These cases involve the just-war condition of proportionality, which says the resort to war is permitted only if the relevant goods the war will secure are proportionate to, or sufficiently large compared to, the evils it will cause. In this assessment the relevant goods don't in my view include all the goods that the war will produce. They include those in the war's just causes plus some other closely related ones, such as deterrence of would-be aggressors. But they don't include the pleasure our soldiers may get from real action, and they also don't include some economic goods. Imagine that our economy, and indeed the whole global economy, is in a recession and that our fighting a war will lift it out of the recession, as World War II ended the Depression of the 1930s. I don't think this economic benefit is relevant to justifying the war; an otherwise disproportionate conflict can't become proportionate because it will boost GDP.[5]

But now imagine that in 1990 Saddam Hussein had occupied not only Kuwait but also the Saudi oilfields and then drastically reduced both countries' oil production, driving up world oil prices

and hurting the economies of African countries. Here the fact that
a war against Saddam Hussein would remove that harm to African
countries, or give them the economic benefit of cheaper oil, does
seem to me a relevant good. How can that be if ending our recession wasn't relevant?

Here's my tentative suggestion. The way war lifts an economy
out of recession is by calling for more industrial, and especially
military, production, where that additional production boosts GDP;
that's certainly how World War II ended the Depression. But industrial production is only a means to the war's just cause rather than
part of it, and that's why this economic benefit doesn't count: it's
caused by an intermediate step. But in the Saddam Hussein case,
the reduction of oil prices follows from our ending his occupations
of Kuwait and Saudi Arabia, which *is* the war's just cause. Since
here the economic benefit follows from something good as an end,
it is relevant.

Here's another pair of examples. To fight the 1991 Gulf War,
the United States put together a large coalition of nations, including Arab ones and, albeit more informally, Israel, and the resulting contacts between the Arab nations and Israel contributed to an
attempt to settle the Israeli-Palestinian conflict through the Oslo
Accords. That attempt ultimately failed, but imagine that it had
succeeded and led to Israeli-Palestinian peace. Even so, I don't think
the good of that peace would have contributed to the proportionality of the 1991 Gulf War, and my reason is that what promoted the
peace was the formation of the coalition, which was a causal means
to the war's just cause rather than any part of it. But now consider the 2003 Iraq War, one effect of which was to stop Iraq's pay-
ments to the families of Palestinian suicide bombers. And imagine
that the result of this was a cessation of suicide bombing and then
Israeli-Palestinian peace. Here I think the good of the peace would
have been a relevant benefit, because it would have followed from
the ending of Iraq's support of terrorism, which is a legitimate goal
of war.[6]

My tentative suggestion, then, based on some tentative intuitions about pairs of cases like these, is that some benefits of war—economic in one case and those of an unrelated peace in the other—can't help justify the war if they follow causally from a means to its ultimate just cause, but they can if they follow from the just cause itself. That's a downstream causal distinction, like the one in Kamm's principle and drawn on the same basis.

This isn't to say it's the same distinction. It concerns the morality of a whole war rather than of an individual act, though I imagine parallel cases can be constructed about individual acts. More importantly, it involves the production of goods rather than of evils. Kamm's principle concerns how the evil of the one death is caused: it's when that evil results from a means to the good of the five being saved that saving the five is forbidden, and when the evil results from the good itself that it's permitted. But my suggestion concerns the production of goods. The question is whether, for example, an economic benefit results from a means rather than from an end that determines whether that benefit can help justify a war. And in non-consequentialist moral views the causation of goods is often treated very differently from the causation of evils. Thus, many such views say it's morally more objectionable to actively cause an evil than merely allow the evil to come about, but they don't say it's morally more creditable to actively cause a good. If you can choose between actively saving one person and letting someone else save five, you should let the other save the five. So the fact that a certain distinction looks or may be important when we're producing goods doesn't imply that it's similarly important when we're producing evils; it may be relevant in one of those contexts but not the other.

Nonetheless, my tentative suggestion is in the same family as Kamm's because it, too, draws a downstream distinction in how a morally significant result is caused, and draws it on the same basis—namely, whether the result follows from something good or only from a means to it. The suggestion that this kind of distinction may matter in the moral assessment of actions was to my knowledge first made explicitly by Kamm and is among her many novel contributions to ethics. Even if it doesn't completely solve the trolley problem—and let's be clear that no one else has done that, in the sense of providing a satisfying justification for our initial intuitive judgments—it's a fruitful distinction to have in mind when exploring the intricacies of non-consequentialist ethics that have been the primary focus of Kamm's brilliant writings.

## Notes

1. F. M. Kamm, *Ethics for Enemies: Terror, Torture, and War* (New York: Oxford University Press, 2011), 142.

2. Judith Jarvis Thomson, "Killing, Letting Die, and the Trolley Problem," *The Monist* 59 (1976): 204–217.

3. Kamm, *Ethics for Enemies*, at 142.

4. Kamm has highlighted the special moral status of neutrals in war, higher even than that of our noncombatants, in "Failures of Just War Theory: Terror, Harm, and Justice," *Ethics* 114 (2004): 650–692, 672–673.

5. See my "Proportionality in the Morality of War," *Philosophy & Public Affairs* 33 (2005): 34–66, at 40.

6. I discussed these two pairs of examples in "Proportionality and Necessity," in *War: Essays in Political Philosophy*, ed. Larry May 127–44 (Cambridge: Cambridge University Press, 2008), at 133–134.

# Solving the Trolley Problem

SHELLY KAGAN

One might despair of ever arriving at a principle adequate to capturing and accommodating our intuitions about the full range of cases that have come to be known as "trolley problems" (roughly speaking,[1] cases where one must choose whether to kill some to save others). But suppose there were such a principle, as indeed I imagine there probably is. For the moment, just call it Q.

Is there such a principle? As I say, I find it plausible to think there is. After all, *something* generates our intuitive reactions to cases. So the odds are there is *some* statement of a rule or law (or a set of rules or laws) that accurately predicts our intuitions. Properly reformulated, this rule could provide the proposed Q. (Here's the idea behind this talk of "reformulating" the rule: start with a rule that accurately predicts the precise circumstances in which we will have the intuition that a given act is permissible; restate it as a moral *principle*, one which correspondingly asserts that acts are permissible in precisely those circumstances. This principle will, by hypothesis, match our intuitions about cases; so that should be the desired Q.)

Admittedly, we might not *always* judge in conformity to Q: perhaps in some situations, or when thinking about certain cases, various psychological factors interfere with our ability to judge in perfect conformity with Q. Even if so, it might still be the case that Q is the best match for our various intuitions. But for simplicity, let us put this complicating possibility aside and suppose we can indeed find a principle—Q—that really does match our intuitions *perfectly*.

More troubling is the possibility that people's intuitive reactions to trolley cases may not all be the same. Perhaps different people will judge some of the relevant cases differently. Then there may not be a single principle that matches everyone's intuitions perfectly; no single Q will fit all. I'll come back to this worry later. But for the time being, at any rate, let us suppose that people's intuitions *are* similar. So we should, in theory, be able to find a single principle, Q, that matches everyone's intuitions.

Suppose, then, that we had Q. Are we done? Have we solved the trolley problem? Far from it! For it might well be that the concepts and distinctions on which the principle Q turns are ones that we are not prepared to embrace, once they are so identified.

That might seem unlikely, since we typically have rather robust intuitions about trolley cases, and we certainly care deeply about right and wrong in matters of killing and letting die. How could it turn out to be the case that we don't care about the distinctions underlying our intuitive judgments?

The answer, of course, is that the distinctions and concepts that underlie our intuitions about the cases might not be ones that seem morally *relevant*, in and of themselves, when we think about them directly.

Suppose, for example, that Q involved elements like this: our intuitions (about which actions are permissible) depend on whether we are making the judgment on a Wednesday or a Sunday, or whether we make it standing up or sitting down, or whether we make it when we are warm or when we are cold (or holding a cup of coffee or a cold drink).

If something like this were the case—if these factors really were what our intuitions turned on—then I imagine that we would resist embracing these factors as morally relevant, and thus we would end up rejecting Q, even if it were a perfect fit for our intuitions about those cases, and no other principle came close to matching our intuitions as well.

To be sure, in the examples I just gave the factors I've identified are about the *judges*, not about the *cases*, and one might hope that Q will take as relevant input only features of the trolley cases themselves (and not features of the person having the intuition). But the same thing could in principle happen even with regard to the cases themselves.

Thus, for example, it might be that Q involved elements like this: whether the act takes place on a Wednesday or a Sunday, whether the person being killed is standing up or sitting down, whether it is warm or cold outside when the agent acts (or whether the victim is holding a cold drink or a cup of coffee).

Here too, I imagine, we would reject Q—even if it matched our case specific intuitions perfectly. The distinctions on which it turns would not be ones we would see our way to endorsing as morally relevant.

To be sure, since we are stipulating that Q matches our intuitions about cases, any distinction important to Q will be "morally relevant" in at least *one* sense of that term: it will be relevant to generating our intuitions about certain important moral questions. But for all that, the distinctions in question might still be morally irrelevant in the sense that we simply cannot see why anything like that should *matter* morally. We may be simply—and appropriately—unwilling to embrace the factors in question as having any genuine moral significance.

What we want from an acceptable moral principle, after all, is not merely that it match our intuitions about particular cases; we also want to be able to see why the various factors appealed to by the principle should matter morally. So if we cannot see, directly, why the factors in question should matter in their own right, then at the very least we need to be able to see how they connect to still other factors, ones whose moral significance we can indeed appreciate directly. In effect, we must be able to provide the principle with an attractive and plausible rationale.

Suppose, however, that neither of these holds for Q. Suppose, that is, that although Q matches our various case specific intuitions, we cannot see why the factors to which it appeals should matter morally, nor can we provide it with a compelling rationale. Then Q will be unacceptable—this, *despite* the fact that it matches our intuitions about the cases. What we will conclude, instead, is that at least some of the intuitions underlying Q are mistaken, influenced by morally irrelevant factors.

Of course, there is certainly no guarantee that Q *will* turn on such morally irrelevant elements. But I suspect that the more complicated Q turns out to be, the greater the danger that it will indeed appeal to features that do strike us as morally irrelevant. And if Q ends up having lots and lots of clauses, or depends on abstruse concepts—or both—it becomes proportionately less likely that a plausible rationale can be provided.

That's the situation I think we actually find ourselves in. I suspect that any principle actually capable of matching our intuitions across the entire range of trolley problems will be a messy, complicated affair, full of distinctions that strike us as morally irrelevant—or at least, will strike us that way once we directly face the question of whether something like *that* could indeed matter morally.

Of course, complexity itself needn't be a problem. An acceptable moral principle might have a large number of clauses and yet it might still be the case that each clause is independently attractive and plausible (or can be adequately motivated). And on the other hand, even a fairly simple principle might turn on a distinction for which no plausible rationale can be provided. Imagine, for example, a principle that permitted killing on all and only sunny days. This would be simple enough, but even if—somehow!—this perfectly matched our intuitions about the relevant cases, we would appropriately reject the principle as turning on a morally irrelevant factor. Absent a compelling rationale, the principle would be unacceptable.

With all of this by way of background, let us turn, now, to Frances Kamm's two difficult but incredibly stimulating lectures on the trolley problem.

I think it fair to say that no one has worked harder to solve the trolley problem than Kamm has. Over the years she has probably examined hundreds of different cases, and she has struggled mightily to produce a principle that matches our intuitions about those cases—the elusive principle that I have been calling Q. In her two lectures, Kamm shares with us a summary of some of her recent thinking about the subject. And one of the most important things she does here is to sketch an outline of her proposed solution to the trolley problem.

Kamm calls her proposal the *Principle of Permissible Harm*. She both introduces the basic distinction lying behind the principle (see especially pp. 62–64, and pp. 66–67) and gestures toward some of the extra complications that she feels would be required for a full and complete statement of that principle. In neither lecture does Kamm provide us with a complete statement of the principle, though she does, I think, say enough to give us at least a rough feel for the basic idea. She also says enough to make it clear that a complete statement of the principle would be a complicated matter indeed. (An earlier work, *Intricate Ethics*, also discusses the Principle of Permissible Harm and gives a somewhat fuller statement of it.[2] But even that version is incomplete, though it takes more than half a page to write down.)

I don't have the space here to consider the various complications that Kamm thinks would need to be incorporated into an adequate statement of the Principle of Permissible Harm. But I do want to raise a question about the central distinction upon which the principle seems to turn.

Let me start, then, by trying to give a rough, intuitive gloss on what I take to be the basic idea (I am skipping many details):

Sometimes someone who is killed is killed by an event that is the very same event as the saving of a larger number of people (the greater good). Then the killing of the one may be justified. But in other cases, the one who is killed is killed by something that is merely a causal *means* to the event that is the saving of the larger number. In such cases killing the one is *not* justified. So the crucial question is whether the event that results in the killing of the one literally constitutes the saving or is merely a means to that saving.

As I understand it, then, Kamm's Principle of Permissible Harm makes essential use of the idea (or something close to it) that some events are themselves the very same event as the saving of the five, the existence of the greater good, while other events are not themselves the saving of the five, but only a causal means to it. Of course, the former events may not be *described* as the saving of the five, but they are—as Kamm puts it—"the noncausal flip side" of the saving of the five: they *constitute* the saving of the five. In contrast, other events are metaphysically distinct from the saving of the five; they are mere means to it. And Kamm's idea is that it makes a significant moral difference if the harm done in a given case is caused by the saving of the greater number *itself* (or its noncausal constitutive flip side), or if, instead, it is caused by something that is itself merely a causal *means* to the saving of the greater number.[3]

I should hasten to admit that this may be too rough an account of the precise distinction that Kamm has in mind. Indeed, this way of putting the idea is somewhat at odds with Kamm's remark (on p. 63) that being the noncausal constitutive flip side of saving the five is "very close" to being the very same event as the saving of the five. This implies, after all, that the event that is the noncausal constitutive flip side of the saving of the five is not, as I have just been suggesting, literally the very *same* event as the saving of the five (albeit under a different description). There is, to be sure, a very close relation between the two events (the latter is partially "constituted" by the former); but it isn't quite identity.

I have to confess, however, that the exact relation that Kamm has in mind—what exactly is involved in one event being the noncausal constitutive flip side of some other event—isn't altogether clear to me. I can think of a few different things that Kamm may have in mind, and she doesn't elaborate. Happily, however, she does imply that the difference between identity, on the one hand, and being the noncausal constitutive flip side, on the other, may not be a morally significant one. And as I have noted, she thinks the two relations (identity and being the noncausal flip side) are very close. So perhaps we won't be far off if we try to understand the key distinction in something like the terms I have offered.

(Whatever it is precisely that Kamm has in mind, there is obviously a fair bit of metaphysics being presupposed here about the proper individuation of events, and that metaphysics may or may not be correct. What's more, even if we grant the metaphysics, it isn't obvious to me that the noncausal constitutive relation always holds in all those cases where Kamm needs to find it. But I will let these two points pass.)

So here, again, is the basic idea underlying Kamm's proposed Principle of Permissible Harm: killing some may be permissible if they are killed as a result of an event that is the very same event as (or the noncausal flip side of) the saving of the many (the greater good); but it will not be permissible if they are killed as a result of an event that is merely a causal *means* to the saving of the many.

Now it should be borne in mind that much of what Kamm is doing here—in trying to lay out the Principle of Permissible Harm—is simply a kind of psychological reconstruction. She is doing her best to identify the various features that actually influence our intuitions about the different cases. From this perspective, presumably, it is not particularly important whether the concepts to which she appeals are familiar ones, or whether they are easy to articulate. Even if we don't recognize them, or find them difficult to grasp, they might still underlie our intuitions. As Kamm remarks at one point, "people may not be able to articulate these proposals, which nevertheless underlie their judgments" (p. 61).

But, of course, Kamm is interested in more than psychology. She is looking for the *correct* moral principle, the one that *accurately* tells us when it is permissible to act. When considered from this perspective, however, it *is* troubling that the key concepts behind the Principle of Permissible Harm are so unfamiliar (in a moral context, at least), and so difficult to articulate. For the simple fact is that the key distinction to which Kamm appeals has no obvious moral significance. When we directly consider the difference between a harm being caused by the saving of the many (or its noncausal flip side) and its being caused by a mere means to the saving of the many, it isn't at all obvious—to me, at least—why a difference like that should *matter* morally. Viewed from this perspective, then, Kamm's proposed principle is in desperate need of a compelling rationale. Unfortunately, this is something that Kamm says very little about.

In fairness, of course, I do want to note that it isn't as though Kamm says nothing at all by way of offering a deeper rationale for the Principle of Permissible Harm. In an important passage (p. 69), she suggests that its central distinction may correspond to a further one—between subordination and mere substitution—which in turn directly connects to deeper moral questions about "persons and their status."

In our lectures, however, Kamm confessedly has little to say about this idea. So let me try to elaborate, I hope sympathetically and accurately, on her behalf.

Intuitively, some ways of treating people involve viewing them as being less valuable than others—as "subordinate" (in Kamm's term). The paradigmatic instance of this, I suppose, is slavery: we subordinate one person to another, treating the subordinate as a mere means to meeting the interests of the slave owner, the "superior." This is, of course, morally abhorrent. Kamm's thought, then, is that *some* ways—perhaps most ways—in which someone might be killed so as to save others will involve this kind of subordination. And as such they will be unacceptable.

But in *some* cases, perhaps, someone can be killed in the course of saving others where this kind of subordination is *not* involved. Of course, the choice will still have been made to kill the one, say, rather than letting the many die (or be killed). So a kind of "substitution" will have been made: the death of the one (or the deaths of the few) will be chosen—substituted—for the deaths of the greater number. But this is "mere" substitution, as we might put it, not subordination. So the objection to killing that is present in normal cases will be absent here, and the permissibility of proceeding will be intelligible.

The thought, then, is that in the standard Trolley Case (where I turn the trolley from the five to the one), we have mere substitution, and so turning the trolley is indeed permissible; but in cases like Topple (where I topple the fat man onto the track, and his weight stops the trolley as he is killed by it), and in many other cases as well, we instead have subordination, and so the relevant acts are forbidden.

Although Kamm doesn't spell this out explicitly (though see pp. 75–76), the suggestion we're discussing is also closely related to a further point, one she emphasizes in the second lecture—namely, that what matters here may be "intervictim" relations, rather than, primarily, relations between the agent and the person killed. In cases of subordination, it isn't that the one killed is subordinated to the *agent,* but rather that the one killed is subordinated to the interests of the *others,* for whose sake the one is killed. It is the relation between the various potential "victims" that is key here, according to Kamm.

That's a promising idea, and surely we can all feel the appeal of the suggestion that something like this is going on in the various trolley cases: perhaps those acts that are intuitively unacceptable can be shown to involve subordination, while those that are intuitively acceptable involve mere substitution.

And obviously enough, Kamm thinks that this is what we actually have. More particularly, she thinks that this is what the Principle of Permissible Harm spells out for us. Not only does Kamm's principle (or a suitably elaborated version of it) sort the cases properly—as we can suppose it does—but Kamm suggests that it does so by way of distinctions and concepts that line up and interact so as to distinguish cases of subordination from mere substitution.

But it is exactly this that I do not see when I try my best to understand the principle. Consider, for example, what Kamm says about the standard Trolley Case as opposed to the *Two* Trolleys Case (where I deflect one trolley to bump a second trolley that would otherwise kill five, but the first kills someone else while it is en route to bumping the second; introduced on p. 61). The former, Kamm assures us, is mere substitution (see, for example, pp. 69, 75–76, and 97 n. 18), the latter, subordination (p. 76).

Why? Because in the former case, it is the noncausal flip side of the saving of the five (that is to say, the turning of the trolley) that is the cause of the death of the one, while in the latter case, the cause of the death of the one (that is, the turning of the *first* of the two trolleys) is the mere causal *means* to saving the five. And according to Kamm, when I kill you by doing something that merely causes the five to be saved, I subordinate you; but when I kill you by doing something that is itself the saving of the five (or is its noncausal flip side), I only substitute (pp. 75–76).

Well, that is what Kamm *says*. But why in the world should we *believe* her? Notice that in Two Trolleys the death of the one is not itself a *means* to saving the five. If it were, we might well agree that this was a case of subordination (one person being *used* to save others). But that isn't what we have in Two Trolleys. Rather, the death of the one is a mere side effect of saving the five. So why, then, is it subordination?

Because, Kamm says, in Two Trolleys the death of the one is caused by something that is itself a mere causal means of saving the five, rather than something that is *itself* the saving of the five (or its noncausal flip side)!

Well, yes, there is that difference, but that wasn't our question. Our question was why this makes this a case of *subordination*—something that we can independently see the moral significance of. What is it that is particularly morally offensive (unacceptable subordination) about killing someone via something that merely causes the rescue, as opposed to killing via the rescue itself?

I just don't see it. Kamm herself offers nothing to support the idea that there is something intelligibly offensive (let alone worthy of the name *subordination*) in the former case (killing via the mere cause of the rescue) but not the latter (killing via the rescue itself). And what I suspect, of course, is that there is *nothing* to say. There is nothing to be said about why *that* difference should matter.[4]

To be sure, we ought to be able to point to a feature that is present in those cases of killing that strike us as permissible, a feature that is missing in the cases of killing that strike us as impermissible. Perhaps Kamm really has managed to identify the feature that explains our intuitions in this way. And having identified this feature, we can slap a label on it. We can *say* that the one kind of case involves "mere substitution," while the other unacceptably involves "subordination." But appearances to the contrary notwithstanding, that is not to offer an independently attractive and intelligible rationale for the principle we have articulated. It is simply to assume that since the principle in question matches our intuitions about specific cases, the factors on which it turns *must* be morally relevant. And that assumption, I believe, is highly suspect.

This, I believe, is the situation we find ourselves in with regard to Kamm's Principle of Permissible Harm. Perhaps the principle does a splendid job of matching our intuitions about cases. At any rate, I am not foolish enough to take Kamm on at her own game, to try to find a counterexample to her proposal, and to offer some alternative Q. No, my complaint is not that the principle doesn't match our intuitions about cases. It is that it cannot be given anything remotely like a plausible rationale. And in the absence of such a rationale, we should reject it.

Of course, this is not to concede that the Principle of Permissible Harm *does* match our intuitions. Indeed, I doubt that it does, at least not for everyone. A very informal survey of students in my upper level normative ethics course at Yale in Spring 2013 suggests otherwise. Thus, to mention only two examples, half my students judged one case (described at the bottom of p. 42) in a manner contrary to the intuition that Kamm is trying to accommodate, and about three fourths judged a second case (described at the top of p. 40) in a contrary manner. While this hardly shows that Kamm's own intuitions are mistaken, it does reinforce the thought that it would be best to shore up the argument for the Principle of Permissible Harm by providing it with some independently attractive rationale.

Admittedly, in principle Kamm might try to dismiss the intuitions of my students—and others who disagree with her—perhaps arguing that her own intuitions are more reliable, having been shaped by years of training and reflection. I would not want to be dismissive of such a claim. But it should be noted, in any event, that Kamm does not in fact privilege her own intuitions in this way in our lectures. On the contrary, although she often simply reports her own judgments about cases, she also makes assertions about what, for example, "people would think" (p. 61) or what "we think" (p. 64), and she talks about "our intuitive judgments" as well (p. 13). So it does seem problematic for Kamm if others fail to share her intuitions; and this makes the failure to provide a plausible rationale for the Principle of Permissible Harm all the more significant.

Nonetheless, it may seem that I have been unfair to Kamm. Although she does offer a few remarks about the difference between subordination and substitution, and how this may provide a rationale for her proposed principle, Kamm is nonetheless quite upfront about the fact that she isn't trying to develop or defend this idea in any detail. She explicitly says that "it is not the point of this lecture to investigate these deeper possible meanings" of the principle, although she certainly recognizes that it is important to do so eventually (p. 69; cf. p. 60). So isn't it unreasonable for me to complain—as I am complaining—that she hasn't spent more time on this issue?

I certainly hope that my doing this is not unfair. For my worry is precisely that the deeper connections that Kamm claims to find are not really there. (Or at least, somewhat more cautiously, it is far from clear that they *are* there.) It is one thing to establish that the Principle of Permissible Harm can be given a plausible rationale and then postpone more careful investigation of that rationale for another occasion. It is quite another matter to rest content, as Kamm does, with a mere gesture in the direction of a potential rationale—if, as I believe, the supposed "deeper meanings" cannot truly be established at all. If the principle really does turn on distinctions that have no independent moral significance—and this is what I take to be the case—then we have reason to worry about it, regardless of how well it matches our intuitions. And what Kamm has to say on this matter is simply not sufficiently reassuring.

Of course, even if I am right that the principle fails to align with a morally relevant distinction (whether subordination versus substitution, or some other), we might still hope that there is some other candidate for Q that meets the double challenge of matching our intuitions about cases (at least, doing so closely enough) and aligning with some morally relevant distinction (whether subordination/substitution, or something else).

But I am prepared to suppose, if only for the sake of argument, that the Principle of Permissible Harm—or at least a suitably modified and even more complicated version of it—*is* the principle that (best) matches our intuitions. That is, I am prepared to believe that Kamm (or future Kammians) will have met the first of these two tasks. And I will readily admit that, given the bewildering array of trolley cases and variants that have been proposed over the years, this is no small feat. It would be a significant achievement indeed to find Q. Nonetheless, if that is all that is successfully accomplished it is not nearly enough. For if the Principle of Permissible Harm is indeed Q, that just makes my skepticism about the second task all the more worrisome. For if the principle is Q, and yet that principle lacks a compelling rationale, then we should come to wonder whether an adequate moral theory will really accommodate quite so many of our intuitions about the various cases.

In short, I suspect that our intuitions about trolley problems respond to factors that simply do not have any genuine moral significance. We cannot give them a rationale. And if that is right, then we cannot fit them into a larger moral discourse that we should be prepared to embrace.

If I am right about this, then any genuine solution to the trolley problem will be one that is more reformist than we might initially have hoped. Perhaps, as Judith Thomson has come to believe,[5] we can retain deontology, but we will have to abandon the intuition that it is permissible to turn the trolley in the standard Trolley Case—thus abandoning the very intuition that got us started thinking about the trolley problem in the first place! Perhaps we will settle for a principle that (roughly speaking) simply rules out killing the innocent. If such a principle can be given a plausible rationale, this may accommodate enough of our intuitions to satisfy us, even if it does not match all of them.

Alternatively, however, and even more radically, perhaps we will need to move somewhat further afield. Taking seriously the thought that an adequate moral theory must involve an adequate rationale, perhaps we will be led to a principle that matches even fewer of our case specific intuitions but which nonetheless can be provided with a rationale that is significantly more compelling. More particularly, perhaps we will ultimately want to abandon deontology altogether and embrace consequentialism instead.

I believe that the latter course is indeed the right choice to make. But that, of course, is a discussion for another day.

## Notes

1. This is indeed rough, and in her lectures Frances Kamm periodically revisits the question of how, exactly, the trolley problem should be delimited; but for my purposes there is no need to try to arrive at a more precise answer.

2. F. M. Kamm, *Intricate Ethics* (New York: Oxford University Press, 2007), pp. 186 n.78 and 188 n.89.

3. Eventually (see pp. 83–91), Kamm suggests that, strictly speaking, the Principle of Permissible Harm doesn't require that the event in question be the same as (or the noncausal flip side of) the saving of the *larger* number (the *greater* good). She suggests, rather, that it may even be permissible to kill *more* than are being saved, provided that this is done as the result of the noncausal flip side of the saving (rather than as a means to the saving). This is a fascinating and important suggestion, but it isn't essential to the point I want to discuss, so I will put it aside.

4. Kamm does have a go at this question in *Intricate Ethics*, pp. 165–167; but if I read that passage correctly, even she acknowledges that the explanation she offers there isn't adequate.

5. See Judith Jarvis Thomson, "Turning the Trolley," *Philosophy & Public Affairs* 36 (2008): 359–374, and her comments in this volume.

I believe that the latter course is indeed the right one to take, but that of course is a discussion for another day.

## Notes

1. This is not a point [illegible] the question of how exactly the trolley problem should be settled, but for our purposes there is no need to try to give a more precise answer.

2. F. M. Kamm, *Intricate Ethics* (New York: Oxford University Press, 2007), pp. [illegible] and [illegible] n.8[illegible].

3. Eventually (pp. [illegible]), Kamm suggests that strictly speaking, the Principle of Permissible Harm should require that the [illegible] be the same as (or the noncausal flip side of) the saving of the larger number (or greater good) [illegible] provided that this is done [illegible] saving. This is [illegible] to the point I want to make, so I will set it aside.

4. Kamm [illegible] *Intricate Ethics* pp. 16[illegible]–167, but [illegible] passage [illegible] that [illegible] increment [illegible].

5. See Judith Jarvis Thomson, "Turning the Trolley," [illegible] 36 (2008): [illegible]–[illegible]74 and her comments [illegible].

# Replies to Commentators

# The Trolley Problem Mysteries on Trial

*Defending the Trolley Problem, A Type of Solution to It, and a Method of Ethics*

## F. M. Kamm

I am grateful to my three eminent and brilliant commentators for the attention they have given to my lectures, and for trying to help me and others see the light. I have tried as best I can to understand, discuss, and meet each of their many challenges. I hope I have succeeded. I have also chimed in on interesting positive suggestions they have made. I will deal with each section of a commentator's response in the order in which it was presented.

## Thomson

### 1.

In section 1 of her comments, Thomson first deals with my concern about how she introduced the term "trolley problem." I am happy that we now agree on this issue to a great extent. As I noted, I came to write Lecture I after I had written an encyclopedia entry on the trolley problem. Part of the assignment I was given was to describe what the problem is and its history. I was surprised at what I found. It seemed that it had not been noticed that there were at least two different references for the term in the work of Thomson, who originated the title. She assigned the term first to Foot's question—that is, why the surgeon (whom Thomson called David) may not operate in the Transplant Case but the trolley driver (whom Thomson called Edward) may turn his trolley though they each kill one to save five. I gave the following quote to support this: "Why is it that Edward may turn that trolley to save his five, but David may not cut up his healthy specimen to save his five? I like to call this the trolley problem, in honor of Mrs. Foot's example." Subsequently, in another article, Thomson applied the term to why a bystander may turn the trolley but the surgeon may not kill one person. I gave the following quote to support that claim: "What I shall be concerned with is a first cousin of Mrs. Foot's problem, viz.: Why is it that the bystander may turn his trolley, though the surgeon may not remove the young man's lungs, kidneys, and heart? Since *I* find it particularly puzzling that the bystander may turn his trolley, I am inclined to call this The Trolley Problem." Thomson now agrees with this history (citing the same quotes) and refers to the first assignment as trolley problem (driver baptism) (TPdb) and the second assignment as trolley problem (bystander baptism) (TPbb). She says that the two problems are intimately related and that her "water-muddying doesn't seem to have done any harm" (p. 116).

However, at least for me, there was confusion created, not by Thomson's earlier articles but by her 2008 "Turning the Trolley." There she says "the (so-called) trolley problem is a nonproblem" on the ground that she believes she has shown there is no TPbb.[1] In that 2008 article she referred to what she now calls TPdb as Mrs. Foot's Problem. Instead, it seems that were Thomson right that there is no TPbb, and we should restrict the application of the term to only these two problems, then TPdb would be the only trolley problem.

However, one of my concerns in Lecture I was that how the term "trolley problem" was introduced need not set the limits on how the term should be used. If TPdb starts the trolley problem, one reason to call the Bystander Case a "trolley problem" is that it was a similar case that differed in one important respect and was thought to be a counter-example to the solution Foot proposed to TPdb. If it were really a counter-example and we found a solution to it, it could help us get the correct solution to the TPdb. Thomson offered a solution to TPbb (that we may redistribute an existing threat by certain means but not create new ones), but suppose a case were offered that modified the TPdb in a different way and was a counter-example to Thomson's solution. (I thought the Lazy Susan Case, in which people are moved away from the trolley, resulting in a new threat of rocks falling on one other person, played this role.) Finding the explanation of this counter-example to Thomson's solution could help to also explain both TPbb and TPdb. This process could continue if a counter case were found to the third solution. In addition, my Driver Topple Case arose by changing the way in which the driver in Foot's case would kill the one person. It seems to be another counter-example to Foot's solution, and it faces us with the problem of explaining why it is permissible for the driver to turn the trolley rather than kill five but not permissible for him to topple the fat man from the bridge so that his body stops the trolley from killing five. This is a new problem that can be seen to arise from combining Foot's Driver Case with part of Thomson's Fat Man Case. A solution to it would help us find a solution to TPdb. Because of how such additional cases are generated, and their role in also providing an explanation of the original trolley problem, I think we should consider all these cases as versions of the trolley problem. (Of course, if some of the supposed counter cases to a solution are not really counter cases, then they may present no problem whose solution helps us with a solution to TPdb.)

## 2.

In section 2 of her comments, Thomson discusses what I think the trolley problem is. She first notes that I say we should include in the trolley problem cases "structurally similar" to TPdb but having nothing to do with a trolley in particular, or even with killing rather than other harms. Some examples I gave were whether a missile or flood may permissibly be redirected from killing or harming less seriously many people toward killing or harming fewer people. I said this close to the beginning of the first lecture, when I had just introduced Foot's original trolley problem case.

Thomson also notes that at the end of Lecture I (p. 47), I say that the trolley problem is "about why it is sometimes permissible to kill, even rather than let die, when we come to kill in some ways and not others." Call this Kamm's Description. Thomson says about this: "I take her to mean: the trolley problem is about when it is permissible to kill and when not, and why." Call this Thomson's Translation. She asks, "How did that happen? How did the particular problem 'Why is it that though the driver may kill one, the surgeon may not' get to *be* the general problem 'When is it permissible to kill and when not, and why?'" (p. 116).

I do not think that Thomson's Translation correctly captures the meaning of Kamm's Description. I certainly do not think the trolley problem is as broad as her translation, for her translation would include whether different reasons for killing, such as self-defense or killing to pursue a just cause in war, and also whether being at fault and deserving punishment could justify killing. But as her quote from me says, I was specifically concerned with whether coming to kill "in some ways but not others" would affect the permissibility of killing, not with all the other factors that could affect permissibility. Furthermore, I gave this description of the trolley problem after having considered a wide range of cases in Lecture I involving different ways of coming to kill only innocent, nonthreatening persons. These cases included redirecting the trolley and toppling a man from a bridge into the path of the trolley. In addition, I gave the description of the trolley problem after having argued that the bystander's turning the trolley was permissible even though his alternative was to let the five die (a conclusion Thomson rejects), but toppling the man was impermissible for both a bystander and the driver even though in the latter case the driver's alternative would be to kill five. So at the end of Lecture I, "in some ways but not others" was meant to refer to these sorts of differences and to reflect my view about permissibility in these cases.[2] In Lecture II, I considered more cases—for example, Lazy Susan Case II, where we are not able to redirect a trolley but are able to redirect people from it though their being away from the threat pushes someone else into the trolley. I thought of this as yet another way in which it might be permissible to kill someone.

It was also because I thought of these cases as arising from the original TPdb in the way described in section 1, and because I thought that all the permissible ways and all the impermissible ways in the cases I considered had a common explanation, that I thought it justifiable to give them the trolley problem label.

I hope this will make clear that my description of the trolley problem should not be construed to mean "When is it permissible to kill and when not, and why?"; that is a more general question than mine.[3]

## 3.

A. The third section of Thomson's comments deals with several concerns I had about the arguments she gave to show that there is no TPbb. She first briefly discusses her Bystander's Three Options Case (in which a bystander may let the trolley go to five, redirect to himself, or redirect to a workman whom she describes as the person on the other track) and her original Bystander's Two Options Case (in which a bystander may let the trolley go to five or redirect to the lone workman). She says the bystander "may not throw the switch so that it kills Workman, because neither he nor Workman is required to pay the cost of saving the five" (p. 117). (In her 2008 article she makes this claim subject to the bystander and the workman not having consented to pay the costs. I shall here assume such absence of consent.)

One concern I have about this summary Thomson gives of her argument is that it seems to best summarize only the second of her two arguments. As I described in Lecture I, her first argument says that in the Bystander's Three Options Case, a bystander may not make someone else pay a cost he himself would not pay to save the five, and since he is not required to pay the cost he may let the five die. If he *cannot* pay the cost because he is in the two-options Bystander Case, he still may not make someone else pay a cost he would not pay if he could. In her second argument, she considers whether an altruistic bystander, who would pay the cost to save the five if he could, may make the workman pay it when the bystander cannot pay it himself in a two-option case. It is at that point that she says that what this altruistic bystander would do is irrelevant; one may not make someone else pay the cost if that person is not required to pay the cost to save the five. I dealt with this second argument separately from the first.

In Thomson's comments she deals with three concerns I raised for her first argument. Having done that, she says: "Kamm goes on in the remainder of her first lecture to produce many arguments against things I said about Bystander; many are just repetitions of arguments that I have already summarized, and the rest, so far as I can see, are irrelevant to whether the bystander may kill the one" (p. 121). What accounts for the repetition of some arguments is that having presented them as objections to her *first* argument, I go on to deal with her *second* argument, and I claim that many of the points I made against the first argument (restating them) also apply to the second one. In addition, while a further section of Lecture I deals with her argument that the driver is required to turn the trolley, a final section presents an alternative argument from Thomson's for the view that the bystander may not turn the trolley. Although I ultimately reject this argument, I don't think it is "irrelevant to whether the bystander may kill the one" because it tries to show that he may not.

Let me now consider Thomson's responses to the three concerns I had with her first argument. She points to my first concern about the permissibility, in general, of moving from what is true in a three-options case to what is true in a two-options case.[4] She says that she did not rely on a general thesis that one can make such a move, but "supplied the three-options case primarily in order to bring out more vividly ... that neither the bystander nor Workman is required to pay the cost of saving the five" (p. 118). I am surprised that she would say that this was the primary purpose of the three-options case, since I believe that most people would agree with her on the basis of even a two-options case that neither person is required to pay the cost. In Lecture I, I myself suggested this by imagining a two-options case in which turning the trolley would be very hard and so break the bystander's back. He is not required to pay this cost to turn the trolley and rescue the five.

It seemed to me that there was another reason why Thomson used a three-options case, since in presenting her first argument she emphasizes that if one can oneself pay a cost to do a good deed, other things equal, one may not make someone else pay it. To make this point it is useful to have a three-options case. Furthermore, in presenting her first argument, she makes this claim—that if one can pay it, one may not make someone else pay it—in advance of saying that the bystander is not required to pay the cost, so it seems to be a separate claim. Indeed, it is just this order of her argument that was my second major concern, which Thomson says she has decided to bypass in her comments. That is, my second concern was that it is not true that if one can pay a cost for a good deed, other things equal, one may not make someone else pay it rather than pay it oneself. For if each were required to pay the cost, and the bystander shirks his duty, it may be permissible for him to make someone else pay the cost—at least if it will save lives. Hence, I said that I thought the claim that neither person is required to pay the cost should precede the claim that one may not make someone else pay the cost if one will not when one can.

So I think that there are reasons for thinking that the Bystander's Three Options Case was taken by Thomson to play a role in drawing a conclusion about the Bystander's Two Options Case besides making vivid that no one was required to pay the cost to save the five.

My third concern was that there is a problem with using either a two- or a three-options case in which a bystander is not required to pay a cost to save the five to support the claim that the bystander may not make the workman pay the cost. This is because the bystander would have to do something to himself that makes him pay the cost as an act of altruism, but the workman would be made to pay the cost by the bystander, not by himself. I said that one could conclude from the bystander's not having to altruistically sacrifice himself to save the five that, other things equal, the workman is not required to altruistically sacrifice himself to save the five. However, the fact that neither is required to pay the cost himself does not alone show that the bystander is not permitted to make the workman pay the cost (or vice versa, were the tables turned). It seemed worthwhile to point out this gap between Thomson's premises and Thomson's conclusion, even if the gap could eventually be filled in (by giving some other reason why one should not make the workman pay the cost). This is especially so because, in her second argument, Thomson claims that even if the bystander would do the altruistic act, the workman should not be made to pay the costs because he may not consent to be an altruist. One of my points was that it would not involve altruistic self-sacrifice from the workman when the bystander makes him pay costs.[5]

Let us now consider the specifics of Thomson's discussion of my third concern in her comments. She first considers my background

discussion of Samuel Scheffler's view that could account for someone's prerogative not to pay a cost without implying the impermissibility of others making him pay the cost.[6] I immediately tried to
make clear that I did not want to depend on such a view by saying:
"Elsewhere I have argued in favor of constraints on imposing costs
(or harms), negative rights not to have costs imposed without one's
consent, and for the connection between constraints and prerogatives" (p. 28). Nevertheless, rather than merely conjecturing that
the gap could not always be filled between self-sacrifice not being
required and the impermissibility of making someone else pay
costs, I said, "However, I think that sometimes it may be morally
permissible to impose costs on others when no one would, or would
be required to, impose them on himself . . ." (p. 28). I tried to give
examples of this.

I think it is important to note that I introduced the term "impose
costs." As far as I can tell, Thomson in her 2008 discussion only
spoke of "making someone else pay the costs." This is why, when
discussing her 2008 views, some of the examples I presented were
meant to exemplify "making someone else pay" and not "imposing" in a strict sense. I will return to this point.

Thomson does not think that the first few cases I give are relevant to showing that it is sometimes permissible to make someone
else pay costs he is not required to pay on his own. She says the fact
that a government may draft someone who need not volunteer does
not imply that another person may draft him, and a business we
harm in competition should be understood to have consented to the
risk of this even though it need not bring harm on itself. I am not
sure that only governments, and not another person, may draft for
some types of services.[7] In the case of business competition, I admit
to having interpreted the absence of consent to pay costs so that it
applied to a particular instance of competitive harm, rather than
to the risk of it, but I also do not think that the permissibility of
competitive harming must depend on conceiving of participants in
business as having consented to a risk of such harm.

For another example, I suggested that we could permissibly protect the five from the trolley with a shield—by which I envisioned that the trolley would hit the area where they are but the shield would absorb the impact—even if we know that when the trolley hits the shield it will be deflected to another person. This is so even though that person would not have been required to shield the five when he knew this would lead to his being killed. Of this case, Thomson says, "what difference could it be thought to make that a person deflects the trolley by putting a shield around the five instead of by throwing a switch" (p. 119), which is just the act whose permissibility is being debated. But I do think there is a difference: a shield protects the five not by deflecting the trolley but simply by absorbing the impact of the trolley that the five would otherwise have absorbed. Even if the trolley did not move away from the five, this would save them. The point here is that placing the shield, unlike flipping the switch, does not save the five by deflecting the trolley even though it results in its deflection. This may be a morally significant difference, so that giving this case does not merely assume what we have to prove—namely, that a bystander deflecting the trolley to save the five is permissible. Similarly, suppose we could just stop the trolley "in its tracks" before it hits the five. I think this would be permissible even if stopping it leads to its starting off in a different direction toward one other person. Indeed, using the shield or stopping the trolley may fit in with the view I describe in Lecture II, according to which (roughly) five being saved (e.g., when the impact is absorbed by the shield) may permissibly cause the death of the one. It certainly seems to me, as I mentioned in Lecture I, that the five could permissibly shield themselves with their arms (supposing they had very impact-absorbing arms), even if they foresaw that the trolley would also be deflected off their arms toward one other person. If they may permissibly do this for themselves, it may be that a bystander may help them do it.[8]

The case of mine involving a person making someone else pay costs that neither person is required to pay, which Thomson discusses last, is what I will call the Drowning Case. Someone is not required to let himself drown so as to save five people, yet it would be permissible for him to let another person drown who morally need not and does not consent to this so as to go and save five other people. I used this case because Thomson had only spoken about "making someone else pay the cost," and I think that refraining from preventing someone's suffering a loss of life in order to save others does involve making him pay a cost. Thomson notes (p. 120) that in Lecture I, I say (p. 30) about this case that "I would permissibly impose a cost on that one by not aiding him" and she argues that refraining from preventing him suffering a loss is not imposing a cost on him. But at the start of the paragraph from which she draws this quote I said that "in cases of letting die, rather than killing . . . , this difference between volunteering and imposing (in a broad sense) holds." I should have made clear that by "in a broad sense" I meant to refer to "making someone pay a cost." As Thomson notes, I go on to emphasize that this is a case of letting someone die, not killing. I also agreed with Thomson that there is a moral difference between killing and letting die, so she wonders why I go on to say that "to show that a bystander may not redirect the trolley to the other person, more has to be said than that, other things equal, he should not make someone else pay a cost that he would not and need not pay himself. For this factor would also imply that he may not let the one die" (in the Drowning Case) (p. 30).[9] I said this because, though I knew that Thomson thought it was a morally important difference between the driver and the bystander that the former would otherwise kill the five and the latter would let them die, it did not seem to me that her phrase "making someone pay the cost" itself drew the killing/letting-die distinction; it seemed to me it could apply to someone suffering a loss by being let die or killed. "Imposing" in a *non-broad* sense would draw the distinction; but as I noted above, I introduced the use of that term in the discussion, not Thomson in her 2008 work.

In her comments, Thomson makes it clear that she is concerned with a "sense of making someone pay the costs" that does involve imposing a cost—in particular, killing someone by contrast to letting him die. She goes on to say that she thinks that it is the moral difference between killing and letting die that makes it the case "that I may refrain from saving one person in order to save five though I would not refrain from saving myself in order to save the five, whereas I may not *kill* the one in order to save five if I would not kill myself in order to save the five. If Kamm thinks that the moral difference between killing and letting die doesn't make that the case, then I find it hard to see what she can plausibly think it does make the case" (p. 121). My response to this is that since I do not agree that a bystander is not permitted to kill one to save five when he does it in a certain way (for example, by redirecting a threat from the five), I do not agree that it is merely the difference between killing and letting die that accounts for the cases in which it is *im*permissible to kill one to save five but permissible to let one die to save five. I think that we have to morally distinguish between different ways of coming to kill someone, and that it will be coming to kill someone in some particular ways rather than others which will make it the case that I may not kill the one to save five even though I may let one die to save five. This is what Kamm's Description (see p. 172) emphasized.[10]

There are several other cases that may lend plausibility to the view that though we are not required and do not consent to pay a cost, others may make us pay it (including strictly imposing it on us). One that I mentioned in Lecture I is not discussed by Thomson, and it involves a clear case of killing. I imagined someone who is morally innocent but poses a mortal threat to another (e.g., he is hurled by a villain and will kill the person he lands on, although he will himself be unharmed). I believe this "innocent threat" need not kill himself or do what will lead to his death to stop his fall.

However, I think it is permissible for a third party to kill him if this is necessary and sufficient to protect the person he would kill.

A second additional case that most people would point to, I think, is collateral harm to innocents in war. For example, it is thought to sometimes be permissible to bomb a military facility in a just war to help a nation that is a victim of aggression, although we foresee killing some innocent civilians as a side effect. This is so although even civilians who might otherwise be required to eliminate the military facility need not do so when they know this will kill them. I did not present this case because I think the justification for such collateral harm is complicated. (I discuss it further in my response to Hurka's comments.)

In a third additional case (suggested to me by Peter Graham),[11] on a track between the trolley headed to one person are five people. If they are hit, they will die but the trolley will stop and the one person will be saved. A bystander could save the five either by stepping in front of the trolley so it hits him or by pulling them off the track. He need not and will not do the former, but it seems permissible for him to pull them off the track even though this leads to the one person being killed by the trolley. So he makes the one person pay the cost of his good deed to the five, though he could have paid it himself, and the one person is not himself required to remove the five people off the track when he will then die. This is a case in which the bystander prevents the one person from being saved, and while for various reasons this may not be a case of killing the one, it also does not seem to be a case of merely letting the one die. (If it were a big rock that would stop the trolley from hitting the one person, removing it would be a case of killing him, I think, even if it would also be a case of preventing him from being saved.[12])

Finally, consider a case (suggested by Shelly Kagan) not involving death. I want to do Joe a favor and so I park his car in a spot Anne would otherwise have used. Neither I nor Anne is required to do Joe a favor at the cost of ourselves losing a parking spot, yet I may impose the loss of a parking spot on Anne.

B. Thomson's comments on Lecture I focus on my criticism of her 2008 arguments for the view that the bystander may not turn the trolley. But I think it is important to remember that Lecture I was also concerned with Thomson's accepting the adequacy of Foot's solution to TPdb, that we can explain both the permissibility of the driver's turning the trolley and the impermissibility of the surgeon's killing in Transplant by the fact that the driver would otherwise kill five people while the surgeon would only let five die. In her comments, Thomson does not discuss the counter-examples I gave to the adequacy of this solution. One case involved the driver having to use a mechanical device to topple the fat man from the bridge to stop the trolley on its way to the five (the Driver Topple Case). I claimed that, even though the driver would otherwise kill five, he is not permitted to topple the fat man in this case. (I was surprised Thomson did not discuss the Driver Topple Case in her comments, since in response to audience questions after Lecture I, she said she thought that the driver may not topple the fat man.[13])

I saw the Driver Topple Case as a counter-example to the claim that the fact that the driver would otherwise kill five could alone explain why he is permitted to kill one by redirecting the trolley. I also thought the case showed that Thomson's claim that the driver must turn the trolley because his not doing so "would itself be unjust, for his only alternative . . . is killing five" was too strong; if avoiding the injustice of killing five were sufficient to explain the permissibility (and obligation) of the driver's turning, it would also justify his toppling the one in the Driver Topple Case. It seemed to me important to add something about the difference in the way he would come to kill the one (by toppling or by redirecting) to the explanation of why the driver may permissibly turn the trolley.

Thomson now says the bystander may not turn the trolley. However, she used to think (and still does, I believe) that *if* the bystander were permitted to turn the trolley, this would be a problem for Foot's solution to TPdb that the driver will otherwise kill more people but the surgeon will not. This is because the bystander's being permitted to turn would show that someone who would only let more die may kill and so the question of why the surgeon may not kill still looms. In the same way, I think that if one showed that the driver who would otherwise kill five may not topple the fat man to stop the trolley, the question of why the driver may permissibly kill one by redirecting the trolley still looms. If the Bystander Case could raise a problem for Foot's solution (whether or not it actually does), then if the driver may not topple the one, this too should raise problems for Foot's solution. And as I said in Lecture I, this issue would be a new part of the trolley problem even if we agreed that a bystander is not permitted to turn the trolley.

Indeed, we might say that the Driver Topple Case helps to "reinvent" the trolley problem for those who think the bystander may neither turn the trolley nor topple the fat man. The question for them is: Why may the driver turn the trolley but not topple the fat man? To reflect their question alone we could present the following variation on my description of the trolley problem: Why is it sometimes permissible to kill when we come to kill in some ways and not in others?

Another case that I raised as a problem for Foot's solution to TPdb that Thomson now favors was the Bystanding Driver Two Options Case. Recall that in this case the driver is thrown from the trolley and is standing by the switch that can turn it away from the five. At the time he must decide what to do, he faces a choice between letting the five die and killing one, even though letting the five die in conjunction with having run the trolley will make him be the killer of the five. I contrasted this case with the one in which the surgeon must decide whether to kill one to acquire organs to save five others whom he himself endangered. I noted that Thomson had once discussed a case like this,[14] and she said the doctor may not kill the one person, just as the doctor in Transplant may not. I agree with this, but I think the bystanding driver may permissibly turn the trolley. If this is right, we have another case in which someone who would otherwise let five die may kill one.

This cannot be so just because he would otherwise be the killer of five, since the same is true of the surgeon who endangered the five patients and yet he may not kill. This led me to believe that it was the difference in the way the one came to be killed in the Bystanding Driver Two Options Case by contrast to the case in which the surgeon endangered the patients that made a moral difference, just as it did when the driver would turn the trolley rather than when he would topple the one from the bridge to stop the trolley.

The two cases in TPdb differ in at least two ways: (1) the alternative for the driver is killing more and for that surgeon merely letting more die; (2) one person is killed by the driver's turning the trolley away from the five and one person is killed in a different way by that surgeon. Foot focused on (1) as the explanation of the difference in permissibility. But it was my view that it might be (2) that is at work, since I presented sets of cases where there is a difference in permissibility owing to how the one is killed even (a) when we hold constant that the alternative to killing one is killing five (that is, I compared driver turning the trolley with driver toppling), and (b) when we hold constant that the alternative to killing one is letting five die (that is, I compared the Bystanding Driver Two Options Case with the surgeon who has to save those he endangered). This supported the view that it is (2) and not (1) that morally distinguishes the case of the driver redirecting from the case of the surgeon killing in TPdb.

Here is one reason why Foot may not have focused on (2). She argued that a doctor who needs to use a gas to save five people may not do so if the gas will unavoidably seep into another room and kill someone who is there.[15] In this Gas Case, unlike what is true in Transplant, the involvement of and harm to the one person is not needed to save the five; the harm to him is a foreseen side effect of the gas, which is the causal means to saving the five. Yet using the gas is still impermissible. Foot may therefore have thought that when another means to saving the five—namely, turning the trolley—also causes a merely foreseen death, the means would not be morally different from the use of the gas, and hence it was not a difference between the way one person comes to be killed in Transplant and the way one comes to be killed when the driver turns the trolley that accounts for the difference in permissibility. However, in Lecture II, I proposed that turning the trolley involves the one coming to be killed in a morally different way from the way the one is killed by the gas. And this reopens the possibility that it is (2) that is responsible for the distinction in TPdb.

Thomson never mentions the Driver Topple and Bystanding Driver Two Options Cases in her written comments, but her discussion of Foot's thesis in section 5 of her comments may bear on their relevance, and I will consider that in the later discussion of her section 5.

4.

A. Thomson's fourth section examines a solution I have proposed to TPdb and other related cases. I gave the following description of one version of a general Principle of Permissible Harm (PPH) that concerns harm to innocent, nonthreatening people:

> Actions are *permissible* if greater good or a component of it (or means having these as a noncausal flip side) leads to lesser harm even directly. Actions are *impermissible* if mere means that produce greater good (like the bomb or second trolley) cause lesser harm at least directly, and actions are *impermissible* if mere means cause lesser harms (such as toppling people in front of a trolley) that are mere means to producing greater goods. (p. 66)

(I said that a more precise version of the PPH could be found in my other work.[16]) I described the principle as "downstreamish" "in that it implies that the lesser, direct harms may permissibly be causally downstream of the greater good, components of it, or means having these as their noncausal flip side" (p. 67). Saying this is (roughly) to say that lesser harms may be justified by goods that cause them rather than by goods they (or mere means having them as direct side effects) cause.

Another way of understanding the PPH is that it distinguishes morally between harm that arises from an "eliminative stage" by contrast to harm that arises from an "opportunistic stage." The eliminative stage involves the threat removed from those originally threatened or those people removed from the threat. By contrast, the "opportunistic stage" involves dealing with entities (including but not limited to people) that are not the threat (or those threatened) but are useful in getting rid of that threat (or removing those threatened). Sometimes using these opportunistic entities causes harm and does so independently of the good (or its component) achieved in the eliminative stage being achieved. (Note that this use of "eliminative" and "opportunistic" differs from another use which contrasts (1) eliminating the threat that a person presents with (2) using a nonthreatening person in a way that requires harm to him because this is useful to stop a threat.)

Thomson understands that the PPH implies that when the trolley is the only threat facing the five, the trolley may be redirected because its being away from the five has the greater good of the five's being saved as its noncausal flip side. (She suggests this makes the trolley being away identical with the five being saved, according to some theories.) This corresponds to most of the first sentence of the PPH. She then raises what she views as a counter case to the PPH as an account of the permissibility of turning the trolley. In her Bat Case, we can save the five by removing the trolley, but we can remove the trolley only by batting it with a heavy bystander. She believes that my PPH yields "that we may kill the one in Bat" and "that won't do."

I agree with her that it is impermissible to turn the trolley in Bat, but I disagree that the PPH implies it is permissible. I think she believes it is a counter case to the PPH because the person who is hit by the trolley is harmed by a means that has the greater good as a noncausal flip side, yet turning the trolley is impermissible. But the PPH does not yield that we may turn the trolley, because the two clauses of its *second sentence* rule out using a heavy bystander to bat the trolley aside and if the trolley may not be turned aside, the five will not be saved as the flip side of doing so. This is because getting the trolley to turn in that way would involve a mere means (namely, picking up and batting a person against a trolley) that (causally) produces a greater good and also directly harms someone (or itself is a harm to him). The fact that this means to the greater good, unlike the moving away of the trolley, does not have the greater good or its component as a noncausal flip side, and that it causes harm to the person used as a bat, makes saving the five impermissible according to the PPH. (Similarly, the PPH would rule out toppling a fat man from the bridge not only so that his body landing between the trolley and the five will stop it. It would also rule out toppling the fat man if his falling on the trolley was required to give the trolley a jolt that redirects it away from the five and toward one other person. This last case is like Thomson's Bat Case in its causal structure.)[17]

I also think it is because Thomson does not consider the two clauses of the second sentence of the PPH that she says it implies the wrong conclusion in my Two Trolleys Case. In this case, we can only remove the trolley threatening the five by turning a second trolley (that would have harmed no one) into the first trolley. However, on its way, the second trolley would kill one person. I think the PPH correctly implies that we may not turn the first trolley away from the five in this case becaues the only way we can do this is by using the second trolley, which is a mere causal means to the greater good and directly causes the death of one person. This is prohibited by the first clause of the PPH's second sentence.

Thomson next considers my Tractor Case: "The five toward whom the trolley is headed also have a deadly tractor headed toward them. If we turn the trolley away, it will hit one person whose being hit will stop the tractor" (p. 68). She believes, though she is not sure, that I hold that turning the trolley is permissible according to the PPH, and should be. In fact, I said the PPH implies we may *not* turn the trolley in the Tractor Case. To clarify this, and because I think that the original Tractor Case and Tractor Case II are important for judging the PPH, let me review what I said. In Lecture II, I introduced the Tractor Case (which I had discussed in earlier work) after having explained why I thought turning the trolley in Thomson's Loop Case (which she discusses in her addendum) is permissible according to the PPH. I asked, "Is it permissible to turn the trolley in the Tractor Case, as it is in the Loop Case?" (p. 68). I argued that in the Tractor Case, the lesser evil was not caused by a trolley whose being away from the five had the greater good or even a component of it as its noncausal flip side because the five were still under the threat of the tractor.[18] Given what Thomson says about the Loop Case, I do not think she would agree with this.

Thomson says (in her addendum) that when we turn the trolley in the Loop Case, we have saved the five even before the trolley hits the one person whose being hit will prevent the trolley's looping back to the five. She says this is because the trolley *will* hit the one and so the trolley will not loop. On these grounds, she thinks my PPH implies it is permissible to turn the trolley in Loop. Hence, in Tractor, she might also say the five are already saved once the trolley is away, given that the one will be hit and this will stop the tractor. If this were so, then the harm to the one person will be causally downstream from the greater good and the PPH should imply turning the trolley is permissible in the Tractor Case.

I find it hard to accept Thomson's analysis of Loop and Tractor, as helpful as it would be for the role of the PPH. It seems to me that the five are not yet saved in Loop and Tractor once we turn the trolley, even if turning the trolley will cause them to be saved. This is, in part, because turning the trolley does not have a noncausal relation to the hitting of the one and the hitting of the one has a causal relation to the trolley's stopping, and so we cannot be absolutely certain that if the trolley is turned, the hitting will be useful in stopping the trolley. Yet I think that, in the Loop Case, even when there is only a good chance that the hit will occur and be effective in stopping the trolley, it is permissible to turn the trolley. In Lecture II, I said this was because when we turn the trolley, we have achieved a component of the greater good—namely, what would be the greater good if only it can be sustained and not undermined by a new threat to the five (the looping trolley) that we create in removing the initial trolley threat.[19] That initial threat would have to be removed, whatever else is also needed, if the five are to survive. This component of the greater good (or means having it as a noncausal flip side) would cause the harm to the one person that can lead to the greater good (i.e., the five surviving because they are free of threats) and so turning in the Loop Case is permissible according to the PPH.

By contrast, it seemed to me that, in the Tractor Case, when we see what is achieved in turning the trolley away, independent of any new threat to the five that turning it creates, we do not yet have even a component of the greater good, at least on one understanding of "component," since the five are still set to be killed by the tractor. Hence, harm to the one would not be downstream from the greater good or a component of it. Furthermore, as noted earlier, in this case it is also not absolutely certain that hitting the one person will cause the tractor to be stopped, so I do not see how we can say we have already achieved the greater good when we turn away the trolley. Yet the one's being hit is needed to produce the tractor's stopping. It is not merely needed to sustain a component of the good already achieved, as in the Loop Case. For this reason I said that "this productive harm is not downstream from a component of the good." I refer to the "possible difference in the permissibility of redirecting in the Loop and Tractor Cases" (p. 68).[20]

Thomson also discusses my Tractor Case II, which is like the original Tractor Case except that the one being hit on the side track has no causal role in stopping the tractor. Rather, the tractor is stopped by a switch that is pressed by the trolley as it turns away from the five. She says correctly that it seemed to me that the PPH would make it impermissible to turn the trolley even though intuitively it is permissible. This case (and especially one in which the trolley presses the switch after it hits the one) showed a possible problem with the PPH, for as in the original Tractor Case, the greater good or even a component of it is no more present when we turn the trolley away than in original Tractor, since the tractor still threatens the five. Nevertheless, I think it is permissible to turn the trolley because the harm to the one person is not causally required to stop the tractor; the morally innocent pressing of a switch by the moving trolley will produce that result, and with the removal of both threats the five will be saved.

I raised Tractor Case II as a problem for the PPH, but I also said that the fact that a principle may require emendations does not mean that its essential message should be rejected. (In science, theories can undergo many emendations without rejecting their central message. Darwinism is a good example.) I did not undertake any emendations in Lecture II because my aim there was to introduce a different approach to the trolley problem than Thomson's or Foot's, not to work it out in all its details. However, in *Intricate Ethics* I had tried to deal with the issues that cases like the Tractor Cases raised. I shall now briefly describe some of what I said there (in part because it also bears on Hurka's comments, as we shall see).

Tractor Case II raises the question of why, in this case, using a means (i.e., turning the trolley) that will kill someone but does not have the greater good or a component of it as its flip side should be permissible when using other means of which this is also true (such as sending in the second trolley or using the bomb that would derail the trolley but also kill someone) is not permissible. One proposal I examined in *Intricate Ethics* was that we should understand the removal of a threat (or the removal of people from a threat though they still face others) as itself a component of the greater good. That is, the five being free of one threat is a component of their being free of all threats. Their being free of all threats (and each component of this) has a noncausal, constitutive relation to the greater good of their being saved. This is unlike the purely causal relation that the bomb going off or the second trolley moving has to the greater good. That is because neither of these is an instance of a threat being removed nor of victims being moved from a threat. This proposal is an alternative understanding of the "component of the greater good" in the PPH, since a component of the greater good could arise even though, independent of our creating new threats by removing a threat, the five are still subject to another deadly threat.

Suppose we took this route to distinguishing turning the trolley in Tractor Case II from, for example, using the bomb in the Bomb Trolley Case. Then the question is why it should not also be permissible to turn the trolley in the original Tractor Case, for under the new interpretation of "component," this is also a case in which a component of the greater good would be causing the lesser harm. In *Intricate Ethics*, I argued that harms that are required to play a further role in producing other components of the greater good, unlike harms that are mere side effects or effects that sustain goods achieved, should already be completely justified, as when they are the result of a good (or means having a noncausal relation to a good) that is greater than the harm that will play the productive role. Removing one threat that secures no one's safety because there are other threats facing everyone is not a component good already sufficient to justify the hit to the one person that is needed to stop the tractor. By contrast, two people being saved from all threats to them would be sufficient to justify harm to someone whose being hit would stop the tractor still headed to three of the five people. In *Intricate Ethics*, I called this amended version of the original PPH the Principle of Productive Purity.[21]

B. Thomson says that she thinks she does not understand what the PPH implies "partly, no doubt, because I don't understand the generalization, though partly also because the cases themselves are hard to get one's mind around" (p. 123). She says this before discussing the Tractor Cases, so I believe she thinks it is hard to get one's mind around those cases, and she also describes the Two Trolleys Case as "complicated." Let me now discuss her concerns with the cases rather than with the PPH itself.

By comparison to all the complicated cases that have been presented in the so-called "trolleyology" literature by many other philosophers,[22] I do not think the Tractor and Two Trolleys Cases are complicated. The Tractor Cases just require us to imagine that there is more than one threat coming at the five and different ways in which the second threat can be stopped. The Two Trolleys Case is one of the cases (like Foot's Gas Case) in which some causal means to a greater good itself has a bad side effect. Recall that the specific reason I introduced the Two Trolleys Case was to respond to Thomson's 2008 suggestion that the reason people (mistakenly) think a bystander may save the five is that doing so only involves turning a trolley. The point was to present another case that also has this property and holds constant many other factors, yet in which it seems impermissible to people to save the five. This suggested that more has to be said to explain why saving the five in the Bystander Case seems permissible to some.

Thomson says that others of my cases are even more ornate (p. 124). To me, "ornate" suggests embellishments that are merely decorative and have no other function, by contrast to "intricate," which does not suggest this. (Compare a surgeon who does intricate surgery with one who does ornate surgery: the former may be doing functionally necessary surgery; the latter is not.) Trolley cases can become intricate because philosophers find it useful to distinguish the role that one factor plays in determining the permissibility of an act by contrasting it with another case that lacks that factor or has another factor that, holding everything else constant, changes the permissibility of the act. One of my cases that Thomson finds ornate (p. 124) employs three options, as did Thomson's Bystander's Three Options Case. In my case, we are to imagine that a driver faces a choice between (a) killing the five, (b)

turning a trolley away from five to a track that runs on a bridge
from where it will topple two people, or (c) pressing a switch that
topples a fat man from a different bridge in front of the trolley to
stop it from hitting the five. The function of the contrast between
(b) and (c) is to show that the PPH implies that it is permissible
to kill more people causally downstream from the greater good in
(b) rather than fewer other people not causally downstream from
the greater good in (c). Why do we imagine a trolley going across
the bridge and toppling two when this seems so bizarre?[23] We do
so because when we use cases to test for the moral significance of
one factor (such as harm being causally downstream from greater
good), we should use a case where it is present and contrast it with
another case where it is not present but try to hold all other factors
constant. So both option (b) and option (c) should involve toppling
someone but (b), and not (c), should involve the trolley's being away
from the five when it causes the deaths. Since we are trying to show
that even when more people will die one way of saving the five is
to be preferred, we also vary the number of victims who will be
killed in options (b) and (c). Because we can manipulate hypothetical cases in this way in order to test for the moral significance of
specific factors, they are in some ways like scientific experiments
done in a lab that do not necessarily use real-world conditions. [24]

An important aspect of the methodology of using hypothetical
cases is at issue here. We must not only hold all the factors of a case
in mind but also have an intuitive judgment about the permissibility or impermissibility of action in the case. I think one should also
try to isolate the factors in the case that account for one's judgment.
Doing this can become increasingly difficult as a case becomes
more complex, but that does not mean one cannot use it as a tool for
discovering the truth. Some hold the view that complicated cases
cannot help us get at the truth. For example, Thomas Nagel, in
discussing his views about a principle of permissible harm based
on the Doctrine of Double Effect, says: "I won't try to draw the
exact boundaries of the principle; though I say it with trepidation,

I believe that for my purposes they don't matter too much, and I suspect they can't be drawn more than roughly; my deontological intuitions at least, begin to fail above a certain level of complexity."[25] In *Intricate Ethics*, I contrasted his view with mine about a principle of permissible harm, saying: "I think that the principle can be drawn more than roughly, and that in doing this we should, if we can, rely on intuitions even at great levels of complexity."[26] (This need not mean that the principle we discover is itself complex, only the cases used in finding it.) Many philosophers (like Nagel and Bernard Williams) use striking cases (like Williams's famous Jim and the Indians Case) but they do not consider many variations on them in which factors they think account for the permissibility or impermissibility of action in the original case are omitted or combined with yet other factors. Such variations can reveal that the factor they thought was responsible for permissibility or impermissibility is, in fact, not responsible.[27]

## 5.

A. Thomson begins section 5 of her comments by saying of the TPdb that "Kamm tells us that that problem really is the problem 'When is it permissible to kill and when not, and why?'" (p. 124). But, as I noted in section 2 of these responses, what I said was that the trolley problem is "about why it is sometimes permissible to kill, even rather than let die, when we come to kill in some ways and not others." I have already said (in section 2 of these responses) that I think Thomson's Translation is too broad and I explained why. I there also noted that I gave my description of what the trolley problem is about after having considered cases (such as Bystander, Driver Topple, and Bystanding Driver Two Options) that I thought were part of the trolley problem, so the description was not intended to just refer to TPdb.[28] So if Thomson now thinks the trolley problem is only TPdb, her question, How did TPdb "get to *be* the general problem, when is it permissible to kill and when not, and why?" has me transforming *less* than I had in mind (i.e., only TPdb) into *more* than I had in mind (i.e., all that is involved in her Translation).

Given her understanding of what I am doing (in her Translation), her answer to her question is that TPdb did not get to be (is not to be identified with) the broader problem. She thinks it is best to understand me as saying that solving TPdb requires solving the broader problem. But given what I actually said the trolley problem is, and the cases on which I based my view, is it wrong to identify what the trolley problem is about with "Why is it sometimes permissible to kill, even rather than let die, when we come to kill in some ways and not others?" Recall that I thought some of the cases I dealt with in Lecture I (such as Bystander and Bystanding Driver Two Options) showed that it could be permissible to kill even rather than let die when we killed in some ways instead of others. And I thought that other cases (such as Driver Topple) showed that it was only permissible to kill one person rather than kill more if the one was killed in some ways and not others. I said that I thought all these "cousins" of Foot's Trolley Case should be considered part of the trolley problem. Furthermore, many of these cases were raised as objections to a certain way of explaining TPdb and were supposed to help us provide a correct explanation of what was going on in TPdb. So the short answer to how TPdb became the trolley problem as I described it is that (i) I identified its cousin cases as parts of the trolley problem, (ii) I judged and raised questions about the permissibility and impermissibility of harm in those cases, and (iii) my description of the trolley problem was based on those judgments and questions.[29]

Of course, Thomson does not think it is permissible to turn the trolley in the Bystander Case, and she may not think that it is permissible to turn it in Bystanding Driver Two Options. If she were right about this, these cases (and the cases with which they are typically contrasted) would be eliminated as parts of the trolley problem. In her comments at least, she does not say whether the driver toppling the fat man is a problem or not by comparison to his turning the trolley. If she thinks TPdb is the only trolley problem, this would explain her thinking that even my actual wording of what the trolley problem is does not capture it, and that the problem I identify could at most be a general problem that we need to solve in order to deal with TPdb.

The PPH and the brief attempt to describe what morally significant ideas may supervene on or underlie it that I presented in Lecture II were indeed supposed to offer an explanation of TPdb. They were also supposed to explain other cases mentioned in Lectures I and II in which we had to decide whether to rescue people from threats when this would kill someone else (such as the Lazy Susan Case and the Loop Case). For reasons given in section 2 of these responses, I considered all these cases to fall under the trolley problem and so the PPH was a proposed answer to the trolley problem. In addition,the formulation of the PPH and the attempt to explain what supervenes on or underlies it seem to me to fall under what Thomson thinks is needed—namely, moral theory rather than merely the consideration of many cases. (I will try to defend this claim further in the next subsection.)

B. The PPH was a principle I had elsewhere proposed and presented in greater detail and subsequent to these earlier publications I had had further thoughts prompted by considering other cases. I presented these newer thoughts in sections 5 through 7 of Lecture II. Thomson thinks these parts of the second lecture involve a "drift along, from hypothetical case to hypothetical case," and "nothing is explained" (p. 125). I do not agree that we merely drift.[30] At the start of section 5 of Lecture II, I stated a clear purpose to what is done: without relying on the PPH, which some might reject, I wanted to continue examining the question of whether those who would otherwise let die are not permitted to kill, by contrast to those who would otherwise kill, holding all else constant. I further wanted to see if judgments about this in certain new cases could be shown to bear on whether it is permissible to turn the trolley in the Bystander Case. I considered two broad categories of cases. The first concerned whether the five people who would otherwise be killed by the trolley may kill someone, and in what way, rather than let themselves die. The second concerned whether one person who would otherwise be killed by the trolley may kill more than one person, and in what way, rather than let himself die. Under each category, I systematically considered the same types of ways of causing harm enumerated by the PPH (e.g., harm caused by good, harm caused by means having good as a noncausal flip side, harm caused by mere causal means to the good, and harm that is a means to the good).

It is true that in these parts I placed less emphasis on explanation and more emphasis on considering cases I thought had not been attended to and then rendering intuitive judgments on them. Though I occasionally suggested how the PPH might explain our intuitive judgments in these cases, I did not belabor the point. However, considering the case in which it seemed permissible for an individual to cause greater harm in order to save himself led me to reconceive the explanatory role of the PPH so that its emphasis on greater good being achieved was separable from its delineation of the ways in which harm might be brought about. Hence, I tried to explain the permissibility of the individual's causing greater harm by suggesting that the part of the PPH that distinguished the permissibility of various ways of killing could sometimes be more crucial than the part that emphasized that greater good would result. Furthermore, I suggested that the first part of the PPH could be combined with a nonconsequentialist prerogative not to maximize the good at great cost to oneself to permit individuals to harm and not only not aid. (I find this result surprising and worth investigating further.) I ultimately tried to show why and how we could use judgments in cases in which individuals acted from a partial perspective (e.g., out of concern for their own interests) to decide what an impartial bystander in the Bystander Case might permissibly do. I said the "partial" cases could bear on the "impartial" ones because, in discussing what the five and the one may do for themselves, I had not relied on any special permission to just do whatever was necessary to save oneself. (For example, using mere means such as a bomb that will directly kill someone else was still prohibited.) Most importantly, if distinctions among permissible and impermissible ways of killing as described in the PPH held up even in the cases involving a partial perspective, this supports their role in explaining such cases as TPdb and TPbb where action from an impartial point of view is assumed. (I shall return to this point.)[31]

In addition, I used the cases in sections 5 through 7 of Lecture II to uncover what I thought might be an alternative to the PPH in explaining the trolley problem. In trying to explain my intuitive judgments in these cases, I focused on the removal of, or escape from, a threat that existed in the environment independently of the actions of those threatened and the effect this removal or escape had on other entities independently in the environment. The fact that the discussion in these parts could be a basis for an alternative to the PPH may not have been made sufficiently clear. I will try to clarify this a bit here.

The comparison of this later discussion in sections 5 through 7 with the discussion of the PPH may show how one can move in different ways from intuitive judgments to identifying the factors that account for the judgments. There is a phenomenon that seems to me similar to the switching Duck/Rabbit gestalt in response to a set of shapes; the same set of intuitive judgments about permissibility may be "carved up" in different ways. For example, when the trolley moves away, one may focus on what remains when it is away (e.g., some good) and see that as what is important in justifying the permissibility of redirecting the trolley. This is what is emphasized in the PPH. Alternatively, one may focus on the movement away of the threatening trolley or some other entity that is in the environment independently of our action that becomes a threat (such as the rocks moved by the lazy Susan). Sometimes the pattern that seems salient in accounting for intuitive judgments is in the positive space (the role of the good) and one ignores the negative space; sometimes the salient pattern is in the negative space (the movement of entities that are in the environment independently of our action that threaten persons).

These two different ways of looking at the data may, however, lead to some different conclusions. In particular (as I noted in Lecture II, n. 24), the downstreamish PPH implies not only that the turned trolley or the rocks that are moved when people escape the trolley may permissibly harm someone. It also implies that people's being saved may itself cause harm without intermediate causes of harm that are entities independently in the environment. For example, suppose five people move away from the trolley (or we move them) and they land on someone standing nearby, killing him. If bringing about this event is, at least intuitively, permissible, it would not constitute an objection to the PPH.

However, suppose some think it is no more permissible for a greater good itself to directly cause harm in this way than it is for a mere means such as the bomb to do so. This would be an objection to the downstreamish PPH. It would also suggest that in the standard Trolley Case we should focus on the means to saving the five (such as the trolley's moving away) in a different way from how the PPH focuses on it. That is, the PPH emphasizes that the trolley may itself kill someone owing to its having a noncausal relation to the five being saved. The bomb may not be used to move the trolley if it would itself kill someone, because it has a mere causal relation to the greater good. But an alternative, less downstreamish way of looking at the (supposed) data is that neither a greater good nor a mere causal means to a greater good independent of its relation to some entity independently in the environment may cause lesser harm. (Examples of what would be ruled out are the five in their escape from the trolley landing on and killing a person, or the bomb's killing someone.) But both the greater good and the mere means may permissibly relate to entities independently in the environment so that these become threats, as when the five escaping the trolley cause the rocks independently in the environment to fall and the bomb that moves the trolley also moves such rocks that kill someone.

This alternative view—call it the Independent Entity View—is not downstream in two ways. First, it prohibits harms that are caused in certain ways by greater good. Second, it permits harms that are caused in certain ways by causal means to greater good. However, it is still a type of solution that focuses on how we would come to kill someone and it is a *non-upstreamish* theory in that it does not permit harms that arise in certain ways to be means to the greater good. So if a mere means to a greater good causes an entity (e.g., rocks) independently in the environment to harm a person, this harm is not permitted to be a further step to producing the greater good that is supposed to justify the harm. However, just as the one's death caused by the trolley's moving away from the five in the Loop Case may be permitted to keep the trolley from looping, the one's death caused by rocks moved by the bomb that moves the trolley away may have the same role.

In sum, the PPH does not differ from this alternative view in the ways it allows and prohibits mere means to lead to harm (since it does not rule out so-called indirect harmful side effects of means to the greater good). It differs from the alternative view in the more generous way it allows (greater) goods to lead to harm. (For more on this issue see pp. 223–24 in my response to Hurka).

C. (i) Thomson's deeper concern in her fifth section is not with drift along cases or even merely lack of explanation of intuitive judgments in many cases. Rather, her deeper concern, put most generally, is whether we really have to consider many cases in order to find a principle (such as the PPH) so that we can then discover what the principle's underlying significant values are, which is a method I suggested. She says that this "certainly doesn't go on in the great works we study in learning how to do philosophy. . . . [I]t is precisely what the morally significant underlying concepts and values *are* that they try to discover. And none of them seems to have thought that, in order to find out what they are, they must first find generalizations of the kind Kamm is in search of" (p. 126).

I see the study of at least some great philosophers somewhat differently. In their pursuit of the morally significant underlying concepts and values, they have often gotten things wrong by not considering cases. Some of the greats tell us that it is maximizing happiness (understood as pleasure and the avoidance of pain) that really matters. Nonconsequentialists commonly draw out the implications of such a view for cases (e.g., Transplant). They do this in part to more completely understand what the view amounts to and also to use the cases in arguing that there is something wrong with the view. This suggests that the problem was that some "greats" did not consider enough cases to begin with and therefore got the morally significant concepts and values wrong.[32] For if we will test theories about underlying concepts and values, at least in part, by their implications for cases, and revise or reject the theories at least partly because of those implications, we might get the same result by first considering cases before we propose a theory that is likely to need revision anyway. Worse still would be to spend time trying to explain more deeply *why* some theory (such as "maximizing happiness is what matters") is correct, before first considering *whether* it is correct by considering its implications for cases, assuming this is (even in part) an appropriate test for whether the theory is correct.

(ii) Thomson narrows the focus of her general concern about considering many cases by contrast to trying to find underlying significant concepts and values when she asks: "*Is* there good reason for thinking that one can't explain why the driver may kill the one whereas the surgeon may not unless we already know when anyone, however situated, may or may not kill a person?" (p. 126). I agree—and never claimed otherwise—that we do not need an answer (if there even is one) to this very general question to decide about the trolley driver and surgeon. I think it is because

Thomson's Translation incorrectly presents my description of the trolley problem as posing the general question that she thinks I disagree with her about this. But Thomson goes on to claim that merely by doing "moral theory" on the single contrast of the driver versus the surgeon we can explain why it is permissible for the driver to turn the trolley and for the surgeon not to, and so solve TPdb. Call this her Ultimate Claim. Before considering how she reaches this conclusion and whether it is true, it is important to note that the venture in moral theory she envisions begins with two cases, rather than with some insight about underlying concepts and values independent of a case. Furthermore, the Trolley Driver's Two Options Case was raised as an objection to another proposed principle—namely, that we may not kill some to save others (which would have implied that the trolley driver may not turn the trolley). The latter principle itself was proposed by some nonconsequentialists to explain why it was impermissible to kill in the Transplant Case, a case that was raised to rebut the principle that we should maximize happiness. If we had not been thinking about cases and moving from one case to another, we might never have gotten to the point of doing moral theory with the Trolley Driver's Two Options and Transplant Cases.

(iii) In trying to support her Ultimate Claim, Thomson considers what she calls Foot's Worseness Thesis: Though (1) killing five is worse than killing one, (2) killing one is worse than letting five die. She says this is standardly interpreted to yield the following Choice Generalization: Though (1') if A must choose between killing five and killing one, then he may kill the one, (2') if B must choose between killing one and letting five die, then he may not kill the one—he must let the five die. She thinks the Choice Generalization is an "overly simple" way of interpreting the Worseness Thesis, which itself is better understood as Worseness* Thesis: Though (1*) an act's being a killing of five counts in favor of its being impermissible more strongly than an act's being a killing of one counts in favor of its being impermissible, (2*) an act's being a killing of one counts in favor of its being impermissible more strongly than an act's being a letting five die counts in favor of its being impermissible.[33] Worseness* Thesis does not rule out any acts and so does not yield Choice Generalization, and "is entirely compatible with there being situations in which we may kill five rather than kill one, and situations in which we may kill one rather than let five die" (p. 127). Thomson says " 'counting in favor of an act's being impermissible' is what moral theorists ascribe when they say ... 'other things being equal, he acted wrongly,' attributing the burden of proof that he didn't act wrongly to anyone who thinks that he didn't" (p. 127). (She notes that Foot herself said "it may make a difference [to whether we may kill someone rather than let others die] whether his presence contributes to the threat to others.") I believe that Thomson thinks that the Worseness Thesis* can lead us to the conclusion that, in Foot's Trolley and Transplant Cases, the factor (for example) of killing one versus killing five makes the trolley driver's turning the trolley permissible because there is no other factor (such as that the five had agreed to be hit or that they contributed to the threat to themselves) that makes this first factor not carry the day. However, in other cases, there may be another factor that defeats the factor in the first clause of the Worseness Thesis*.

At this point, I should note an alternative view about what moral theorists ascribe when they say "other things being equal, he acted wrongly." Thomson says that they are ascribing that more counts in favor of an act's being impermissible, attributing the burden of proof to those who say otherwise. Presumably, the burden of proof could be met by presenting some factor that defeats (by outweighing or undermining) the significance of the factor that points to an agent's doing wrong even though the factor is still present. But I believe that sometimes when moral theorists say that one factor counts more strongly in favor of impermissibility than another factor "other things equal," they mean that in cases where everything else is the same, one factor will count more strongly in favor of impermissibility than another. For example, in discussions of whether letting someone die is less seriously wrong than killing someone, we try to equalize for such factors as intention, cost to avoid the act, and so on, so that it is only the degree to which killing and letting die count toward the impermissibility that we are measuring. Similarly, it might be claimed that holding constant the way in which someone comes to be killed (e.g., as a mere means to the greater good), killing five counts more strongly in favor of impermissibility than killing one. I think we should keep in mind in the discussion that follows that there are two different senses of "other things equal." I shall call Thomson's use "other things equal (1)" (where this amounts to "unless there is a special defeating factor") and the second use "other things equal (2)" (where this amounts to "holding all other factors constant in contrasting cases").[34]

Thomson also thinks the Worseness* Thesis tells us (as the Worseness Thesis does not) why it matters whether an act is a killing of one or of five, and why it matters whether an act is a killing of one or a letting die of five. (I think she means that the Worseness* Thesis, for example, points to a factor in an act of killing one that, other things equal (1), makes that killing worse than letting five die—namely, its having the factor of being a killing of one, which counts more strongly in favor of impermissibility than the factor of being a letting die of five counts in favor of its impermissibility.) She says, "there isn't anything in either of Kamm's lectures that sheds any doubt on it" (p. 127) (where the "it" refers, I believe, to the claims in Worseness* that the factor of being a killing of one counts less strongly in favor of impermissibility than an act's being a killing of five does, and the factor of being a killing of one counts more strongly in favor of impermissibility than an act's being a letting die of five does). Presumably, Foot would point to these factors in explaining TPdb because she would think in this case other things are equal (1) and so the factors account for the permissibility and impermissibility of acts.

In fact, I do believe that it is not these factors that make the killing permissible in Foot's Trolley Case and impermissible in Transplant. This is not because I disagree with drawing a distinction between acts and factors, as in the contrast between the Choice Generalization and the Worseness* Thesis. Elsewhere in discussing what I believe to be the moral difference between killing and letting die, I have emphasized that to say that there is a moral difference between killing and letting die is not to say that there is a moral difference between every instance of killing and letting die; and the fact that in some cases the differential significance of the factors of killing and letting die (i.e., the factors per se) makes no moral difference to what is done does not show that these factors never make a moral difference to the permissibility of acts.[35] The per se moral difference might not make a difference to the permissibility of acts because other things are not equal (1) or (2).[36] Furthermore, the PPH could be rephrased in "factor language" so that it implies, among other things, that an act's being a killing in some particular way (though not others) of one person counts more strongly in favor of its impermissibility than an act's being a letting die of five counts against its impermissibility, other things equal (1), but an act's being a killing in some other way of one person does *not* count more strongly in favor of its impermissibility than an act's being a letting die of five counts in favor of its impermissibility, other things equal (1). If this were true, it would not be true that "there isn't anything in either of Kamm's lectures that sheds any doubt on [the Worseness* Thesis]" (p. 127). I shall provide further defense of this claim below.

Notice also that one need not translate a principle into the language of factors in order for the principle itself to be true only if other things are equal (1). There might be cases where something else overrides the PPH, as when one has promised the one person not to kill him under any circumstances or promised to kill the one person only by toppling him from the bridge.

Sir David Ross was an early defender of the idea of *prima facie* duties, which are also considerations that determine what we should do only if no other considerations opposing them give us more reason to do something else. He thought we could identify several *prima facie* duties, but the decision about what to actually do in a situation where several pull in different directions is a matter of "perception," not given by a principle. Similarly, the fact that something is a killing is a *prima facie* consideration against doing it, but there may be considerations that weigh against this. However, suppose we could reduce the reliance on mere perception by discovering a more complex factor that already embodies the weights of several simpler factors. Then we will have made an advance, even if this factor is also *prima facie* with respect to still other factors. Whether Foot is right or not about the factors that Thomson sees her as identifying to explain TPdb, one way of seeing what Foot (according to Thomson) is doing is trying to go beyond the claim that being a killing is a factor that counts against an act. If her view implies that killing one as the alternative to letting five die counts against an act more than does killing one as the alternative to killing five, she would identify a complex factor of killing as the alternative to letting die that counts against permissibility, and that factor is not going to be outweighed by as many other factors as the simple factor of killing.

The PPH I proposed also allows us to go beyond merely saying that killing counts against an act but may be outweighed by other factors. The PPH can be seen as identifying a complex factor that counts against permissibility—killing that is not causally downstream of a greater good—that is not going to be outweighed by as many other factors (e.g., producing a greater good) as the simpler factor of killing would be. In creating the more complex factor, we could be seen as specifying in a principled way a general factor that has *prima facie* moral significance in order to reduce the reliance on Rossian perception in decision making.[37]

So I am not opposed to pointing to factors; rather, I do not believe it is the particular factors in the Worseness* Thesis that explain TPdb. This is because I think (a) there are other cases in which these factors are present but they do not explain permissibility and impermissibility; (b) this is not due to the presence of factors defeating those in the Worseness* Thesis (inequality (1)) but due to the presence of other factors that do determine permissibility and impermissibility; and (c) those other factors are also present in the TPdb cases.[38] Hence, for me, one crucial question is whether pointing to other cases besides those in TPdb can help us decide which factors are crucial in accounting for TPdb. I think Thomson believes that other cases in which the factors she points to in the Worseness* Thesis are shown not to be crucial for permissibility or impermissibility not only cannot show that the factors never make a moral difference, because there could be special defeating (outweighing or overriding) factors in the other cases (a claim with which I agree), but that other cases cannot show that the factors do not account for the moral difference between killing in Transplant and killing in Foot's Trolley Case. I disagree with the latter claim. Hence, even if I agreed with there not being anything in my lectures that sheds any doubt on the factors in the Worseness* Thesis sometimes having moral importance, I think there are things in my lectures that shed doubt on their making the difference in permissibility between Transplant and Foot's Trolley Case and so explaining TPdb—and also things that shed doubt on the truth of the Worseness* Thesis itself.

To see why I believe this, first consider that Thomson in her earlier work thought (and continued to think in her 2008 article) that *if* it were permissible to turn the trolley in the Bystander Case, this would present a problem for Foot's account of the difference between the Transplant Case and her Trolley Driver's Two Options Case. But given what Thomson now says in her comments, should she not instead say that even if the bystander may kill one rather than let five die, (i) this would not show that killing one does not count more strongly in favor of impermissibility of an act than letting five die does, other things equal (1); and (ii) it would not show that this factor does not account for why the doctor in Transplant may not kill. For according to Thomson's discussion of the Worseness* Thesis, there might be some factor in the Bystander Case that makes other things not equal (1) and so overcomes the weight of killing one versus letting five die. Yet, presumably, Thomson thinks that if the bystander were permitted to turn the trolley, this would not be because the case has such a special factor distinguishing it from Transplant and defeating the moral role that killing one versus letting die has in Transplant. This is partly why she would think it could be a counter-example to Foot's explanation of TPdb.

In a sense, my claim is that there is a factor in the Bystander Case that makes it not equal (2) to the Transplant Case even though both involve killing one rather than letting five die, but this factor is not some special defeater that outweighs the role of the killing one versus letting five die factor, which according to Foot and Thomson is playing the decisive role in explaining the moral difference between the Transplant and Trolley Driver's Two Options Cases (in the way that the one's consent to be killed would outweigh it). Rather, my claim is that the factor of being killed causally downstream from the greater good that is present in the Bystander Case is absent in Transplant, and so makes the two cases not equal (2). Further, this factor is also present in Foot's Trolley Driver's Two Options Case. And if this factor did make the killing in the Bystander Case permissible when killing in Transplant is not, it may be it (not that the driver will kill one rather than kill five) that also makes turning in the Trolley Driver's Two Options Case permissible when killing in Transplant is not. This is a different explanation of TPdb, and it supports the PPH because it attributes an explanatory role to parts of the PPH.

Thomson now says that killing in the Bystander Case is impermissible, so this argument will not appeal to her. (Nor will the idea that there is a defeating factor in that case that accounts for permissibility.) However, I used other cases to make the same point. Suppose killing in the Bystanding Driver Case (which is the Bystanding Driver Two Options Case) were permissible even though his alternative is to let five die. It might be said that here the fact that the driver would otherwise become the killer of the five (through having started the trolley and then letting the five die from it) is a factor that defeats the significance of the factor that he would kill one rather than let five die, making other things not equal (1). This would be consistent with the latter factor still doing the work to distinguish morally between Transplant and Foot's Trolley Driver's Two Options Case. However, Thomson does not think that it is permissible for the bad surgeon (who is morally responsible for the five being ill) to kill the one so as to save the five in that variation on Transplant. If this is right, the fact that an agent would otherwise be the killer of five would not itself defeat the killing versus letting-die factor in the case of the bad surgeon. My suggestion is that it is the difference in how the one would come to be killed in the Bystanding Driver Case by contrast to how the one would come to be killed in the case of the bad surgeon that accounts for the difference in permissibility of killing the one in these two cases. This could be reinforced if the bystanding driver who was permitted to turn the trolley was not permitted to topple the one person from the bridge to stop the trolley's hitting the five, since this way of coming to kill the one is comparable to the way the one would be killed in the case of the bad surgeon and the Transplant Case. Furthermore, the difference in how the one would come to be killed in the Bystanding Driver Case by contrast to how the one would be killed in the case of the bad surgeon also distinguishes the Trolley Driver's Two Options Case (in which the one is killed as a side effect of means having a noncausal relation to the greater good) from the Transplant Case (in which the one is not killed in this way). So my claim in the PPH was that it is this factor of how the one comes to be killed that accounts for the moral difference between the Trolley Driver's Two Options Case and the Transplant Case, not the fact that killing five counts more toward impermissibility than killing one and killing one counts more toward impermissibility than letting five die.

The Bystanding Driver Case may convince those who agree with me that it is permissible to kill in this case but not in the Transplant Case or the case of the bad surgeon . However, Thomson may not think killing is permissible in the Bystanding Driver Case. That is why the Driver Topple Case that I also presented is important in the discussion. For I believe it is a point of agreement between Thomson and myself that killing is impermissible in this case. While Thomson does not mention or discuss this case in her comments, in the seminar after the first lecture she indicated that she thought the driver may not topple that person in front of the trolley to stop it from killing the five.[39]

In the Driver Topple Case, as in Foot's Trolley Driver's Two Options Case, the driver faces a choice of killing one rather than killing five. Is there some factor in the Driver Topple Case not present in Foot's Trolley Driver's Two Options Case that could be defeating the factor of killing five's counting more for impermissibility than killing one, so that not all things are equal (1) (as would be true if the five had consented to be killed in the Driver Topple Case)? I do not think so. Rather, my view in the PPH was that the fact that the one would *not* be killed causally downstream from the greater good (or its component or means having these as a non-causal flip side) makes it impermissible to kill the one person as the alternative to killing the five. This factor is absent in Foot's Trolley Driver's Two Options Case, and its absence does not merely remove a defeater of killing five's counting for the impermissibility of an act more than killing one does. Rather, the absence in Foot's Trolley Driver's Two Options Case of the killing of one *not being* causally downstream from greater good involves its replacement by the killing of the one *being* causally downstream from the greater good (or means having it or its component as a noncausal flip side). This factor, I thought, accounts at least in part for the permissibility of killing in Foot's Trolley Driver's Two Options Case.

However, we need to do more to show that this factor on its own, not in combination with the killing of one being the alternative to killing five, explains the permissibility of killing in Foot's Trolley Driver's Two Options Case. To see why, consider the following question: Does the "killing *not* being causally downstream from greater good" factor in the Transplant Case account for the impermissibility of killing in that case independent of the alternative being letting five die? This depends on whether we think it is permissible to kill in the Bystander and Bystanding Driver Cases (but not in the Transplant Case and in the case of the bad surgeon). Suppose Thomson were right that it is impermissible to kill one rather than let five die in both the Bystander and Transplant Cases because of its being worse, other things equal (1), to kill one rather than let five die. Then the factor of *how* the one comes to be killed would have no role in accounting for impermissibility in these cases. However, if there is still a moral difference between killing in Foot's Trolley Driver's Two Options Case and in the Driver Topple Case, the fact that a person would be killed causally downstream from the greater good as the alternative to killing more people would still provide a more accurate description of the factor that accounts for the difference between Foot's Trolley Driver's Two Options Case and her Transplant Case.[40]

Next, suppose we think it is permissible to kill in the Bystander and Bystanding Driver Cases, but not in Transplant. Then the very same factor—a distinctive way of coming to kill someone— that is needed to explain the distinction between permissibly and impermissibly killing one when the alternative is to kill five will be needed to explain the permissibility of killing one rather than letting five die in Bystander and Bystanding Driver but its impermissibility in Transplant. That means that the two different alternatives to killing one—namely, killing five and letting five die—would drop out as explanations for differential permissibility in TPdb.

In short, while Thomson says that nothing I say counts against the Worseness* Thesis, I think that against its first clause I did show that killing five does not count more in favor of impermissibility than killing one, other things equal (1). Rather, killing five counts more in favor of impermissibility than killing one, other things equal (1), only when we kill one in some ways but not in others (where the ways in question might be those roughly distinguished by the PPH). This is shown by the Driver Topple Case. It is also shown by the three-options case I gave (Diagram 12) in which even the trolley driver should turn a trolley away from five to two rather than topple one person to stop the trolley from hitting five. It may be that when other things are equal (2), killing five counts more in favor of impermissibility than does killing one. That is, it may be true that if we would come to kill five in the same way as we would kill one (e.g., as a mere means), thereby holding other things equal (2), killing five does count more in favor of impermissibility, other things equal (1). But coming to kill five in one way could count less in favor of impermissibility than coming to kill one in another way—that is, not holding other things equal (2).

If what I said supports the permissibility of killing in the Bystander and/or Bystanding Driver Cases (without also supporting killing in Transplant or in the case of the bad surgeon), then what I said holds against the second clause of the Worseness* Thesis. I would have shown that killing one does not count more in favor of impermissibility than does letting five die, other things equal (1), when we come to kill in some ways but only when we kill in other ways, perhaps as (roughly) described by the PPH. Intuitively, it seems permissible to kill in the Bystander and Bystanding Driver, and I argued in Lecture I that Thomson's argument from the claim that someone need not sacrifice himself to save others does not show that we may not impose the same loss upon him for this purpose, even when we do no injustice in not saving those others.

(iv) Now we come to Thomson's final points in her defense of the Ultimate Claim that we do not need to consider many cases but need to provide a moral theory to explain TPdb, and we can do this by considering only TPdb. As we have seen, Thomson thinks that Foot is pointing to factors to explain why killing is permissible in Foot's Trolley Driver's Two Options Case but not in Transplant—namely, (1) that killing five people counts more strongly against an act than killing one; and (2) that killing one counts more strongly against an act than letting five die, other things equal (1). We might consider this the first part of providing a moral theory. Thomson says of these factors that they show us what must be explained by a deeper moral theory (e.g., how killing differs from letting die so as to make clause (2) be true). Her additional claims are that (i) finding this further theory need not involve considering cases other than Foot's Trolley Driver's Two Options and Transplant Cases; and (ii) once we have this further theory we will thereby know why the factor to which Foot points in clause (2)—the relative weights of killing one and letting five die with respect to impermissibility—does not conduce to impermissibility as strongly in other cases, and why in other cases certain other factors could outweigh or undermine the moral significance of the factor to which Foot points in clause (2) though they do not in Foot's cases.

My response to these points begins by considering Thomson's claim that to do moral theory about the trolley problem does not require considering many cases. I think that it is part of doing moral theory first to find out what factors are important in Foot's cases, as well as second to explain why they are important. As I mentioned earlier, I think that we need to consider cases other than those in TPdb to find out what factors are important in Foot's cases. If we begin doing the second step of moral theory on Foot's cases before considering the Bystander Case, and the

Bystander Case would make problems for the factor Foot thinks is morally important in distinguishing the Transplant Case from the Trolley Driver's Two Options Case, we will have misidentified the factor for whose significance we need to provide the further moral theory. Similarly, if we are only concerned with the factor that makes it permissible to turn the trolley in the Trolley Driver's Two Options Case, we will not identify completely the right factor if we do not consider cases like Driver Topple. Foot herself was aware that in considering only her Transplant and Trolley Driver's Two Options Cases, some might think that the important factors were the difference between the surgeon's intending harm to one person while the driver only foresees the harm. To eliminate this factor as the significant one (and whose significance needs to be explained by a deeper moral theory), she considered another case—the Gas Case—which was supposed to show that it can be wrong to harm people even if we do not intend but only foresee the harm. This was intended to show that the question remained why the driver did no wrong when he turned the trolley foreseeing harm to the one person, given that it would be wrong to use the gas. So Foot herself felt the need to consider another case in order to deal with the Transplant and Trolley Driver's Two Options Cases.[41]

Next, suppose that on the basis of considering other cases we reject the factors to which Foot points, and we are now looking for other factors that explain TPdb. If we just focus on Foot's cases in TPdb to locate those factors, we may find something that is sufficient but not necessary to account for permissibility or impermissibility. For suppose that someone thinks (as Thomson once did) that the important factor in the Trolley Driver's Two Options Case (and the Bystander Case) that weighs in favor of permissibility is that we are better redistributing an already existing threat by doing what violates no one's rights.[42] It might be that the factor is sufficient but not necessary to explain the permissibility of the driver's turning the trolley. We might come to think this by considering another case, like the Lazy Susan Case, in which someone may permissibly kill one not by better redistributing an already existing threat but by removing people from an already existing threat which in turn causes a new threat to kill one person. Suppose we think that even though it does not have the factor Thomson pointed to, what is going on in the Lazy Susan Case and in Foot's Trolley Driver's Two Options Case is morally fundamentally the same. We might then come to find a more general factor that conduces to permissibility. We will have contributed to moral theory by locating a new factor that seems to make a moral difference and whose significance we can try to explain with a deeper moral theory. Suppose we reject a factor as the one on which we should focus in doing further moral theory because it falls under a more general factor. This is not the same as rejecting a factor because its absence makes no moral difference even when no more general factor under which it falls is present and even when there is no other factor that is defeating it (and so things are not equal (1)).

So finding the explanatory factor in Foot's cases about which we should do deeper moral theory (not only rejecting a factor as the one on which we should focus) may require considering other cases. I used many cases to search for the factors that are significant in TPdb. At a certain point, I came up with the factors described by the PPH that distinguish different ways of coming to kill someone that bear on permissibility and impermissibility.[43] Since I think that finding factors (or principles containing them) is one part of doing moral theory, and that Foot and Thomson were doing moral theory in trying to isolate such factors, I think I was also doing part of moral theory in doing this.

Suppose we have what we think is the explanatory factor (or factors). Will we need cases other than the Transplant and Trolley Driver's Two Options Cases to arrive at the deeper theory that accounts for the moral significance of the factor? I am tempted to say that once we have the factor, we do not need to even think about these two cases. We just have to consider the factor itself. Of course, Thomson and I disagree about what the factor is for which we need the further theory. She thinks the further theory we need is about why killing differs morally from letting die. As important as I think a theory about this issue is, I do not think it is the theory that we need to explain the trolley problem. This is because I think that the alternative to killing one being killing more versus letting more die is not crucial, and that different ways of killing the one are crucial even when doing so is the alternative to killing more. I think we need further theory about the factors in the Principle of Permissible Harm (or an amended version of a theory that focuses on how we come to kill). My suggestion in Lecture II that what underlies (or supervenes upon) the PPH is the importance of the distinction between substituting people and subordinating people can be seen as an attempt to point in the direction of a deeper moral theory.

In Lecture II, I also tried to place the PPH within the scope of what I called theories that focus more on inter-victim relations and less on agent-victim relations. (The first type of theory does not make an action's permissibility vary with who the agent is, whether he is someone who would otherwise kill or someone who would otherwise let die. Instead, it focuses on the different relations that are established between people affected by an act, depending on how we come to harm someone, whether it is done by an agent who would otherwise kill or by one who would let die.) I think that discussion is also part of moral theory.

Neither Foot nor Thomson provides the complete deeper theory needed to explain the significance of the killing/letting-die distinction in their discussions of the trolley problem.[44] Hence, I would be no different in this respect in discussing the trolley problem if I did not provide a complete theory of the moral significance of different ways of coming to kill that the PPH (or improved principles like it) distinguishes.

Put to one side the differences between Thomson and myself about the explanatory factor and the type of deeper moral theory needed. Regardless of what the explanatory factor is, suppose we know it and even have a theory about why it is significant. Will we then also know why that factor weighs more strongly in some cases than in others, what other factors can defeat it, and that the defeating factors are not present in Foot's cases, as Thomson claims? Might we still have to consider other cases to know, for example, what other factors can defeat the explanatory factor or reduce its conducing to permissibility or impermissibility? Without considering intuitive judgment in cases, might we, for example, fail to recognize that some variant of a factor that ordinarily defeats the explanatory factor does not? I'm not sure but I suspect so.

(v) As I described earlier, in sections 5 through 7 of Lecture II, after having given my version of two steps in moral theory that I think Thomson describes—formulating the PPH and trying to isolate values I thought might underlie it—I went on to consider other cases. These were the ones in which five people and one person who would otherwise let themselves die are, I thought, permitted to kill other people. I think it is especially these cases that Thomson thinks can do nothing to show that the factors in the Worseness* Thesis do not weigh in favor of or against permissibility and do not determine permissibility and impermissibility in TPdb. Since the cases involve people (either five or one) trying to save themselves, some might think that these are clearly cases in which a defeator is present and other things are not equal (1), because there are special agent-relative permissions to kill rather than let die. If this were so, the permissibility of killing rather than letting die in these cases would tell us nothing about whether killing as the alternative to letting die counts toward impermissibility in TPdb. It would also tell us nothing about what may be done in the Bystander Case that would make that case a counter-example to Foot's solution to TPdb. However, I said:

Are there implications *from* what the five and the one to whom the trolley is originally headed are permitted to do rather than let themselves die *for* what a mere bystander is permitted to do rather than let others die? Why should we think there are any implications? In thinking about what it is permissible for the one or the five to do, we have not relied on any view that implies that people who are themselves threatened may do just anything they need to do to save themselves. Hence, our conclusions ... may generalize to the bystander who would kill rather than let die. (pp. 87–88)

In other words, I thought that in large part the permissibility of people who are themselves threatened to kill others would not be because of some special factor in these cases outweighing the role of the factors on which Foot focused. The permissibility was instead largely due to the presence of factors different from those to which Foot pointed—namely, how the others would be killed—that are also present in TPdb cases. I did think that a special agent-relative permission is at work when someone may permissibly kill more people to save fewer people, and I noted that achieving a *lesser* good at the cost of greater harm should conduce to the impermissibility of an act for an impartial bystander in a way it need not for one person when the trolley threatens only him. However, the fact that achieving a lesser good can take precedence over causing greater harm only when the greater harm comes about in a certain ways (e.g., in a causally downstreamish way) speaks for the general significance of the parts of the PPH that bear on ways of killing, separate from the part that is concerned with achieving greater good at the cost of lesser harm. If there were no general significance to different ways in which harm comes about (so that these distinctions did not also apply to Foot's cases), it would be harder to explain why even the one and the five toward whom the threat is headed are constrained by the PPH's limits on how someone may come to kill others.

# Hurka

## 1.

The first part of Hurka's discussion deals primarily with the degree to which a principle I have suggested to account for certain moral differences in various trolley cases has counterintuitive implications in cases other than the trolley problem as he understands it. He takes the trolley problem to ask "why it's impermissible to save five people by throwing a fat man in front of a trolley but permissible to save them by diverting the trolley to another track where it will likewise kill one person" (p. 136). (He does not tell us whether he thinks this is a problem only for a bystander or also for the driver.) He describes my Principle of Permissible Harm (PPH) as distinguishing between causal means to a greater good causing a lesser evil and greater good itself, and means having a noncausal flip side relation to the greater good causing lesser evil.

A. I have the following thoughts about Hurka's presentation of the PPH. His description of the PPH is roughly right. However, it is important to distinguish what is a *mere* causal means to a greater good from a causal means to one greater good that also has another greater good as its noncausal flip side. The use of the latter means to the first greater good may be permissible. (See n. 17 for an example of this.) Further, the PPH allows that components of the greater good (or means having these as noncausal flip sides) rather than the greater good itself (or means having this as a noncausal flip side) may permissibly cause lesser harm. The PPH also distinguishes between mere causal means to a greater good that (to put it roughly) directly causes a lesser evil and a mere causal means that indirectly (via entities independently in the environment) does so. Use of the latter may be permissible when the former is not.[45]

Hurka describes the PPH as "downstream" because he thinks it distinguishes moral permissibility of acts on the basis of what happens downstream from what we do. He says: "[I]t doesn't consider how *you* relate to [the one's] death. Instead, it focuses on a causal distinction that arises later in the causal process, after you act. That's one reason for calling it a 'downstream' principle: its vital distinction occurs after or downstream from you" (p. 136). I used the term "downstreamish" to describe the principle for a different reason—namely, because (roughly) it is concerned that lesser evil be causally downstream from the greater good or some component of it. So, the way in which Hurka applies the term "downstream principle" may be different from the way in which I use it. (If he means the principle distinguishes morally among acts even though in all of them an agent will kill, that is true. But it still is not the way in which I used "downstream.") Hurka says that my downstream principle is unlike "traditional deontological principles," which he says "concern your relation to an evil: they say it's more objectionable to cause than to allow an evil or to intend than merely to foresee it" (p. 142). I would say that my PPH is also concerned with your relation to an evil, though with how you cause it rather than simply with your causing it. That it is more objectionable to intend rather than merely to foresee an evil is one way of stating the Doctrine of Double Effect (DDE). Those who defend the DDE have had problems dealing with cases in which it seems clear that it is no less permissible to act even with a wrong intention (e.g., fight a just war or kill only defensively merely as an excuse for one's intention to kill people). To deal with this problem, some have suggested that one is not permitted to do what could *only* be done by someone with a wrong intention, but one may do what an agent with a good intention would be permitted to do even if one has a wrong intention. This revised DDE is a deontological principle does not concern *your* relation to an evil as Hurka conceives it (i.e., whether you in particular intend it).

B. Hurka notes that I reject the Doctrine of Double Effect insofar as it focuses on a particular agent's intention in acting to determine permissibility of the act, even though the DDE so understood could distinguish morally between toppling the fat man and redirecting the trolley. I reject it because it gives answers that conflict with intuitive judgments in other cases. Hence, he says, my methodology commits me to rejecting the PPH if it, too, conflicts with intuitive judgments in cases other than the trolley problem (as he understands it). I do not object to this methodological requirement of consistency. However, I would note that one of the other cases I used to argue against the DDE was the Bad Man Trolley Case, which I think is a trolley problem case.

Hurka also raises a second methodological point. He claims that intuitive judgments we have about "real-life" cases should weigh more than those we have about cases that are high on a scale of "ingenuity." In speaking of my Lazy Susan Case, he says: "Even if, once I've understood how it works, I share Kamm's intuition . . . I'm not very confident about that intuition just because the example is so far from reality" (p. 139). I do not agree with this methodological point. After all, turning a trolley from five people to one and pushing a fat man into a trolley to save five from it are not things that have often (if ever) been done in "real-life" cases, and yet Hurka does not say he is less confident of his intuitions in those cases. And some cases that would seem "ingenious" if merely hypothetical have occurred in reality (e.g., the *Palsgraf* case often studied in law school).[46] "Real life" provides an existential property, but it does not in any other way affect the properties of a case, and finding out that what we thought was a real-life case is only imaginary should not affect our intuitive judgment. Putting aside this difference between us, let me consider the cases outside of the trolley problem (as he understands it) in which he thinks that our intuitive judgments conflict with the PPH.

The first set of cases involve war. Hurka notes that the ethics of collateral harm in war would not distinguish between the permissibility of side-effect harm to civilians that is caused by (a) parts of a bomb that we use to blow up a munitions factory, or (b) parts of the munitions factory itself as it explodes. Yet the bomb is a mere causal means to achieving a greater good even if it is assumed that the munitions being blown up is the greater good. Hurka thinks that (a) and (b) are both permissible or both are impermissible.

The second set of cases for which he thinks the PPH gives results that conflict with intuitive judgments are outside of war and involve my Bomb Trolley Case. In this case, we can stop the trolley only by setting off a bomb that we know will itself kill one bystander. The PPH implies this is impermissible. It also implies that it is permissible to use a bomb that harms no one to stop the trolley's hitting the five when the trolley's stopping causes a part of the trolley to fly off and kill a bystander. Hurka finds it implausible to draw a moral distinction between these two cases.

In response, let me say that I do not share Hurka's intuitive judgments about the Bomb Trolley Case and the case in which the trolley's stopping kills a bystander. As I noted in Lecture II, I specifically introduced the Bomb Trolley Case because unlike toppling the man from the bridge so that he will be hit by the trolley, the bomb causes merely foreseen involvement and harm to the bystander that has no useful role in stopping the trolley. In this respect it is similar to the turning trolley in the basic Trolley Case, which causes the merely foreseen death of a bystander that has no useful role in stopping the trolley. Hence, I felt it was most important to explain why turning the trolley was permissible when intuitively I judged it impermissible to set off the bomb. Since I do not accept that the PPH has a counterintuitive implication for the Bomb Trolley Case, I am not defending the principle despite what I think are counterintuitive implications. The latter would violate the first methodological constraint of consistency Hurka mentions (p. 221).

Furthermore, I constructed the Bomb Trolley Case so that it would have the same causal structure as another case of Philippa Foot's (that she used to argue against the DDE) that I referred to as the Gas Case. In this case, we need to use a gas to save five people, but the gas will unavoidably seep next door and kill another immoveable person. Foot's judgment was that (contrary to the DDE) this was impermissible even though the death was merely foreseen and a greater good stood to be achieved. (I agreed with Foot about this case. Given what Hurka has said, I assume he disagrees with Foot.) However, I also believed that Foot failed to construct an important variant on this case, so I imagined the following case: We can save the five people using a gas that will hurt no one but we know that the five being saved and so breathing normally will move germs in the atmosphere so that the germs kill one bystander. Call this Gas Case 2. I thought it would be permissible to save the five people in this case. I thought that this helped show the moral difference between a mere causal means to a greater good harming a person and the greater good itself causing the same harm, as the PPH implies. As suggested by my elaboration in these responses (pp. 198–200) of sections 5 though 7 in Lecture II, one concern I now have with the construction of Gas Case 2 is that it is germs in the environment independently of what we do that kill the one person, not the five breathing normally in itself. As noted earlier, the PPH does not rule out that, in order to bring about a greater good, it might be permissible to use even mere causal means that also produce harm indirectly, as when our bomb going off disturbs some rocks that are in the environment independently of what we do and they cause someone's death.[47] So we have to determine which of the following differences matter morally: the difference between (a) a mere causal means and a greater good causing a lesser evil, or the difference between (b) direct and indirect harm (in the sense described in endnote 16) causing lesser evil. To do this we might consider the following additional contrasting cases to Foot's Gas Case:

(1) The greater good directly causes the side-effect harm (because the normally expanding chests of five people saved crush one other person when they all share cramped quarters).

(2) The gas we use to save the five itself will harm no one. However, its being in the air will move germs and these germs will kill one other person.

If it were permissible to operate in (2) and in Gas Case 2 but not in (1), the principle we would develop would be different than if it were permissible to operate in all the cases. Hurka, however, seems to deny the moral relevance of the direct versus indirect role of mere means (in the way I distinguish them) in causing harm.

Now, let us consider Hurka's concern about the PPH being inconsistent with the permissibility of many cases of collateral harm in war. In my writing on war, I have often pointed to Foot's Gas Case as showing that a typical justification for collateral harm based only on the DDE is inadequate. Hurka assumes that collateral harm due to even direct harm from mere means is permissible in war and outside of war (assuming the means satisfy such conditions as proportionality, necessity, etc.), I thought justifying such collateral harm in war was problematic, given that I agreed with Foot about its impermissibility in her Gas Case. In an early paper on war,[48] I tried to account for the permissibility of some collateral harm within the confines of the PPH. I there raised many of the same concerns that Hurka raises in his comments. I said that one question the PPH approach raises is whether destruction of a military facility is a greater good or only a mere causal means to the greater good of achieving a just peace. I suggested that one might view the destruction as having the good of certain soldiers not being killed as its noncausal flip side (because weapons otherwise produced in the facility won't exist). Alternatively, I suggested that getting rid of some munitions is a component of the greater good of peace reigning. (In other works, I had already considered cases in which a component of the greater good and not the greater good itself could permissibly cause lesser harm.[49]) I also suggested that it might suffice for employing the PPH to identify a goal whose achievement on its own justifies causally downstream collateral harm regardless of whether the goal is a greater good. So while the goal of setting off a bomb in itself would not justify collateral harm, getting rid of munitions might. This means that greater good may be only one goal of many whose achievement might permissibly cause lesser harm.

In later work,[50] I suggested that harming civilians collaterally in war might be permissible even when a mere causal means directly causes the harm if the civilians are citizens of an unjust aggressor. This is because they are liable to bearing risks of such harm in order to stop their country from being unjust. But I noted (as Hurka does) that neutrals are not liable to harm on this ground. Indeed, I argued that neutrals in war are not even subject to being harmed as a result of warring opponents' redirecting threats to them, even when their being harmed would reduce overall harm to civilians. So neutrals seem to be more immune to such redirected threats than ordinary people in non-war contexts (such as the Trolley Cases).

In sum, I do not think the PPH conflicts with intuitive judgments in non-war contexts. Furthermore, it may not apply in war contexts because those who may be harmed collaterally in war are in several ways different from ordinary innocent people, and the PPH is intended to apply only to harm to such ordinary innocents.


## 2.

The second part of Hurka's discussion deals with the plausibility of the PPH and its implications for the trolley problem itself (as he understands it). He begins with a third methodological point: that principles should not only account for intuitive judgments but also be morally plausible in their own right. I agree that either the principles should be plausible in their own right or be shown to follow from or express underlying considerations (concepts, values) that are morally plausible in their own right. I have said, in *Intricate Ethics*, among other places:

> In general, the approach ... I adopt may be described as follows: consider as many case-based judgments ... as prove necessary, don't ignore some just because they conflict with simple or intuitively plausible principles ... work on the assumption that some other principle can account for the judgments ... be prepared to be surprised at what this principle is ... consider the principle on its own, to see if it expresses some plausible value or conception of the person or relations between persons. This is necessary to justify it as a correct principle, one that has normative weight, not merely one that makes all of the case judgments cohere ... this is only a working method. It remains possible that some case judgments are simply errors. [51]

In *Intricate Ethics* and in Lecture II, I suggested that the underlying morally significant point of the PPH might be the distinction between subordinating people and substituting people. I argued that subordination could occur without using harm to someone as a mere means if use or survival of mere causal means to the good of others took precedence over the persons directly harmed. (I also argued that requiring harm to someone as a causal means does not always involve subordination, as in the Loop Case.) This attempt at identifying intuitively morally significant ideas underlying or supervening on the PPH may not succeed. If so, I would pursue the search further before rejecting the PPH (or a principle like it) if it is in accord with intuitive judgments. This is in part because if only the PPH were in accord with intuitive judgments, they too would have to be rejected as errors if we rejected the principle.

Having argued that the PPH has incorrect implications for cases other than the trolley problem, Hurka then argues that it either does not account for our intuitive judgments in the trolley problem or does so by drawing arbitrary distinctions and not by relying on factors at a deeper level that might have moral significance on their own. He seems to accept that greater good or means having it as a noncausal flip side being the cause of lesser evil is in itself a morally significant factor. However, he claims, this is not what occurs even in the basic Trolley Case. A greater good is something that has moral significance on its own. I say that the five being saved is such a greater good and also relative to one person's dying. But Hurka claims that I use the term "greater good" ambiguously. He says: "On one reading, this good matters morally in itself, but the trolley's moving away is only a causal means to it and her principle forbids diverting the trolley. On the other reading, the trolley's moving away isn't a causal means, but the so-called greater good doesn't matter in itself and is itself only a means to what does" (p. 146). (I assume that in the last sentence his "means" refers to causal means, by contrast to means that have greater good as a noncausal flip side.)

Let us consider the complaint based on using the first reading of "greater good." Hurka imagines a case in which the trolley is turned at 8:00 when it otherwise would have traveled on another track hitting the five at 8:10. He thinks the greater good you achieve can't be their being alive between 8:00 and 8:10, since even if you don't divert the trolley, they'll be alive at those times. The greater good you achieve must be their being alive at 8:10 and after. But this can't just "be" the trolley's moving away, or be something the trolley's moving away has as its noncausal flip side, because they are not contemporaneous. He says: "nothing that happens at 8:00 can be identical to or constituted by something that happens at 8:10" (p. 145). (It seems that if the trolley would have hit the five at 8:00 had it not been turned, Hurka would accept that their being alive at that time and after can be the flip side of turning the trolley. It is not clear he should accept this, because their being alive later than 8:00 or 8:10, which is an important part of the greater good, would not be contemporaneous with the trolley's turning away, either. I shall return to this point.) He concludes: "The trolley's moving away at 8:00 must therefore be a causal means to the five's being alive at 8:10" (p. 145). And the PPH does not permit mere causal means to a greater good to cause lesser evil (at least when it does so directly and not by affecting something in the environment independently of our actions).

My response to this has several components.

First, that the five would have been alive between 8:00 and 8:10 independently of what we do does not itself show that we are not responsible for their being alive during this interval. For example, that someone else would have provided life support to Joe from 8:00 until 8:10 had we not done so does not show that we did not actually save Joe's life from 8:00 until 8:10 if we provided him with life support. (I do not mean to say that turning a threat away earlier than it actually threatens someone is like providing life support. I only wish to raise a question about a counterfactual principle that seems to underlie this one argument of Hurka's—namely, that if someone would have otherwise been alive at a certain time even if one had not acted, one's action could not have been what made him be alive at that time.)

Second, Hurka thinks that the fact that the five's being alive at 8:10 and onward is not contemporaneous with the turning away of the trolley at 8:00 means that the turning of the trolley is a causal means to their being alive later (and long enough for this to be a greater good relative to the death of the one person). Suppose the trolley's turning away at 8:00 also flipped a switch at 8:00 that stopped a death ray that would have killed the five at 8:10. Then I would agree that its turning away was, at least in part, a causal means to their being alive at 8:10. This is because the trolley's flipping the switch functions, in part, in the same way as the bomb's going off in the Bomb Trolley Case when it causes the diversion of a threat from the five, and the bomb is a causal means to their being alive. But in Hurka's case, the trolley's turning away at 8:00 affects the five only by making it be true (by entailing) that it is not headed toward them at times after 8:00 including 8:10, whose flip side is that they are alive at 8:10. So in this case, I think it is not appropriate to describe the trolley's turning at 8:00 as causing the trolley's not heading toward them at close to 8:10, its not hitting them at 8:10, and the flip side of this, namely their not being hit and so alive at 8:10.

Of course, in a different type of case, turning a trolley at 8:00 could *cause* the trolley not to hit them at 8:10, in the way that a bomb that moves the trolley would cause it not to hit the five people. This would be so if, for example, the trolley's turning at 8:00 were necessary but not sufficient for it to be away from them at 8:10 (and thereafter), but its turning also caused a device to malfunction that would have turned the trolley back toward the five at 8:10.

I think that Hurka's case supports the view that there are more noncausal relations an outcome can have to means than merely a flip side or constitution (if the latter must be simultaneous with the means). This would imply that the PPH is an instance of a more general type of principle.

Third, Hurka does not raise the objection to my view that the first instant of the five's not being hit is only a means to the rest of the time that is necessary for that survival to be a greater good. However, I myself noted (in response to the point raised by Derek Parfit) that, strictly speaking, the flip side of turning the trolley is that instant and that instant is not the greater good. In that sense, turning the trolley even at 8:10 in Hurka's case could not have the greater good as a noncausal flip side. In response to this point, I argued that the instant that is the flip side is not only a causal means to the greater good of the longer time alive, it is also a component of it (i.e., a component of the rest of what is expected to be the long enough time alive).[52] The PPH allows that the removal of a threat may have a noncausal relation only to a component of the greater good, and also that the removal of the threat or the component of the greater good can also play a further causal role in producing the greater good.

So it still seems to me that the trolley's moving away that causes the death of the one does not have a merely causal relation to the greater good in the way that a bomb that turns the trolley away, and whose parts also cause the death of the one, has a causal relation to the greater good.

Now, let us consider the complaint based on the second account of "greater good" that Hurka locates in my discussion—namely, "the five being saved" understood as the "five's being saved from the threat of the trolley." On this account of the greater good, he argues, turning the trolley is not a mere causal means to the greater good because the five being saved from the trolley happens at the same time as the trolley moves away (in the original Trolley Case). However, he says: "on this reading the greater good isn't something that matters morally in itself; on the contrary, it matters only as a means" (p. 145). (I assume his claim here is that being saved from the trolley is only a causal means (by contrast to means having a noncausal relation) to what does matter morally in itself—namely, the greater good of the five being alive for a significant time.) Hurka's point is that being saved from the trolley does not mean the five will continue to live. For example, in the case he gives, there will be a rockslide that will kill them at 8:10 anyway. He says: "That the five are saved from the trolley matters only if it causes them to be alive at 8:10, and the same is true of their being free from any other threat . . . : all of these matter only as means to something like their being alive" (p. 145). Hurka thinks that all these means to the five being alive (i.e., removing various threats to them), insofar as they will kill one other person, are in principle no different from a bomb that would move the trolley and also kill the one person. It is only a distinction between causal means #37 (the bomb) and causal means #38 (moving the trolley), he says.

My response to this concern has several components.

First, the Trolley Case that I primarily dealt with in my lectures was specifically described as one in which the five faced no other threats to them, so the removal of the trolley would assure their continuing alive long enough to be the greater good. (However, I did describe the Tractor Cases, in which other threats are present.) So, at the very least, in a case in which the trolley is the only threat and it is turned away at the very instant it would hit the five, it seems that Hurka would accept that the trolley's turning away constitutes the greater good (what really matters). Likewise, suppose there were many threats, each was turned away at the instant it would hit, and the removal of none of the threats would also be a causal means to the removal of another of the threats (e.g., its moving away does not trigger the other threats' moving away). Then the removal of none of them would be even a partial causal means to the greater good that really matters, in the way that a bomb exploding to derail the trolley would be a causal means to what matters. The fact that removal of all the threats would be necessary, because the removal of any one individually would not be sufficient for the five's being alive for long, does not mean that the removal of each is a mere causal means to what really matters in this case.

Second, suppose that the trolley threat is removed some time before it would hit the five (e.g., at 8:00, when it would hit at 8:10). I argued earlier that I did not think this alone implied that the trolley's being removed had a mere causal relation to the five's being saved. But if there are also other threats to the five, it cannot be true that removing the trolley has a noncausal relation to the greater good, for there may be no greater good if the other threats will still occur. (This is what I meant when I said, in first discussing the Tractor Case in Lecture II, that when we turn away the trolley, independent of any new threat we create in doing this, we do not have even a component of the greater good because the five are still under the tractor threat.) Nevertheless, the removal of all of these threats even some time before they would kill the five could have a noncausal relation to the greater good's coming about if the removal of one of them would have such a relation when it was the only threat (as I argued earlier).

In sum, Hurka's arguments are that turning the trolley away is no different from any other means (like the bomb that moves the trolley) to saving the five and therefore there can be no moral significance to the trolley's causing the death of the one by contrast to the bomb's causing the death. But I do not think Hurka successfully shows that there is no difference between these different means, and the difference between them may explain different intuitive moral judgments.

Third, intuitively, a difference between the trolley turning (even in the case where there is another threat headed to the five) and the bomb going off is that only turning the trolley constitutes one threat that was facing the five no longer facing them. The question that Hurka would press is how this relates in any special way to the greater good. (Similarly, moving people away from the trolley constitutes their being away from one threat. But when they still face the tractor threat, the question arises of how their being away from the trolley relates to the greater good.) In first discussing the Tractor Case, I took a position somewhat like Hurka's, in that I thought that one threat being away was not even a component of the greater good when the other threat was still facing the five. (I did not think, however, that this meant that removal of one threat had a mere causal relation to the greater good.) However, in my response to Thomson, I described an alternative view (pp. 189–91): the permissibility of turning the trolley in other Tractor Cases (in which the trolley moving away presses a switch that turns the tractor away) might lead one to think that the five no longer facing one of the threats to them is itself a component of the greater good, which consists of their facing no threats (which has their continued survival as its flip side). (As I also noted in my response to Thomson, if we adopt this view of a component of the greater good, we need to explain why it would be impermissible to turn the trolley in the original Tractor Case.)[53]

Of course, the difference between means that have a mere causal relation and those with a noncausal relation to the greater good or a component of it may still not amount to a difference that justifies some killings when others are not justified. But Hurka seems willing to grant that a special relation of means to greater good, if it existed, might be the sort of distinction that could sometimes justify those means killing some people to save other people.

### 3.

The final part of Hurka's discussion focuses on what he thinks are clear cases in which a good causing something can make a moral difference by contrast to a mere means to the good causing the same thing. His cases by contrast to mine involve causing an additional good, not a harm. He is concerned with whether a good produced by another good, rather than by a mere means to a good, can figure in a proportionality calculation against evils that will result from pursuing a just cause in war.[54] I have the following concerns about his discussion.

First, his initial case involves Iraq's unjust invasion of Kuwait, which causes economic problems for Africa; defeat of Iraq will help African economies. Hurka thinks such economic benefits may permissibly weigh against the evils caused by the war in a proportionality calculation required to justify war against Iraq. By contrast, Hurka believes the fact that defeating an unjust enemy (e.g., Germany in World War II) will lift the world out of an economic depression does not weigh similarly because it is through war production, a mere means to winning the war, that economic benefits would arise.

I disagree with this reasoning. It seems to me that in deciding whether war with Iraq is justified it would be permissible to weigh the recovery of African economies in a proportionality calculation even if they arose solely from war production undertaken in Africa. This is because the economic harm to Africa (that would be undone) would have been caused by the actions of Iraq on account of which the war is fought. By contrast (by hypothesis), the world-wide depression was not caused by the country we would fight (e.g., Germany in World War II). Furthermore, even if it were the greater good of winning the war (rather than means to it) that alone caused a recovery from the worldwide depression, this recovery should not count in a proportionality calculation in the decision to go to war. Hence, I think this case of Hurka's does not support the distinction between greater good (or a good) and mere means causing another good effect.

Second, the next set of cases that Hurka presents distinguish between (a) resolution of the Palestinian-Israeli conflict as a result of winning an unrelated war that has a just cause and that, as a side effect, eliminates terrorist supplies needed to keep the conflict going; and (b) such resolution as a result of interaction between Arabs and Israelis in conducting the unrelated war. He thinks the resolution in the first case could count in a proportionality calculation against the evils of the war because the resolution would result from achievement of the war's just cause, but not count in the second case because it results from a mere means to the achievement of the just cause.

One concern I have about these cases is whether the achievement of the just cause causing a good effect is necessary in order to justify counting that effect in a proportionality calculation. For suppose we foresee that not long after we win the just war that also eliminates the terrorist supplies, the opponent defeated in the war will rise up again so that victory is short-lived. However, the connections that made it possible for terrorists to be supplied will be irrevocably broken and so Palestinian-Israeli peace will be longlasting. Furthermore, we foresee that we will succeed in a new war against the original opponent and achieve its permanent defeat. Suppose that the period of victory after the first war is short enough that it alone would not constitute a good worth achieving relative to other bad effects of the war. Would it still be permissible to count the resolution of the Israeli-Palestinian dispute in a proportionality calculation in deciding to fight this war, given that we know we will defeat the opponent's new uprising? If it were permissible, it could be because the short-lived victory over the opponent is a component of, not merely a causal means to, the greater good (not yet achieved) of eventual long-term defeat of unjust forces. (So we would not get the same proportionality result if, instead of defeating the original opponent in the second war, we were enabled by the first war to defeat a different unjust opponent.)

## Kagan

Like Thomson and Hurka in their comments, Shelly Kagan discusses an important issue concerning methodology: the use of hypothetical cases to derive principles, discovering what deeper ideas supervene on or underlie the principles, and whether the principles (or other ideas to which they are related) are inherently morally significant. Kagan points to several issues: (1) not all people may share my intuitive judgments about cases; (2) the principle I suggested (the PPH) does not adequately capture our intuitive judgments and has other (e.g., metaphysical) problems; (3) the distinctions among cases to which the principle points (a) are not intuitively morally significant in themselves and (b) do not connect with any intuitively morally significant ideas. It is (3) on which Kagan focuses, for he believes that even if everyone had the same intuitive judgments about cases, and even if a principle correctly captured all these intuitive judgments, if the principle has no morally compelling rationale for the distinctions it draws, the principle should be rejected. If there is no other principle that captures the intuitions and has a morally compelling rationale, the intuitive judgments, however firmly held, should also be rejected as revealing moral truths about what is and is not permissible.

With respect to (1), Kagan suggests that if others disagree with one's intuitive judgments, it would help to settle a dispute at this level if one had the deeper rationale for a principle that accounts for one's judgments. I agree with this, but wish to suggest that there are other things one can do in the face of conflicting intuitive judgments. For example, one might see how those who make the opposing intuitive judgment would decide a closely related case; if their intuitive judgments are inconsistent with each other, this might speak to a need to revise one or another judgment. One might also try to get a description of the case from those with an opposing judgment that highlights factors in the case as they see it. If they fail to even notice some factor that one thinks is significant, one might construct another case that truly lacks this factor and ask if they think the second and original cases are alike. If they sense that the two cases are different, one might be on the way to getting them to at least see a factor they had missed, whether or not they agree it is morally important. The fact that they did not detect the factor's presence originally may suggest that they are not as good at understanding what is going on in a case as they should be. (This may be true, however, only if the factor is in fact morally significant.)

Further, we might try to get those with an opposing judgment to identify those factors they take to be the only morally significant ones in the case and that account for their moral judgment. One could then try to consider whether other factors are important as well. Here is an example. Daniel Kahneman and Amos Tversky presented people with sets of cases that they thought are alike in all morally significant respects but that differ in "framing effects" which should be insignificant for drawing a moral conclusion about the cases. In one case, a store owner does not raise wages to compensate as inflation goes up, while in the other she lowers wages when there is no inflation. Kahneman and Tversky think that the fact that the workers in these two cases wind up in the same economic condition makes the owner's not raising wages to compensate for inflation and reducing wages in the absence of inflation morally equivalent. They think the economic outcome of the workers is what is morally significant and judging the cases differently would be due to framing effects. However, in the first case, a business owner has no causal responsibility for an economic force (such as inflation) and so she may have no moral responsibility to compensate for it. In the second case, she instigates a decline in wages. This may be a morally significant factor distinguishing the cases.[55]

We might also try to see whether the factor that those with an opposing judgment identify as morally important is so. At a purely case-based level, one might remove only that factor from the case and see if judgment changes in the altered case. If it does not, the moral significance of that factor is called into question even without considering its merits on its own. For example, some think that it is the "up close and personal" pushing of the fat man from the bridge by a bystander (so that he falls in front of the trolley) that would make toppling him impermissible by contrast to mechanically turning a trolley away when it will kill one person.[56] But if mechanically turning a second trolley that would have harmed no one so that it topples a fat man in front of the first trolley in order to stop it seems no more permissible, then pushing him up close and personal will not be the morally significant factor in topple cases.

In other words, there may be ways to deal with disagreements about intuitive judgments without providing a morally compelling rationale for a principle that accounts for one's own judgments.

With respect to (2), I am willing to believe that there may be problems with my formulation of the PPH. As Kagan notes, it has undergone various revisions, in part in order to try to accommodate judgments about new cases, and I offered only a rough version of it in the early part of Lecture II.[57] However, as I noted in my response to Thomson, I do not think this is inconsistent with the PPH's being headed in the right direction. In addition, in sections 5 through 7 of Lecture II, I suggested a way of conceiving of trolley problem cases that did not depend so heavily on the PPH but, rather, emphasized causing entities in the environment independently of us and our use to become threats when some other good was at stake. (However, the cases I considered in those sections were constructed so as to capture distinctions the PPH draws concerning how harm comes about.[58]) In particular, I discussed cases where there was no greater good that would lead to lesser evil—namely, the cases in which one person would have to turn the trolley away from himself or take other action that would kill a greater number of people.

Now let me consider (3), both (a) and (b), the primary focus of Kagan's discussion. He thinks the PPH fails with respect to (a) (i.e., distinctions it points to are not intuitively morally significant in themselves) and (b) (i.e., distinctions it points to do not connect with any intuitively morally significant ideas). He thinks that the PPH failing in these respects is important because he believes that it is crucial to find a rationale for such a principle that is morally significant. As shown by the quote from *Intricate Ethics* I presented in my response to Hurka, I agree with Kagan that one's job is not over when one has found a principle that accounts for intuitive judgments if the distinctions it draws are not themselves morally significant or not connected with morally significant ideas. However, I am very wary of the direction in which Kagan takes this view. Assuming for the sake of argument that the PPH alone accommodates all our intuitive case judgments, he says:

> [I]f the principle ... lacks a compelling rationale, then we should come to wonder whether an adequate moral theory will really accommodate quite so many of our intuitions about the various cases....
>
> Perhaps we will settle for a principle that (roughly speaking) simply rules out killing the innocent. If such a principle can be given a plausible rationale, this may accommodate enough of our intuitions to satisfy us, even if it does not match all of them.
>
> Alternatively, ... perhaps we will be led to a principle that matches even fewer of our case-specific intuitions but which none-theless can be provided with a rationale that is significantly more compelling.... [P]erhaps we will ultimately want to ... embrace consequentialism instead. (p. 164)

Essentially, what Kagan's last step does is make the intuitive compellingness of a general rationale (understood independently of what it implies for cases) the sole criterion of a correct theory, because he considers rejecting a principle that accounted for some intuitive case judgments and had an "adequate rationale" in favor of a principle that accommodated (perhaps) none of our case judgments on the grounds that its rationale was significantly more compelling. This approach would mean that the implications that the most compelling (considered on its own) principle had for cases could never serve as grounds for rejecting or modifying the principle. This completely eliminates a role for the methodology of cases as counter-examples to a principle. We have moved from having to give a rationale for case-based judgments (with which I agreed) to retaining a rationale that is at odds with all case-based judgments.

One question that is raised by the direction in which Kagan takes the search for a rationale is why we should trust our intuitive judgment about the moral adequacy or compellingness of a rationale considered on its own more than we trust the adequacy of our intuitive judgments in cases. Many of those who originally intuitively judge that maximizing happiness is the most plausible rationale for ethics come to reject this intuitive judgment in part because of what they find to be its morally implausible implication for cases. Similarly, the Kantian view that we must not manipulate rational agency sounds plausible until we think of a case in which we could stop an unjustified attacker either by lying to him (manipulating his rational agency) or shooting him and thus paralyzing him. Intuitively, it is morally preferable to lie than to shoot.[59] Admittedly, those who rely on such intuitive case judgments also look for an explanation and justification for these case judgments by seeking rationales that differ from the original ones proposed. This leaves it open that while judgments about cases can trigger a search for other intuitively plausible rationales, these other rationales could be discovered independently of the consideration of the cases. However, the critical point is that case judgments are an important bar that rationales must hurdle, not merely devices that can trigger their discovery, and that our intuitive judgments about cases are often more to be trusted than intuitive judgments about the moral compellingness of rationales. When we debate about consequentialism and Kantianism and the correctness of their deepest rationales, I doubt that we can decide which rationale is the correct one (if either) without considering what the rationales imply about cases.[60]

I believe that in some of his work Kagan takes a much more positive attitude toward case-based intuitions and resistance to rejecting a principle that accounts for them, even in the absence of a deeper rationale for the principle. For example, in "What's Wrong with Speciesism?"[61] he argues against Peter Singer's view that most of us are speciesists in Singer's sense and that our attitudes favoring humans spring from a mere prejudice without a rationale. Kagan argues that our intuitive judgments are best captured by a principle he describes as Modal Personism. (What this is need not concern us here.) He believes that it is not obvious that Modal Personism is a plausible position to hold, but goes on to say:

> At the very least ... insofar as it can accommodate many of our deeply held intuitions about the proper treatment of marginal cases—impaired humans and the like—I think there may well be a great deal to be said for it.... [R]ejecting speciesism ... will run afoul of an even larger number of our intuitions. That obviously won't settle the question of which view is the correct one to take but it does show that we should not be so quick to dismiss Modal Personism. It seems to me a view worth taking very seriously indeed.

He concludes:

> My own inclination is to hold off judgment, until Modal Personism has been worked out with greater care.... I would be more comfortable ... if we could go beyond the mere appeal to brute intuition ... offering an account of why Modal Personism should

matter in the way we may intuitively think it does.... But it is one thing to ask for such an account, quite another to dismiss the view.[62]

Even when he assumes (for the sake of argument) that the PPH captures our intuitions, he does not seem to grant it the same status as Modal Personism. Given these other things he says, one would expect Kagan to have suggested that I might settle for the PPH (assuming it captures intuitive judgments in cases) before simply "giving up" intuitive judgments in some or all cases for what seems like a more intuitively compelling principle.

The question also arises what "giving up" an intuitive judgment for the sake of what seems to be a more compelling rationale amounts to. (This is different from giving up an intuitive judgment because one comes to make a different judgment when one reconsiders the factors in the case.) On one possible view, "giving up" an intuitive judgment is not the same as no longer having it. Rather, it is something like continuing to see a stick bent in water while knowing that this is an illusion, in virtue of commitment to a rationale that implies the intuitive judgment is wrong. One question is whether the compelling rationale provides (or is associated with an explanation that provides) an error theory explaining why we continue to have the intuitive judgment even though it is wrong, in the way science explains our optical illusion. According to the theory of reflective equilibrium, at least, a deeper rationale we accept even when it conflicts with some intuitive judgments need neither prove (or be associated with an explanation that proves) that these intuitive judgments are wrong nor provide an error theory for them. The deeper rationale need only be more plausible than the intuitive judgments about cases with which the rationale conflicts. But given that the intuitive judgments are not shown to be wrong, it is possible that we will still hope to find another deeper rationale that is as compelling and does not require that we give up these intuitive judgments. In a sense, we may not be "in equilibrium" at all but always looking out for something better. (Notice that we need not be on the lookout for only another rationale that is compatible with *both* the earlier rationale and the case judgments that are less plausible than it. Even if the first rationale is more plausible than the case judgments, the plausibility of a new rationale combined with those case judgments could be greater than the first rationale with which they are both inconsistent.) My own sense is that without an explanation showing that the intuitive judgments about cases are erroneous, we should often resist "giving them up" and seek further for their rationale.[63]

Finally, let me consider the reason why Kagan thinks one deeper rationale for the PPH—the difference being substitution and subordination—that I offer does not succeed. It is not that he thinks the rationale is not morally significant in its own right. His objection to it is that it does not account for an intuitive case judgment that I have in the Two Trolleys Case—namely, that it is impermissible to redirect the second trolley so that it derails the original trolley headed to the five when the second trolley will kill one person. Since the PPH accounts for this intuitive case judgment, he thinks the rationale I suggest cannot be the PPH's rationale. In this case, a mere means to the greater good directly causes the lesser evil. As such, its causal structure is like (i) my Bomb Trolley Case in which we use a bomb to stop the trolley, though the bomb will kill someone; and like (ii) Foot's Gas Case. Kagan does not see how using this means subordinates the person who will die to the people who would be saved. My thought was that we would never choose to use a device that would harm a person by contrast to not harming that person when we face these two options on their own. So it is the means serving the greater number of people that could give it greater weight relative to the bystander's not being harmed by it. This reason for changing the weight given to the means seemed to me to smack of subordination of one to the five, at least in this context. Another attempt I made to justify how I applied the subordination description was to consider a case that did not involve using a means with a harmful side effect. It involved saving a means that we need in order to save five people rather than destroying it with a redirected trolley, when doing this would involve killing someone else by redirecting the trolley toward him instead. This is what is at stake in the Bystander Saving-by-Letting-Die Case (given at the end of Lecture I). In that case, I thought we ought not to turn a trolley away from eight people toward killing one person when we could instead send the trolley toward a path; it would be subordinating not to do this just because we would otherwise use the path to save five other people.[64]

## Notes

1. Judith Jarvis Thomson, "Turning the Trolley," *Philosophy & Public Affairs* 36 (2008): 367.

2. If I had not assumed particular judgments about permissibility in cases, I would have described the trolley problem as *"whether* it is sometimes permissible to kill, even rather than let die, when we come to kill in some ways and not others." For a difficulty with doing this, see n. 29.

3. Sometimes philosophers have said to me that they were discussing the trolley problem when they were discussing only the question of whether it is permissible to kill one to save five in the way the surgeon would. I do not think this considered by itself is the trolley problem.

4. This concern about using a three-options case was that in it, when one faces a choice between one's paying a cost or someone else's doing so, there may be a factor present that makes it impermissible (in the first instance, at least) to make someone else pay the cost. But this need not imply that in a two-options case the same factor is present. For example, it might be held that if one can save the five without infringing anyone's rights, one should do that before doing what infringes someone's rights, and while one would infringe the workman's rights, one cannot infringe one's own rights. However, when there is no possibility of saving the five without infringing someone's rights because one is not able to pay the cost oneself, it is permissible to do that. (Peter Graham offers this explanation for why he agrees with Thomson that it is wrong to turn the trolley on the workman in a three-options case but not

wrong to turn it on him in a two-options case. See his "Thomson's Trolley Problem" (unpublished manuscript).

5. In his *The Ends of Harm* (Oxford University Press, 2011), Victor Tadros suggests that the difference between turning the trolley toward oneself and turning it toward someone else is that one would use oneself as a mere means to save others but not use the other person as a mere means because he dies as a mere side effect of the trolley's hitting him. I do not think Tadros's suggestion is correct. When we turn the trolley in our direction, we also foresee that we will die as a mere side effect of the trolley's turning. Our being hit is not causally necessary to stop the trolley in the way in which the fat man's being in the trolley's path is, and it is using our self as we would use the fat man that would make us use our self as a mere means to saving the five, I think.

6. See Samuel Scheffler, *The Rejection of Consequentialism* (New York: Oxford University Press, 1982).

7. In my "Harming Some to Save Others from the Nazis," in my *The Moral Target* (New York: Oxford University Press, 2012), I consider the permissibility of an oppressed group doing this to some of its members to save others. But if a government at least may make people pay costs they are not required to volunteer to pay, this raises the interesting possibility that a bystanding government could permissibly redirect a missile sent by another country from a larger to a smaller population even if a bystanding person would not be permitted to.

8. I will discuss the move from self-help to help by a bystander further in this response.

9. Keep in mind that I raised this concern in response to Thomson's first argument, which focuses on not making someone pay a cost one would not oneself pay. This accounts for why the concern is not phrased as "to show that a bystander may not redirect the trolley more has to be said than that . . . he should not make someone else pay a cost that that person is not required to pay," which was the view she supported in her second argument.

10. Thomson also says that she is puzzled by what is added in my saying at the end of my discussion of the Drowning Case (in connection with examining her first argument), "If one has an independent argument for the permissibility of letting someone die to save others, one cannot show it is impermissible to do so merely because one would permissibly not let oneself die to save others," when I had already said that more had to be said to show that one may not let another person die to save five than that one would not let oneself die for that purpose. I did not think the quoted remark was mere repetition because I was imagining a case in which one already had an argument

that made it permissible to let someone die, and I was claiming one could not defeat that argument by the new consideration. This was by contrast to what I had already said, which was merely that the fact that I did not have to sacrifice myself could not establish that I was not permitted to sacrifice another. The latter claim does not involve having some positive argument for letting someone die. I made the quoted remark because I think it is also relevant to the following situation involving a killing case: Suppose one thinks one has an argument for doing what causes collateral harm to civilians in a two-options case (in which we either bomb a military facility causing collateral deaths or do not bomb.) Suppose that a pilot would not do what would lead to collateral harm to himself by taking a different route that would allow him to successfully bomb but also lead to his being gravely harmed. Some may want to take this as grounds for thinking that, after all, the original argument for bombing was not good. I think this is incorrect.

11. It is also in his "Thomson's Trolley Problem."

12. Graham has also raised as counter-examples to Thomson's view cases in which we kill a person in a group whose members would all soon die in any case in order to save others in the group. He thinks this is permissible even if the one person does not consent and is not required to die for the others. I assume that Thomson is concerned with killing people who would otherwise go on living for a significant time if they were not killed, and so I would not rely on a case like this as a counter-example to her 2008 view.

13. See audio recording of the lectures, comments, and post-lecture discussions at tannerlectures.berkeley.edu/2012-2013/.

14. In Judith Jarvis Thomson, "The Trolley Problem," *Yale Law Journal* 94 (1985).

15. I discussed this point that Foot made in "The Problem of Abortion and the Doctrine of the Double Effect" in Lecture I.

16. For example, my *Morality, Mortality,* vol. 2 (New York: Oxford University Press, 1996), chap. 5, and my *Intricate Ethics* (New York: Oxford University Press, 2007), chap. 5. In *Intricate Ethics,* I explained what I meant by ruling out mere means that cause harm "at least directly." I did not mean that a very complicated "Rube Goldberg" type of mere means causing harm would be permissible when greater good would result. Rather, I focused on whether mere means we introduce or use in an environment (complicated or not) to save some people itself causes harm by contrast to its causing harm by affecting what is in the environment independently of what we introduce to save the people. The former is ruled out by the PPH, while the latter need not be. (Lecture II, endnote 12 should have included "use in an environment".) The

more precise version of the PPH also refers to lesser harms that are aspects of (rather than causally downstream from) greater goods, and it employs a modal condition. The body of the PPH given in Lecture II refers to "the bomb or second trolley" to remind the reader of some cases I had discussed in Lecture II leading up to the principle.

17. Suppose the history of how the person had come to bat the trolley away was not as in Thomson's case where we just picked him up to be used as a bat. Rather, by innocent means we turned a second trolley away from killing ten people and that redirected trolley unavoidably pushes a person into the first trolley headed to five so that his batting it redirects it from those five. In this revised case, the harm to the one who bats the trolley is downstream from the greater good of the ten being saved (or means having that as its noncausal flip side). Hence, when the person comes to bat the trolley in this alternative way, it is permitted by the PPH.

18. Cases like Tractor are just the sort Hurka points to in one part of his comments, as we shall see.

19. I spoke of it as the "structural equivalent" of the greater good. In earlier work, I distinguished it from components of the greater good, such as the trolley's being moved only slightly to the right so that one of the five is saved. In *Intricate Ethics*, I argued that often turning the trolley would also be permissible in the latter type of case, assuming the greater good would eventually come about in an acceptable way (that I described). For more discussion of these issues, see *Intricate Ethics*. In Lecture II, I tried to simplify, as the Tanner Lectures were for a more general audience.

20. In her addendum, Thomson notes that in the seminar following the two lectures, many who thought it permissible to turn the trolley in the Bystander Case did not think it permissible to turn it in the Loop Case. Let me clarify my response to those people because Thomson says she did not understand it. I focused on what I thought these people's concern might be. I suggested that they thought that in Loop, we would have to intend that the one person be harmed but not so in Bystander, and they thought such an intention made turning impermissible. (While I share Thomson's view that intention does not usually bear on permissibility, I simply took their concern with intention as given.) I argued that the fact that someone would turn the trolley because they thought the one person would be hit, given that his being hit was necessary to save the five, did not imply that they intended his being hit. Acting because some effect will occur need not mean that one intends that the effect occur. For example, suppose the person who turned the trolley in Loop did intend that the one person be hit. Then it would be inconsistent of him to save the one

person if only after he turns the trolley does it become clear that it is possible to remove the one person from off the track. But turning in the Loop Case would be consistent with saving that one person if it unexpectedly becomes possible to do so, rather than intentionally leaving him to be hit in order to save the five. (For more on this, see chap. 4 of *Intricate Ethics*.)

In her addendum, Thomson gives her own response to those who gave a split decision on Bystander and Loop. While she does not think it is permissible to turn in Bystander, she thinks that *if* one thinks it is permissible, one should also think it is permissible to turn in Loop. In defense of this, she says that it would be odd if a bystander hesitated to turn the trolley solely because he was uncertain whether or not the track looped. I am not sure I agree. (Notice that Thomson's argument would also apply to someone who was uncertain whether he was in the Bystander Case or the Tractor Case.) My own view is that this would be a case of acting under uncertainty. If it is more reasonable for a bystander to believe he is in Loop than in a non-looping case, and he were right to think that turning in Loop is impermissible, he should not turn. If it is more reasonable for him to believe he is in a non-looping case, he may turn. It does not seem odd that he should do what he can to find out which situation he is in if he thinks turning in Loop is wrong. Suppose it turns out that a bystander was actually in a Loop Case when it was reasonable for him to believe that he was in a non-looping case. Thomson thinks that if it is true that one should not turn in the Loop Case, this bystander will have done the wrong act in turning the trolley. This may be true on a so-called objective view of permissibility, but some hold that one has acted permissibly if one acts in the light of what it is reasonable to believe. And on this view, the bystander in question will not have acted impermissibly. (This view is consistent with its being permissible to stop someone from doing what it is permissible for him to do because his doing it is not objectively permissible.) Thomson also imagines a case in which others intervene to make it the case that there is a loop on the track after the bystander has acted on the assurance that no loop will be made. She says this "thereby mak[es] it have been all wrong for him to turn the trolley." But when others intervene in this way (even for good reason) after the bystander has acted, it seems even less plausible to say it was wrong of him to have turned the trolley.

21. In Lecture II, I raised another concern about the PPH, that what it would allow was not always permissible (by contrast to its not allowing what was permissible, as in Tractor Case II under one understanding of "component"). This was because not all greater goods or their components could justify lesser harms due to them. In particular, it might be that sometimes there is

nothing morally wrong with the greater number of people being harmed (as when the greater number had agreed to be harmed) or not aided (as when the trolley would lead to their deaths by disconnecting a life-support machine whose assistance they had no right to have continued). I discussed such a case, Bystander Saving-by-Letting-Die, at the end of Lecture I. Some might also suggest that only greater goods that involve reducing greater harm rather than providing "pure" benefits could justify the lesser harms. For a view like this, see Seana Shiffrin, "Wrongful Life, Procreative Responsibility, and the Significance of Harm," *Legal Theory* 5 (1999): 117–48. However, Shiffrin's view would not affect the PPH's implications for the standard trolley cases including Bystander where we do eliminate greater harm.

22. This includes the case by Alexander Friedman that I discussed in Lecture II, n. 12.

23. I think it was J. M. Fischer who first used a case in which the trolley was sent across a bridge.

24. Peter Unger made use of more complicated multiple-option cases in his discussion of the trolley problem because he thought they would show that we should always choose the option that kills the fewest people, given that we are going to kill some anyway, regardless of how we come to kill them. I disagree with Unger's conclusion, but I understand why multiplying the options served a function given what he was trying to show. Unger's discussion occurs in his *Living High and Letting Die* (New York: Oxford University Press, 1996), 88–114, 152–154. I critically examine his views in chap. 6 of *Intricate Ethics*. For more on the methodology of using cases, see my "Moral Intuitions, Cognitive Psychology, and the Harming/Not Aiding Distinction" in *Intricate Ethics*; and "Explaining, Justifying, and Finding Oneself" in my *Bioethical Prescriptions* (New York: Oxford University Press, 2013). See also the responses to Shelly Kagan's comments that follow.

25. Thomas Nagel, *The View From Nowhere* (New York: Oxford University Press, 1986), 179–180. This quote also appears in my *Intricate Ethics*, 4.

26. *Intricate Ethics*, 5.

27. See n. 32 for an example.

28. In Lecture II, I considered other cases, such as Lazy Susan II, that I think should be put in the category of the trolley problem.

29. As I noted earlier (in n. 2), I phrased my description so that it reflected some of my judgments about permissibility and impermissibility. Independent of these judgments, the description could be revised to say, "whether it is sometimes permissible to kill, even rather than let die, when we kill in some ways rather than others." One difficulty with this revision is that it

suggests there would be a trolley problem even if it were not permissible for the driver to turn, any more than for the surgeon to kill, and even if the bystander or bystanding driver were not permitted to turn, and so on. There being a *problem* seems to depend on making certain judgments of permissibility and impermissibility that seem inconsistent with each other and so need explanation.

30. Though I am not necessarily opposed to drifting.

31. Thomson points out that I gave no summary at the end of these sections of Lecture II. That is true, but I used what I had said to try to derive a conclusion about the Bystander Case. She mentions a table at the very end of the lecture, apparently thinking that it was intended to summarize Lecture II. That was not its purpose. It only summarizes factors relating to a new issue I raised in the last part of Lecture II (section 10)—namely, whether what a bystander is permitted to do depends on whether people in danger face a threat that is still controlled by the person presenting the threat to them. However, there is another table (table II.1, p. 91) at the end of section 9 (which is the last part of Lecture II that Thomson discusses) that I said "provides a template for some distinctions covered in this discussion as they pertain to the Trolley Problem" (p. 90). That table organizes the important types of cases discussed in Lecture II up to that point by type of agent involved and type of action taken to stop a threat either to the agent or to others. It uses abbreviations for types of cases. I thought these would be clear, given that they followed discussion of the cases, but let me here clarify them. The horizontal axis of the table refers to the type of agent(s) in a case: those acting to prevent a threat to self or others and acting from a partial or impartial perspective. The vertical axis describes what the agent(s) in a case would do. Under "Remove persons," a case may involve either (a) an agent removing a person (including himself) who faces a threat because he is between it and other people, or (b) an agent removing a person who faces a threat when his being removed causes a new threat to others. In the next option listed, a case involves an agent shielding a person (including himself) from a threat, though this results in the same or new threat to others. The final option listed in the table is to redirect a threat.

32. Similar things could be said about some nonconsequentialist theorists who think that not intending harm is the crucial negative value underlying deontological constraints on action. To support their view, they may focus on the difference in permissibility in a case in which it is impermissible to deliberately make a child suffer in order to achieve a good by contrast to a case in which it is permissible to make him suffer as a side effect of means needed to achieve a good (as Thomas Nagel does in his *The View from Nowhere*). But

their value seems to imply that if an agent does the act that both achieves the good and has suffering as a side effect while intending to cause the suffering, he is not permitted to do the act. This seems wrong. It is through not considering more cases that they may rest content with attributing moral import to the wrong factor.

33. I note in passing that clause (2*) in the Worseness* Thesis suggests that something being an act of letting five die does count in favor of its impermissibility. Some (not I) might object to this claim, whereas they would not object to clause (2) in the Worseness Thesis because killing one may be worse than something that is not bad at all.

34. Here is another concern about the phrasing of the Worseness* Thesis and what Thomson says about it. Consider an example. It could be the case that an act's being the breaking of a promise to meet someone for lunch counts more strongly in favor of its impermissibility than an act's being the failure to do something supererogatory to save a life (e.g., give up one's own life to save another) counts in favor of its impermissibility. As noted, Thomson says, "counting in favor of an act's being impermissible is what moral theorists ascribe when they say ... 'other things equal, he acted wrongly.'" But in the example I gave, one could say that more counts in favor of an act's being impermissible in being a breaking of a promise than in being the failure to do a supererogatory act without ascribing this because one thinks that other things being equal, someone acted wrongly if he broke the promise to one person in order to supererogatoriliy save the life of another. It is not at all impermissible to fail to do the supererogatory act, and yet it is morally acceptable to break the promise in order to do the supererogatory act. (I first made this point in my "Supererogation and Obligation," *Journal of Philosophy* 82 (1985): 118–138.) This is one reason why, if the two clauses in the Worseness* Thesis are to account (even) for the permissibility of killing in Trolley Driver's Two Options Case, it should be made clearer in this case how having more *all told* (i.e., no outweighing factors are present) to be said in favor of the impermissibility of killing five than of the impermissibility of killing one leads to the judgment of the permissibility of killing one.

35. See, for example, "Killing and Letting Die: Methodological and Substantive Issues," *Pacific Philosophical Quarterly* 64 (1983): 297–312; *Morality, Mortality*, vol. 2; and a brief summary of the latter in "Nonconsequentialism," in *The Blackwell Guide to Ethical Theory*, 2nd ed., Hugh LaFollette and Ingmar Persson (Malden, MA: Blackwell, 2013). In those discussions, I argued that the killing/letting-die distinction was morally important when our killing takes from someone his life that he would have had independently of our

providing it to him at the time and which he was entitled to keep. When we let someone die, the person loses out on only what he would have had through our providing it by our efforts, and these efforts are what we are entitled to decide about. Insofar as I emphasized the role of what we and others are entitled to, I agree with Thomson that rights are important in explaining the moral significance of the killing/letting-die distinction. Furthermore, in Lecture II, section 4, I also specifically attended to how one could (1) retain the idea that whether one kills or lets die can be morally relevant factors in relation to permissibility while thinking that (2) whether killing one in a certain way (as described in the PPH) is the alternative to killing more people rather than to letting more people die need not be a morally significant factor in relation to permissibility. (It might still matter in relation to obligation.)

36. Suppose an aggressor is attacking us. It may make no moral difference whether we kill him or let him die if either is necessary and sufficient to stop his attack. This is because, even if all other factors are equal (2), the fact that he is an aggressor is a defeator making other things not be equal (1).

37. I described the desirability of this sort of process in the introduction to *Morality, Mortality*, vol. 2.

38. I have elsewhere argued that when a factor that is present in one case is also present in another case and weighs in favor of permissibility in the first case, it is still possible that it does not weigh in favor of permissibility in the second case. I said this was possible because of some particular "contextual interaction." That is, given the specific factors in the second case not present in the first case, the same factor might not have the sample functional role. I referred to this as the Principle of Contextual Interaction. For my first mention of this, see my "Killing and Letting Die: Methodological and Substantive Issues" in *Pacific Philosophical Quarterly* 64 (1983): 297–312. I also discuss it in *Morality, Mortality*, vol. 2. But there is a burden of proof on showing that there is such contextual interaction, and in the absence of proof we may assume there is no such interaction present.

39. See audio at tannerlectures.berkeley.edu/2012-2013/. However, Thomson does mention in her comments another case of mine that makes the same point as Driver Topple—namely, the one in which the driver can save the five from the trolley either (a) by turning a switch to the right, which will turn the trolley away from the five onto a track that goes up a bridge where the trolley will topple two people as a side effect, or (b) by turning the same switch to the left which will cause one other person to be toppled from a bridge in front of the trolley to stop it. I said that in this case, too, the driver should not minimize the number that he kills because only in the former option is the one's

death causally downstream from the greater good (or means having it or its component as a noncausal flip side). Thomson does not say if she agrees with me. Nevertheless, it shows that she is aware of cases that raise the question of whether killing more than one counts more strongly in favor of impermissibility than killing one does when we do not hold equal the factor of how the death of the one will come about (i.e., that other things are not held equal (2)). My answer to this question is the heart of my conclusion on page 212.

40. It might seem this is not so, for the following reason. If killing in Bystander and Bystanding Driver Two Options were impermissible, merely pointing to killing one as the alternative to letting five die would be both sufficient and necessary to explain the impermissibility of killing in the Transplant Case. But explaining in this way the impermissibility of killing in Transplant is compatible with its also being impermissible to kill in Foot's Trolley Driver's Two Options Case, and so it is not sufficient to show a difference in permissibility between the two cases. After all, the factor of killing one rather than killing five when present in Driver Topple is not sufficient to make it permissible to kill one in that case, and this is not merely because some special factor in Driver Topple is defeating the weight of the killing one versus killing five factor (as would happen if one had promised not to kill one person on the bridge). It is because of the moral significance of the way in which we come to kill in Foot's Trolley Driver's Two Options Case that killing is permissible in it but not in Driver Topple. So if it were true that we may not kill in Bystander or Bystanding Driver, it is still true that a better explanation of why it is permissible to kill in Foot's Trolley Driver's Two Options Case and not in Transplant would be that it is worse to kill five than to kill one when the one's death would be causally downstream from a greater good (or means having it or its component as a noncausal flip side) but it is worse to kill one rather than let five die, other things equal (1).

41. It is worth noting that Foot assumed that the fact that acting with foresight to harm bore on impermissibility in the Gas Case meant it might bear on impermissibility in the Trolley Driver's Two Options Case. If she thought the Gas Case was a special case, because other things were not equal (1), she would not have used it as a counter-example to the intention/foresight explanation of TPdb. (This is like what I earlier argued Thomson must have assumed in thinking the permissibility of turning in the Bystander Case would be a counter-example to Foot's explanation of TPdb.)

42. See her "Killing, Letting Die, and the Trolley Problem," *The Monist* 59 (1976): 207–217.

43. Though considering other cases led me to modify the PPH further, as I noted earlier. See *Intricate Ethics* on this. And I also suggest a somewhat different approach in sections 5-7 of Lecture II.

44. They (and I) have tried to do so elsewhere. For references to my work, see n. 38.

45. See n. 16 for a fuller description of this distinction.

46. See *Palsgraf v. Long Island Railroad Co.*, 248 N.Y. 339, 162 N.E. 99 (N.Y. 1928). In *Palsgraf*, two railroad guards attempting to help a passenger board a moving train seem to have caused the passenger's package to fall. The package contained fireworks, which exploded on impact with the ground and likely caused scales at the end of the platform to fall, injuring the plaintiff Palsgraf.

47. I discussed this in *Intricate Ethics*. See also n. 16 for what I mean by "indirect."

48. "Justifications for Killing Noncombatants in War," *Midwest Studies in Philosophy* 24 (2000): 219–228.

49. See, for example, *Morality, Mortality*, vol. 2. I dealt with it again in *Intricate Ethics*.

50. In "Failures of Just War Theory," *Ethics* 114 (2004): 650–692.

51. In *Intricate Ethics*, 5.

52. See *Intricate Ethics* and Lecture II, p. 64.

53. See Lecture II and my response to Thomson, pp. 169–218, for earlier discussion of the Tractor Cases and possible emendation of the PPH in light of them. Further discussion also occurs in *Intricate Ethics*.

54. It is not clear in Hurka's account that achieving the just cause has to be a greater good than the good it would cause. However, it seems problematic if the achievement of a just cause that is not a very important good has very bad side effects and these bad side effects are to be outweighed in a proportionality calculation by a very great good that is merely a side effect of the just cause. It seems this greater good would have too big a role in justifying going to war.

55. I discuss this case and more from Kahneman and Tversky in *Intricate Ethics*, chap. 14.

56. In Thomson's original case, the fat man was pushed up close and personal.

57. I said some more about revisions to it in my discussion of responses to Thomson and Hurka. See also *Intricate Ethics*.

58. There is additional discussion of this alternative in my response to Thomson.

59. I also discussed the role of cases in my response to Thomson on "the greats."

60. For earlier discussion along these lines, see my discussion of Peter Unger's *Living High and Letting Die* in my *Intricate Ethics*. Also see my discussions of methodology of cases more generally in "Moral Intuitions, Cognitive Psychology, and the Harming/Not Aiding Distinction" in *Intricate Ethics* and "Explaining, Justifying and Finding Oneself" in my *Bioethical Prescriptions*.

61. "What's Wrong with Speciesism?," pp. 16–17 (unpublished manuscript, presented at the University of Toronto).

62. I thank Shelly Kagan for permission to quote from his unpublished paper.

63. Not to be too dramatic, it may be better to "go to the stake" rather than simply renege on or deny one's intuitive judgment. I once described someone's sensing moral importance in factors that others take to be insignificant as something like the Princess's response to the pea. Perhaps the Princess will have to turn into Joan of Arc.

64. For discussion of parts of these comments, I am grateful to Shelly Kagan, Jeff McMahan, and Larry Temkin. For help in preparing this book (under time constraints) I am grateful to the editor, Eric Rakowski, and for the production assistance of Margaret Collins, Lisa MacPhee, and Jenn Valois. I also thank Martin Jay, Peter Ohlin, and Jay Wallace for their help.

# Index of Names

Printed in the USA/Agawam, MA
September 20, 2022

798755.033